2022
Securities
Licensing

SERIES 22
EXAM STUDY GUIDE
+ TEST BANK

SECURITIES LICENSING SERIES

The Securities Institute of America proudly publishes world class textbooks, test banks and video training classes for the following Financial Services exams:

Securities Industry Essentials Exam / SIE Exam

Series 3 exam

Series 4 exam

Series 6 exam

Series 7 exam

Series 9 exam

Series 10 exam

Series 22 exam

Series 24 exam

Series 26 exam

Series 39 exam

Series 57 exam

Series 63 exam

Series 65 exam

Series 66 exam

Series 79 exam

Series 99 exam

For more information visit us at: www.securitiesCE.com

2022
Securities
Licensing

SERIES 22
EXAM STUDY GUIDE
+ TEST BANK

Direct Participation Programs
Limited Representative

The Securities Institute of America, Inc.

ISBN (Paperback): 978-1-937841-45-4
ISBN (ePub): 978-1-937841-46-1

Contents

CHAPTER 5
DPP OFFERINGS AND SUITABILITY   87

About the Series 22 Exam

ABOUT THE SERIES 22 EXAM

Congratulations! You are on your way to becoming a Registered Representative licensed to conduct business in direct participation program securities. The Series 22 exam will be presented in a 50 question, multiple-choice format. Each candidate will have a total of 2 hours and 30 minutes to complete the exam. A score of 70% or higher is required to pass. The Series 22 is as much a knowledge test as it is a reading test.

TAKING THE SERIES 22 EXAM

The Series 22 exam is presented in multiple-choice format on a touch screen computer known as the PROCTOR system. No computer skills are required and candidates will find that the test screen works in the same way as an ordinary ATM machine. Each test is made up of 50 questions that are randomly chosen from a test bank of thousands of questions. Each Series 22 exam will have several practice questions, which do not count towards the final score. The test has a time limit of 1 hours and 30 minutes, which is designed to provide enough time for all candidates to complete the exam. Each Series 22 exam will be comprised of questions that focus on the following areas:

Seeks business for the broker-dealer from customers and potential customers	17 questions	34%
Opens accounts after obtaining and evaluating customers' financial profile and investment objectives	4 questions	8%
Provides customers with information about Investments, makes suitable recommendations, transfers assets and maintains appropriate records	27 questions	54%
Obtains and verifies customers purchase instructions and agreements; processes, completes and confirms transactions	2 questions	4%
TOTAL	50 Questions	100%

HOW TO PREPARE FOR THE SERIES 22 EXAM

For most candidates the combination of reading the textbook and using the exam prep software is enough to successfully complete the exam. It is recommended that the individual spend at least 60 hours preparing for the exam by reading the textbook, underlining key points and by taking as many practice questions as possible. We recommend that a student schedule their exam no more than one week after completing your Series 22 exam prep.

TEST-TAKING TIPS

- Read the full question.
- Identify what the question is asking.
- Identify key words and phrases.
- Watch out for hedge clauses, i.e., except & not.
- Eliminate wrong roman numeral answers.
- Identify synonymous terms.
- Be wary of changing answers.

WHAT TYPE OF BUSINESS MAY BE CONDUCTED BY A SERIES 22 REGISTERED REPRESENTATIVE

A Series 22 registered representative may conduct business in offering of direct participation programs including:

- Direct participation programs (real estate, oil and gas, and Equipment Leasing)
- Limited Partnerships
- Limited liability companies
- S corporations

WHAT SCORE IS NEEDED TO PASS THE EXAM?

A score of 70% or higher is needed to pass the Series 22 exam.

ARE THERE ANY PREREQUISITES FOR THE SERIES 22 EXAM?

In addition to passing the series 22 exam candidates must also successfully complete the Securities Industry Essentials exam /SIE. Unlike the SIE exam candidates must be sponsored by a finra member firm to take the series 22 exam. You may take either test first but, you must successfully complete both to become registered

HOW DO I SCHEDULE AN EXAM?

Ask your firm's principal to schedule the exam for you or provide a list of test centers in your area. You must be sponsored by a FINRA member firm prior to making an appointment. The Series 22 exam may be taken any day that the exam center is open.

WHAT MUST I TAKE TO THE EXAM CENTER?

You should only take a picture ID with you. Everything else will be provided, including a calculator and scratch paper.

HOW LONG WILL IT TAKE TO GET THE RESULTS OF THE EXAM?

The exam will be graded as soon as you finish your final question and hit the "submit for grading" button. It will take only a few minutes to get your results. Your grade will appear on the computer screen and you will be given a paper copy from the exam center. If you do not pass the test, you will need to wait 30 days before taking it again. If you do not pass on the second try, you'll need to wait another 30 days. After that, you are required to wait 6 months to take the test again.

About This Book

The writers and instructors at The Securities Institute have developed the Series 22 textbook, exam prep software, and videos to ensure that you have the knowledge required to pass the test and to make sure that you are confident in the application of the knowledge during the exam. The writers and instructors at The Securities Institute are subject-matter experts as well as Series 22 test experts. We understand how the test is written, and our proven test-taking techniques can dramatically improve your results.

Each chapter includes notes, tips, examples, and case studies with key information; hints for taking the exam; and additional insight into the topics. Each chapter ends with a practice test to ensure that you have mastered the concepts presented before moving on to the next topic.

About The Securities Institute of America

The Securities Institute of America, Inc. helps thousands of securities and insurance professionals build successful careers in the financial services industry every year. In more than 25 years we have helped students pass more than 250,000 exams.

Our securities training options include:

- Classroom training
- Private tutoring
- Interactive online video training classes
- State-of-the-art exam prep test banks
- Printed textbooks
- ebooks
- Real-time tracking and reporting for managers and training directors

As a result, you can choose a securities training solution that matches your skill level, learning style, and schedule. Regardless of the format you choose, you can be sure that our securities training courses are relevant, tested, and designed to help you succeed. It is the experience of our instructors and the quality of our materials that make our courses requested by name at some of the largest financial services firms in the world.

To contact The Securities Institute of America, visit us on the Web at: *www.securitiesce.com* or call 877-218-1776.

Definition of Terms

INTRODUCTION

In order to successfully complete the Series 22 exam, it is important to have an in-depth understanding of the terms relating to direct participation programs and to understand how these terms will be tested on your exam. In this chapter we detail a number of the terms that you are going to be tested on on your exam.

1031 EXCHANGE

Internal Revenue Code 1031 allows investors to exchange certain types of properties without recognizing a capital gain or capital loss on the exchange. The property exchange must include properties of like-kind and must be held for investment purposes or for the use in the taxpayer's business or trade. A 1031 exchange is applicable to investments in real estate. Investments in securities such as stocks, bonds, interest in limited partnerships, or other evidence of ownership interest or indebtedness do not qualify for the 1031 Exchange exemption.

AFFILIATE

An affiliate is an individual who is controlled by or who controls a broker-dealer or a sponsor of a direct participation offering. Your exam may refer to a broker-dealer as a FINRA member or simply as a member. Affiliates also include:

1. A person who beneficially owns or who has the right to acquire 10% or more of the voting interest in a member or a sponsor.

2. A person who has the right to vote 10% or more of the voting interest in a member or sponsor.

3. A partner, officer, or director of a member or sponsor including individuals providing similar functions at a member firm or sponsor.

4. Immediate family members of officers, directors or affiliates as outlined above will also be deemed to be affiliates of the member or sponsor

5. Any entity which is owned or controlled by affiliates as detailed above will also be deemed to be an affiliate of the member or sponsor.

AGENT

An agent or registered representative is a natural person who represents an issuer or a broker-dealer in the purchase and sale or the attempted purchase and sale of securities.

ALTERNATIVE MINIMUM TAX AMT

The IRS has designed a different set of rules to ensure that high-income earners do not significantly reduce their overall tax liability by taking advantage of certain tax benefits. The Alternative Minimum Tax is designed to ensure that high-income earners pay a minimum amount of tax on their overall income. The AMT is a tentative tax calculated by eliminating or reducing certain exclusions and deductions. Certain tax preference items may be added back to the high-income earner's taxable income. Tax preference items that may be added back to the income to calculate the alternative minimum tax are accelerated depreciation or depletion, net income from oil and gas, investment tax credits, and interest income on private-purpose municipal bonds such as industrial development bonds.

APPLICABLE TRADE OR BUSINESS

An applicable trade or business is any activity conducted on a regular continuous and substantial basis consisting in whole or in part of raising or returning capital and investing in or disposing of specific assets or developing specified assets.

AT RISK

The term "at-risk" is used to describe the partner's capital contribution, plus the partner's proportional liability for the limited partnership's or LLC's liabilities. Qualified non-recourse loans are specifically excluded from the calculation of "at-risk."

BOOT

The term boot is used to describe the value of a non-like-kind property received as part of a 1031 exchange. The fact that the exchange includes a non-like property does not disqualify the exchange, it merely results in a partially tax-deferred exchange. That is to say that the exchange will not be 100% tax-deferred.

BROKER-DEALER

A broker-dealer is a person or a firm that maintains a place of business and effects transactions in securities markets for its own account or for the account of others. A broker-dealer must be registered with the SEC and in the states where they have an office or transact business with retail customers.

CARRIED INTEREST

A carried interest is an interest awarded to the sponsor of the program in exchange for their management of the program. The carried-interest is a participation in the profit or cash flows of the program awarded to the sponsor that have been received, not in exchange for a capital contribution, but in exchange for the efforts of the sponsor.

CASH FLOW

For the purpose of the Series 22 exam, cash flow is cash provided from operations minus expenses, and prior to deducting depreciation, depletion or other non-cash allowances. The deduction of all cash expenses including wages, insurance, debt service, capital improvements, repairs, maintenance and replacements will be made to determine funds from operations. Should the partnership have outstanding leases made to builders, sellers, or other parties, cash flow will also include lease payments received on net leases prior to depreciation.

CAPITALIZATION RATE

A program's capitalization rate is a method used to determine the value of a property based on its net operating income. The future cash flows to be received are discounted to a present value to determine an appropriate valuation for real estate. The capitalization rate is determined by dividing the price of the property by its net operating income. Higher capitalization rates imply a higher expected rate of return and imply a higher degree of risk.

CASH AVAILABLE FOR DISTRIBUTION

Cash available for distribution is the amount the partnership has available to distribute to interested parties. Cash available for distribution is the amount generated from cash flow minus any sums that have been set aside for repairs, maintenance, or reserves to provide such repairs and maintenance in the future.

CERTIFICATE OF LIMITED PARTNERSHIP

A certificate of limited partnership must be filed in the state of formation by any limited partnership. A certificate of limited partnership filed with the state will include the name of the partnership, the name and business address of each general partner, the registered office of the limited partnership, the mailing address for the limited partnership as well as the latest date of termination for the partnership. Once a certificate of limited partnership has been filed with the state and the partnership has been formed, many states require the limited partnership to advertise its formation to the public in the newspaper or through other publicly available means. Should any of the above information change, an amendment to the certificate of limited partnership will be filed with the state department.

CLOSING DATE

The closing date for a limited partnership is the date when the investor's interest in the limited partnership becomes effective. This date may be the day when the subscription agreement is accepted by the general partner or it may be a date stated in the subscription agreement or in the offering documents.

CONTROL

The term control as used in connection with an entity means any person or entity who owns a beneficial interest of 50% or more of the outstanding voting securities of a corporation or has a right to 50% or more of the profits and losses of a partnership or other non corporate entity.

DELAWARE STATUTORY TRUST

A Delaware statutory trust/DST is an alternative form of ownership to tenants in common. The Delaware statutory trust is an unincorporated entity or association created by a trust or other controlling agreement. The trust is then operated to own, invest, manage, control, or operate real property or a business interest. The formation of a Delaware statutory trust provides a great deal of flexibility regarding the rights, powers and privileges of both the trustee and the beneficiaries. The parties to the Delaware statutory trust define the relationship, terms and conditions as they so choose. The trust will provide liability protection for both the trustee and the beneficiaries. Unless the controlling document states otherwise, the beneficiaries of the Delaware statutory trust will enjoy the same protection as the stockholders in a corporation. Investors in a DST will receive their proportional distribution of income, gains and deductions. An important feature for this type of trust is that it allows an owner of real property to exchange that property for an interest in the trust without being subject to capital gains tax on the exchange. If an investor in real estate has elected to exchange his / her interest in a real property for an interest in a Delaware statutory trust, the investor's cost basis for the property becomes the investor's cost basis for his / her interest in the DST. For example, if an investor has depreciated a $1 million building over the course of many years to $200,000, the Investor's cost basis for the trust would also be $200,000. Many large DSTs are operated by large professional property management companies allowing an investor to enjoy the benefits of real estate investing without the management responsibilities. Some DSTs have certain limitations regarding the operation that investors should be aware of, Including:

Once the offering of the trust has been closed, the trust may not raise additional funds from current or new investors
- If the property is sold, the proceeds must be distributed to the participants in the trust and the proceeds may not be reinvested in other properties

- If a mortgage has been obtained to finance property acquisition, the mortgage may not be refinanced. Additionally, the trust may not borrow new funds unless the trust has defaulted on a mortgage or is about to default on a mortgage.

- The trust is required to distribute all income over and above expenses and required operating reserves on a regular basis

Should any of the limitations place the trust at a substantial risk, the DST may convert to a limited liability corporation in an effort to mitigate the risks associated with the limitations of a Delaware statutory Trust. The limited liability company created during the conversion is known as a springing limited liability company.

DEPRECIATION

Depreciation is an accounting method used to amortize the purchase price of an asset over the estimated useful life of the asset. Depreciation is a non-cash charge that reduces the value of a fixed asset on the balance sheet of the entity. The depreciation is then taken as a deduction to taxable income on the income statement. There are several types of depreciation schedules that may be used to reduce the value of an asset over time. Two of the more popular methods are straight-line depreciation and modified accelerated cost recovery. With the straight-line method, the price of the asset is depreciated in equal amounts over its useful life. When modified accelerated cost recovery is used, a large percentage of the asset's price is recovered in the early years of its use. This creates large deductions in the early years and smaller deductions in later years of the asset's useful life.

DEPLETION

Depletion is an accounting method used to reduce the value of natural resources carried on the balance sheet. Natural resources such as gas and oil cannot be depreciated; these resources must be depleted. The depletion allowance is used to reduce the value of the reserves to reflect the fact that, at some point, all of the natural resources will have been extracted, and the reserves extinguished. Depletion, like depreciation, is a non-cash charge that reduces the value of the natural resource on the balance sheet with the resulting depletion charge being taken against income to reduce tax liability.

DIRECT PARTICIPATION PROGRAM

A direct participation program, also known as a DPP or simply as a program, is an entity which provides for the complete flow through of all economic events and tax consequences. For the Series 22 exam, a direct participation program includes any program regardless of its structure, whether a limited partnership, an S corporation, a limited liability company, a business development company or a program that is made up of multiple legal entities or structures. A direct participation program may be formed as the legal entity to distribute interests in agricultural concerns, cattle feeding, cattle growing, oil and gas operations, equipment leasing, real estate development , financing and management, commodity pools, or securities investments. Excluded from the definition of a direct participation program are real estate investment trusts / REITS, corporate pension and profit-sharing plans, individual retirement accounts, tax sheltered annuities, investment companies, and insurance company separate accounts.

DISSENTING LIMITED PARTNER

Any person who is the owner or holder of a beneficial interest in a limited partnership subject to a proposed rollup transaction in which the partnership will be combining or merging with another limited partnership, who at the time votes are solicited files an objection to the proposed roll up or merger transaction.

EQUITY INTEREST

An equity interest as used in conjunction with a direct participation program refers to any person who has an interest in the capital, profits or losses of that partnership. The term equity interest when used in connection with a corporation refers to anyone who owns the stock of the corporation or who has a right to acquire shares of that corporation. A person will also be considered to have an equity interest in a corporation if that individual owns any security which would give them the right to convert, exchange or exercise another security into the stock of that corporation.

FAIR-MARKET NET WORTH

A partnership's fair-market net worth is the total market value of the partnership's assets minus any outstanding liabilities. The partnership's fair market net worth is determined based on the fair market value of its assets without regard to the partnership's actual cost and excluding any tax deductions or depletion allowances taken by the partnership.

FIRST-USER

First user is a term associated with a depreciation schedule. First user is the first fiscal year when a depreciable asset is put into use and the time when depreciation may begin.

FUNDS FROM OPERATIONS

When reviewing the financial performance of a limited partnership, funds from operations will provide investors with the details of the partnership's economic performance. Funds from operations are calculated by adding depreciation, amortization or depletion allowances back to the earnings of the partnership. Once the appropriate add-backs have been calculated, any capital gains realized on the sale of assets are subtracted to determine funds from operations for the partnership.

GENERAL PARTNER

The general partner of a limited partnership is the individual or entity who provides management expertise and is responsible for the day-to-day operations of the limited partnership. While the general partner may be a natural person, more often than not the general partner is a corporation or other legal entity that is designed to provide a level of legal protection to the natural persons who operate the partnership.

GENERAL PARTNERSHIP

A general partnership is a venture between one or more parties and allows all partners to make management decisions and to enter into legally binding contracts on behalf of the partnership. All general partners are jointly and severally liable for all of the obligations of the partnership unless otherwise stated in the partnership agreement. All of the income will be distributed to the partners and the partners will pay taxes on their individual return.

GRANTOR TRUST

With a grantor trust, the creator of the trust retains control of the assets in the trust. Grantor trusts may be set up as revocable or irrevocable trusts. In the case of a revocable grantor trust, the creator of the trust is deemed to be the owner of the assets and will report the income on his / her tax return. A revocable trust will also be deemed to be part of the grantor's estate at the time the grantor passes away. Should the grantor trust be established as an irrevocable trust, the grantor may retain the ability to pass income through to his / her own tax return and the assets will not be deemed to be part of the grantor's estate, provided the grantor meets certain minimum IRS requirements. The establishment of the irrevocable grantor trust which allows the grantor to retain the income and the assets to be seen as separate from the grantor are sometimes referred to as intentionally defective grantor trusts. The type of grantor trust established will be set forth in the trust instrument or trust deed.

JOINT VENTURE

A joint venture is a business entity that has been created by two or more parties. The parties to the joint venture share in the ownership, management, returns, and risks of the operation or entity. A joint venture may be an incorporated or unincorporated entity and is usually designed to carry out a particular business goal. Joint ventures are organized on a temporary basis and will terminate upon the completion of the objective or upon agreement of the owners.

LIMITED LIABILITY COMPANY

A limited liability company is a hybrid entity that allows for the flow through of taxes and significant flexibility for the members of the limited liability company. Unlike a limited partnership, where the limited partners are precluded from exercising any management control over the partnership, limited liability company members may operate, manage or control the limited liability company and still enjoy asset protection. The financial and management arrangements agreed to by the members of a limited liability company will be set forth in the operating agreement. The terms and conditions spelled out in the operating agreement are of particular importance to investors who are considering becoming a member of the limited liability company. These financial and management aspects are of particular importance when determining suitability.

LIMITED LIABILITY PARTNERSHIP

A limited liability partnership, as the name implies, affords the partners protection from liabilities of the limited liability partnership. However, this form of business structure may only be used by professional organizations such as accountants, attorneys, architects, and physicians.

LIMITED PARTNERSHIP

A limited partnership is a type of unincorporated direct participation program created through the association of limited partners and one or more general partners. The limited partnership must conform with the state regulations where the partnership is organized as well as the revised Uniform Limited Partnership Act.

LIMITED PARTNER

A limited partner is an investor in a limited partnership who has provided capital to the partnership in exchange for an economic interest in the partnership. A limited partner's liability is generally limited to the amount of the partner's investment. A limited partner may not exercise any management over the partnership's operations, nor may they seek to control the actions of the general partner. If a limited partner exercises management over the partnership's operations or controls the general partner, the limited partner will lose their classification as a limited partner and will be deemed to be a general partner of the partnership.

LIMITED PARTNERSHIP AGREEMENT

The limited partnership agreement is the foundation for the limited partnership. It spells out the business purpose of the partnership and all of the terms under which the partnership will operate. The agreement will be signed by both the general and limited partners to ensure all parties understand their rights and responsibilities. The partnership agreement will state the terms and conditions for the following:

1. The acceptance of limited partners.
2. The acceptance of substitute limited partners or additional limited partners.
3. The withdraw a capital by a limited partner.
4. The allocation of profits and losses.

5. How distributions to the limited partners will be made.

6. Any priority among partners.

7. The powers of the general partner to manage and control the partnership.

8. The powers of the general partner to acquire and sell property on behalf of the partnership.

9. The voting rights of the limited partners.

10. The requirement of the general partner to maintain books and records for the partnership.

11. The requirement of the general partner to provide periodic performance reports to the limited partners.

12. The amount of time required to be committed by the general partner to the management of the partnership.

13. The compensation to be paid to the general partner for its management services.

14. The acceptance of a substitute general partner or the assignment of the general partner's interest in the partnership.

LIMITED PARTNERSHIP ROLL-UP TRANSACTION

A limited partnership or direct participation roll-up transaction is any transaction which combines or reorganizes one or more limited partnerships directly or indirectly where investors will receive new securities or securities in another entity. Additional transactions that would meet the definition of a DPP roll-up transaction include:

1. Any transaction where the limited partners voting rights are subject adverse change or reduction.

2. Any transaction where the term of the existence of the partnership is amended.

3. Any transaction that impacts or changes management's compensation.

4. Any transaction that impacts or changes the investment objectives of the partnership.

5. Any transaction where investors do not have an option to receive or retain the same terms of ownership as the original issue.

A DPP roll-up transaction does not include any transaction where the interests of the limited partners are repurchased, recalled or exchanged under pre-existing terms of the partnership clearly defined at the time the partnership was organized. Additionally, a DPP rollup transaction will not include:

1. Any operating policy or practice of retaining cash for distribution or reinvesting proceeds from a sale of partnership assets or financing activities.

2. Any transaction involving the combination of or reorganization of one or more limited partnerships in which an unaffiliated party succeeds the interest of the general partner or sponsor if at least 66 2/3 % of the outstanding partnership units approve the transaction.

MANAGEMENT FEE

A management fee is a fee to be paid to the sponsor, general partner, or their affiliates for the management, administration, and operation of the partnership.

MASTER LIMITED PARTNERSHIP

A master limited partnership combines the tax benefits of a partnership with liquidity provided by the public exchanges. The MLP must receive at least 90% of its revenue from production, processing, storage, or transportation of natural resources such as oil and gas. An MLP will also qualify if it owns real property designed to produce rental income, or in some cases, if it provides financial management services. Master limited partnerships are required to make quarterly distributions to limited partners in the form of dividends.

MASTER TENANT

A master tenant is often used as part of a Delaware statutory trust where the trust leases the entire property to a master tenant. The master tenant in turn then manages, operates and subleases the property to the ultimate tenants who will occupy the property. By using a master tenant, the owners of the Delaware statutory trust remove themselves from the day-to-day operations of the rental property.

MODIFIED FUNDS FROM OPERATIONS

To determine a limited partnership's modified funds from operations one must first calculate the partnership's funds from operations by adding depreciation, amortization, or depletion allowances back to the earnings of the partnership. Once the appropriate add-backs have been calculated, any capital gains realized on the sale of assets are subtracted to determine funds from operations for the partnership. From this number, funds from operations will be adjusted for the acquisition expenses of the other property, non-recurring charges or impairments, non-recurring gains or losses, adjustments to above or below-market leases or mark-to-market gains or losses on assets

ORGANIZATION AND OFFERING EXPENSES

The organization offering the expenses of a partnership include all expenses incurred in creating and preparing the direct participation program for registration and distribution of partnership interests. These expenses include all forms of compensation paid to underwriters broker-dealers and their affiliates in connection with the sale of partnership interest to investors.

PERSON

The term person refers to any entity that may enter into a legally-binding contract and may transact business in securities markets. The term person includes any of the following:

- Natural person
- Corporation
- Trust
- Government organization
- Partnership
- Joint stock company
- Sole proprietor
- Association
- Unincorporated organization

Those individuals who have passed away, who are deemed to be mentally incompetent or who have not yet reached the age of majority are not deemed to be persons because they may not enter into a legally-binding contract.

PARTICIPANT

A participant in a direct participation program is a purchaser of an interest of beneficial ownership in the direct participation program.

PAYOUT RATIO

The partnership's payout ratio is determined by looking at the distributions made to partners in relationship to the funds from operations. The higher the payout ratio, the greater the percentage of the partnership's funds from operations that are being distributed. Income-oriented programs will have a much higher payout ratio than those that are designed to produce capital appreciation.

PUBLICLY TRADED PARTNERSHIP/PTP

A publicly traded partnership effectively acts in the same capacity as a master limited partnership. However, the publicly traded partnership may be organized as a limited liability company, whereas a master limited partnership is always organized as a limited partnership.

QUALIFIED INSTITUTIONAL BUYER

A qualified institutional buyer or a QIB is an institution that has at least one hundred million dollars in investable assets. A broker-dealer meets the definition of a qualified institutional buyer if it has $10 million in investable assets. Qualified institutional buyers made purchase shares of restricted securities prior to the expiration of the six-month holding period under Rule 144.

QUALIFIED PURCHASER

A qualified purchaser is an individual, family-owned business, or trust with 5 million dollars in investments.

REAL ESTATE INVESTMENT TRUST

A real estate investment trust or REIT is an entity that is organized to manage, operate or finance real estate. The REIT is organized under Internal Revenue Code Subchapter M and allows for the flow through of net investment income to the investors. The REIT may be organized as a trust, a corporation or as an unincorporated entity. Unlike a direct participation program, the REIT does not pass through losses, deductions, or credits

REGISTRATION STATEMENT

An issuer's registration statement, formerly known as an S-1 or as an S-1a is the full disclosure document for the SEC. When an issuer wishes to sell securities to the public, they must file a registration statement with the SEC. The registration statement will be on review with the SEC for a minimum of 20 days; this is known as the cooling off period. During the cooling-off period, sales may not take place. Once the SEC is satisfied with the submission of the registration statement, it will issue an effective date.

SECURITY

As defined by the partnership code of the Internal Revenue Service, a security is any of the following: a share of corporate stock, partnership interest, beneficial ownership interest in a partnership or trust, note, bond, debenture, any evidence of indebtedness, interest rate, currency, equity, notional principal contract, interest in or derivative financial instrument in any security or any currency, or a position in a non security established to hedge a security.

SOLICITATION EXPENSES

Solicitation expenses include any direct marketing expenses incurred by the FINRA member in connection with a DPP rollup transaction. A member's legal fees, phone bills, fact sheets, expenses and direct compensation paid to agents or other members for solicitation all constitute solicitation expenses.

SPONSOR

The sponsor of a direct participation program is any person or entity that directly or indirectly provides management services to the direct participation program. The sponsor may be a general partner or other entity contracted to provide such services to the program or partnership. The sponsor may also be the entity who acquires the property and subsequently forms the program for the distribution of interest in the property to investors.

SPECIFIED ASSETS

As defined by the Internal Revenue Service, specified assets include securities, commodities, real estate held for rental or investment, options and derivatives, cash, cash equivalents, and an interest in a partnership

SUBCHAPTER S CORPORATION

A entity organized as an S corporation allows for the flow through of income to the shareholders. The income distributed to the shareholders will be taxed as ordinary income to the recipient. Interest in an S corporation may be distributed as part of a direct participation program. Ownership in an S corporation is limited to 100 shareholders and the S corporation must be organized as a domestic corporation within that state.

SUBSCRIPTION AGREEMENT

The subscription agreement is the document in which a limited partner or investor irrevocably subscribes to purchase the limited partnership interest, shares, units or participation in the offering, in exchange for a stated capital contribution. As part of the subscription agreement, the subscriber represents that he/she has the business and financial knowledge required to evaluate, understand and absorb the risks of the investment. Additionally, the subscriber is required to represent that they are purchasing the interest for their own investment purposes and that he/she has no need for liquidity. The subscription agreement is also the document where the investor attests to the fact that he / she meets the definition of accredited investor or higher. If the subscription agreement is accepted by the general partner or by an authorized officer of the general partner, the general partner will countersign and accept the subscription agreement. The investor's interest in the partnership, limited liability company, S corporation or other entity will become effective on the closing date.

SUBSTITUTE LIMITED PARTNER

The transfer of an interest in a limited partnership is very limited. Once a limited partner has purchased his/her interest in the partnership, it may not be transferred without the consent of the general partner. Should the partnership allow for the transfer of partnership interests, any successor partner to whom an interest is transferred from the existing partner will become known as a substitute limited partner. The substitute limited partner will have to document to the general partner that he/she understands and can afford the risks associated with the investment.

TENANTS IN COMMON

An entity organized as tenants-in-common is specifically designed as an investment in real estate. Many real estate investors who have purchased real estate as rental properties often find themselves facing large tax liabilities when they go to sell the property. A tax-free 1031 exchange requires the investor to find a property of equal value to invest in to avoid paying capital gains taxes on the property sold. Entities organized as tenants-in-common provide a vehicle for real estate investors to defer taxation by pooling their proceeds from the sale of real estate to purchase a larger investment property. Owners of an entity organized as tenants-in-common own an undivided fractional interest in the entire property or portfolio of properties are held as tenants-in-common.

TRANSACTION COSTS

The transaction costs incurred in connection with a DPP roll-up transaction include the printing and mailing of proxy statements, prospectus and any other written communication required to be prepared in connection with the transaction. Transaction costs also include:

1. Legal fees not associated with the solicitation of votes
2. Advisory fees
3. Appraisal fees
4. Accounting fees
5. Travel costs
6. Independent committee expenses

Any expenses that would normally be incurred by the member are not included in the transaction costs associated with the DPP roll-up transaction.

TRIPLE NET LEASE

With a triple net lease, the tenant pays a pro rata share of property taxes, common area maintenance, and insurance providing the landlord with a "net" rental income. Triple net leases are traditionally commercial leases and are quoted as a base rent, plus a charge for taxes, common common area maintenance, and insurance.

Pretest

1. Jim is a limited partner in steady rentals limited partnership. Jim has made a substantial capital contribution and is concerned that he may be liable for more than his contribution. Which of the following would be excluded when determining Jim's value-at-risk?

   a. His proportional capital contribution in relation to the total assets of the partnership.

   b. An unsecured promissory note for which he is contingently liable.

   c. A secured promissory note for which he is contingently liable.

   d. An unsecured promissory note which only allows the creditor to seek recourse from the partnership itself.

2. A real estate limited partnership is reviewing several opportunities to purchase rental units. During the evaluation process the general partner is looking at the capitalization rate for each property. As it relates to the capitalization rate, which of the following is correct?

   a. The lower the capitalization rate, the higher the expected return.

   b. The lower the capitalization rate, the greater the risk associated with the investment.

   c. The higher the capitalization rate, the lower the expected return.

   d. The higher the capitalization rate, the greater the risk associated with the investment.

3. A general partner of an oil and gas limited partnership receives a 15% ownership stake in the partnership without providing any capital to acquire the stake. Which of the following would best describe the general partner's ownership?

    a. A management fee.

    b. A carried interest.

    c. An overriding royalty.

    d. A royalty interest.

4. Which of the following would best describe cash flow for an oil and gas limited partnership?

    a. Cash from operations minus expenses, minus depreciation.

    b. Cash from operations minus, expenses minus depletion.

    c. Cash from operations minus expenses, prior to deducting depreciation.

    d. Cash from operations minus expenses, prior to deducting depletion.

5. As it relates to the operation of a limited partnership which of the following choices best describes the partnership's closing date?

    a. The date when an an investor's interest in the partnership becomes effective.

    b. The date upon which the operations of the limited partnership will cease.

    c. The date upon which the limited partnership acquires property for the benefit of the partners.

    d. The date upon which the general partner is appointed to act for the benefit of the partnership.

6. Which of the following statements is correct as it relates to the benefit of a Delaware statutory Trust?

    a. It allows an investor to exchange an interest in real property for an interest in another real property on a tax free bases.

    b. It allows an owner of real property to exchange a property for an interest in the trust without being subject to capital gains.

    c. It allows investors to easily exchange the interest in the DST for other investments in real estate.

    d. It allows the beneficiaries to enjoy asset protection but the trustee can be held liable for the obligations of the trust.

7. A dissenting limited partner would best be defined as:

    a. A limited partner who opposes the merger of a partnership with another.

    b. A limited partner who opposes the acquisition of a large property.

    c. A limited partner who has a conflict with the general partner's business practices.

    d. A limited partner who has a conflict with the operation of the partnership.

8. XYZ Mining and ABC Landco have decided the time is right to begin to mine the gold from the ground owned by ABC. ABC and XYZ have decided to pursue the operation together and to share in the management and ownership of the effort. The two companies have decided to form an unincorporated entity to begin operations. Which of the following best describes the entity formed by ABC and XYZ?

    a. A direct participation program.

    b. A limited partnership.

    c. A joint venture.

    d. A general partnership.

9. A large entity has been formed to operate a vast portfolio of commercial real estate. The entity will have its interests listed on the New York Stock Exchange and will provide for favorable tax treatment of distributions and tax benefits. This entity is most likely formed as:

    a. A real estate investment trust.

    b. A master limited partnership.

    c. A direct participation program.

    d. A Delaware statutory Trust.

10. A large well-known mining operator has acquired an interest in a gold producing property with substantial reserves. Upon acquiring the property the entity forms a limited partnership and places the property in the partnership. Partnership interests are then sold to limited partners. Which of the following best describes the role of the mining operator?

    a. General partner.

    b. Master tenant.

    c. Sponsor.

    d. Organizer.

Direct Participation Programs

INTRODUCTION

Direct participation programs (DPPs) and limited partnerships (LPs) are entities that allow income, expenses, gains, losses, and tax benefits to be passed through to the investors. There is generally no active secondary market for these investments, so it's important that investors understand the risks and can afford the risks associated with DPPs and LPs. Series 7 candidates can expect to see several questions on this material on their exam.

LIMITED PARTNERSHIPS

A limited partnership is an entity that allows all of the economic events of the partnership to flow through to the partners. These economic events are:

- Income
- Gains
- Losses
- Tax credits
- Deductions

There are two types of partners in a limited partnership: limited partners and the general partners. The limited partners:

- Put up the investment capital.
- Losses are limited to their investment.
- Receive the benefits from the operation.
- May not exercise management over the operation.
- May vote to change the objective of the partnership.
- May vote to switch or remove the general partner.
- May sue the general partner, if the general partner does not act in the best interest of the partnership.

A limited partner may never exercise any management or control over the limited partnership. Doing so would jeopardize the partner's limited status such that he or she may be considered a general partner.

The general partner is the person or corporation that manages the business and has unlimited liability for the obligations of the partnership business. The general partner may also:

- Buy and sell property for the partnership.
- Receive compensation for managing the partnership.
- Enter into legally binding contracts for the partnership.

The general partner also must maintain a financial interest in the partnership of at least 1%. The general partner may not:

- Commingle funds of the general partner with the funds of the partnership.
- Compete against the partnership.
- Borrow from the partnership.

It is important to note that there are no tax consequences at the partnership level. In order to qualify for the preferential tax treatment, the DPP or LP must avoid at least two of the six characteristics of a corporation. These characteristics are:

- Continuity of life
- Profit motive

- Central management
- Limited liability
- Associates
- Freely transferable interest

Several of the characteristics cannot be avoided, such as associates and a profit motive. The hardest characteristic to avoid is centralized management in fact this cannot be avoided as someone must operate the partnership. The easiest two characteristics of a corporation to avoid are continuity of life and freely transferable interest. The LP can put a termination date on the partnership, and substitute limited partners may not be accepted or may only be accepted once the general partner has agreed.

STRUCTURING AND OFFERING LIMITED PARTNERSHIPS

The foundation of every limited partnership is the partnership agreement. All limited partners must be given a copy of the partnership agreement. The partnership agreement will spell out all of the terms and conditions, as well as the business purpose for the partnership. The powers and limitations of the general partner's authority will be one of the main points detailed in the partnership agreement. Prior to forming a limited partnership, the general partner will have to file a certificate of limited partnership in the state in which the partnership is formed. The certificate will include:

- Name and address of the partnership.
- A description of the partnership's business.
- The life of the partnership.
- Size of the limited partner's investments (if any).
- Conditions for assignment of interest by limited partners.
- Conditions for dissolving the partnership.
- Conditions for admitting new limited partners.
- The projected date for the return of capital, if one is set.

A material change to any of these conditions must be updated on the certificate within 30 days.

Most limited partnerships will be offered to investors through a private placement. All investors who purchase a limited partnership through a private placement must receive a private placement memorandum. Private placements, with very limited exceptions, may only be offered to accredited investors. However, a few limited partnerships will be offered to the public through a standard public offering. All investors who purchase a limited partnership though a public offering must receive a prospectus. If the partnership is sold through a syndicator, the syndicator is responsible for filing the partnership documents. The maximum fee that may be received by the syndicator is limited to 10% of the offering. If a secondary market develops for a partnership, the partnership will be known as a master limited partnership (MLP). All investors wishing to become a limited partner must complete the partnership's subscription agreement. The subscription agreement will include:

- A power of attorney appointing the general partner.
- A statement of the prospective limited partner's net worth.
- A statement regarding the prospective limited partner's income.
- A statement from the prospective limited partner that he or she understands and can afford the risks related to the partnership.

TYPES OF LIMITED PARTNERSHIPS

A limited partnership may be organized for any lawful purpose. Most commonly, limited partnerships are set up to:

- Invest in real estate.
- Invest in oil and gas wells.
- Engage in equipment leasing.

There are several types of real estate partnerships. They include:

- Existing property
- New construction
- Raw land
- Government-assisted housing
- Historic rehabilitation

Type of LP	Risk	Advantages	Disadvantages	Tax Benefits
Existing property (purchase income property)	Low	Immediate, predictable cash flow	Rental problems and repairs	Deductions for mortgage interest and depreciation
New construction (build units for appreciation or rental)	Higher	Potential capital gains, low maintenance	No deduction for current expenses and no promise of rental or sale	Deduction of expenses and depreciation only after completion
Raw land (purchase land for appreciation)	Highest	Only appreciation potential	No tax deductions or income	No tax benefits
Government-assisted housing (low-income housing)	Low	Government rent subsidies and tax credits	High maintenance costs and risk of a change in government programs	Tax credits and any losses on the property
Historic rehabilitation (restore sites for use)	Higher	Tax credits	Financing trouble; no rental history	Tax credits, deductions, and depreciation

There are several types of oil and gas partnerships that an investor may participate in. They are:

- Income programs
- Developmental programs
- Exploratory drilling or wildcatting

Intangible drilling costs are usually 100% deductible in the year they are incurred. Intangible drilling costs (IDC) include:

- Geological surveys
- Wages
- Supplies
- Insurance
- Well casings (Well heads have salvage value. Well casings may or may not have salvage value.)

Investors in oil and gas programs will be given a depletion allowance for the decreasing reserves.

Type of LP	Risk	Advantages	Disadvantages	Tax Benefits
Income (buys existing wells)	Low	Immediate, predictable cash flow	Reserves run out or prices fall	Depletion allowance
Developmental (drills near proven reserves)	Higher	Higher probability to find reserves than wildcatting	Not many fields ever produce	Immediate deductions for IDCs
Exploratory/wildcatting (drilling to find new reserves)	Highest	Huge payoff if significant reserves are found	Not many fields ever produce	Immediate deductions for a high level of IDCs

OIL AND GAS SHARING ARRANGEMENTS

Once the oil or gas partnership has been formed and has begun operating, the limited partners and the general partner will share in the income and tax benefits generated by the partnership according to the sharing arrangement laid out in the partnership agreement. There are several types of sharing arrangements. They are:

- Functional allocation
- Reversionary working interest
- Disproportionate working interest
- Net operation profits
- Carried interest
- Overriding royalty interest

Functional allocation: This is the most common sharing arrangement. The limited partners receive the deductions for the IDC and the general partner receives property write-offs. The revenue is shared between the limited and general partners.

Reversionary working interest: The limited partners bear all of the costs of the program. The general partner will receive no payments until the limited partners have gotten their investment back.

Disproportionate working interest: The general partner receives a large portion of the revenue but only bears a small portion of the costs.

Net operating profits: The limited partners bear all of the cost of the partnership. The general partner bears no costs but is entitled to a percentage of the net profits. This arrangement is only available for partnerships sold through a private placement.

Carried interest: The limited partners receive the IDC and the immediate write-offs. The general partner will share in the tangible drilling costs and will receive property depreciation benefits.

Overriding royalty interest: The holder of an overriding royalty interest has no partnership risks but receives a royalty from the partnership.

EQUIPMENT LEASING PROGRAMS

Equipment leasing programs are formed to purchase equipment with the intention of leasing it to a corporation. The program generates income from the lease payments received from the corporation. Investors will receive tax benefits from operating expenses, depreciation of equipment, and any interest expenses paid by the program.

TAX REPORTING FOR DIRECT PARTICIPATION PROGRAMS

Direct participation programs are organized as either limited partnerships or as subchapter S corporations. These entities allow for the flow-through of income and losses, and the DPP has no tax consequences. The DPP will only report the results of its operation to the IRS. The responsibility for paying any taxes due rests with the partners or shareholders. DPPs allow the losses to flow through to the investors. Losses from DPPs can only be used to offset the investor's passive income. Investors may not use the losses to shelter or offset the ordinary income. Investors should not purchase DPPs simply for the tax benefits; they should purchase them to earn a return. Any DPP that is found to have been formed simply to create tax benefits may subject the investors to strict penalties. Investors could owe back taxes, fines, or be prosecuted for fraud.

LIMITED PARTNERSHIP ANALYSIS

Before investing in a limited partnership, investors should analyze the key features of the partnership to ensure that the partnership's objectives meet their investment objectives. Investors should review:

- The program's economic viability.
- Tax considerations.
- Management's ability.
- Lack of liquidity.
- Time horizon.
- Whether it is a blind pool or a specified program.
- Internal rate of return (IRR) the IRR is used to measure the estimated present value of the future income and asset value. The IRR will allow the investor to measure DPP programs against each other.

A blind pool is a partnership where less than 75% of the assets that the partnership is going to acquire have been identified. In a specified program, more than 75% of the assets that the partnership is going to acquire have been identified.

A partnership's internal rate of return is the discounted present value of its projected future cash flow.

TAX DEDUCTIONS VS. TAX CREDITS

Tax deductions that are generated by partnerships are used to lower the investor's taxable income. A tax credit results in a dollar-for-dollar reduction in the amount of taxes due from the investor.

OTHER TAX CONSIDERATIONS

If a limited partnership has used up all of its deductions and has a gain on the sale of a depreciated asset, the sale above the asset's depreciated cost basis may subject the limited partners to a taxable recapture. This is known as the crossover point. The crossover point is also the time when the partnership begins to generate taxable income to its partners. There are two types of loans that a partnership may take out: nonrecourse loans and recourse loans. With a nonrecourse loan, if the partnership defaults the lender has no recourse to the limited partners. With a recourse loan, in the event of the partnership's default the lender can go after the limited partners for payment. A recourse loan can increase the investor's cost base. Partners must monitor their cost base and adjust it for:

- Cash or property contributions to the partnership.
- Recourse loans.
- Any cash or property received from the partnership.

Investors are responsible for any gain on the sale of their partnership interest in excess of their cost basis.

DISSOLVING A PARTNERSHIP

A partnership will terminate on the date set forth in a partnership agreement, unless earlier terminated. A partnership may dissolve if a majority of the limited partners vote for its dissolution. If the partnership terminates its activities, the general partner must cancel the certificate of limited partnership and liquidate the partnership assets. The priority of payment will be as follows:

- Secured lenders.
- General creditors.
- Limited partners' profits first, then return of investment.
- General partner for fees first, then profits, then return of capital.

Pretest

DIRECT PARTICIPATION PROGRAMS

1. A type of expense and profit sharing arrangement where the limited partners absorb all of the expenses and the general partner does not receive payment until the limited partners have recovered their costs is known as:

    a. disproportionate sharing.

    b. net operating profit interest.

    c. reversionary working interest.

    d. overriding royalty.

2. A customer seeking tax advantages from her investment in a DPP would most likely invest in:

    a. raw land real estate programs.

    b. developmental oil and gas programs.

    c. rental properties.

    d. historic rehabilitation programs.

3. While investing in a DPP, an asset is sold at a price above its depreciated basis and all tax credits have been used up. This is known as which of the following?

    a. Inversion

    b. Coaxial

    c. Crossover

    d. Conversion

4. A limited partner may do all of the following, EXCEPT:

    a. switch the general partner.

    b. vote to add a new general partner.

    c. advise the general partner.

    d. sue the general partner.

5. A participant in a limited partnership that has no partnership risk but receives payments is said to have a(n):

    a. reversionary interest.

    b. credit secured interest.

    c. overriding royalty interest.

    d. net income interest.

6. Which one of the following could result in additional payments being required by a limited partner?

    a. A recourse loan.

    b. A limited partnership may never require the limited partners to make additional payments.

    c. Additional cash requirements.

    d. A nonrecourse loan.

7. Your real estate limited partnership has taken out a recourse loan as an investor. Which of the following are true in this case?

     I. You can't be held liable.

    II. You can be held liable.

    III. It can't increase your cost basis.

    IV. It can increase your cost basis.

    a. I and III

    b. I only

    c. II and IV

    d. I and II

8. List the following in order from the least important to the most important factors when considering investing in a DPP.

    I. Tax considerations

    II. Profitability

    III. Liquidity

    IV. Safety

    a. III, II, I, IV

    b. III, IV, I, II

    c. II, I, IV, III

    d. IV, II, III, I

9. In a DPP, all of the following may be depreciated, EXCEPT:

    a. buildings.

    b. machinery.

    c. equipment.

    d. raw land.

10. When investing in a wildcat oil and gas program, most of the tax credits are generated by:

    a. depletion.

    b. depreciation.

    c. intangible drilling costs.

    d. management expenses.

Additional Types of DPPs

INTRODUCTION

In this chapter, we're going to take a deeper look at real estate and oil and gas partnerships. We will also review a number of the different types of direct participation investments that go beyond the oil and gas and real estate programs. The Series 22 exam will cover a number of direct participation programs, including those designed to invest in agricultural interest, livestock, entertainment, equipment leasing, commodity pools, asset backed securities, structured finance and venture capital.

UNDERSTANDING DIRECT PARTICIPATION PROGRAMS

In order to understand the performance risks and opportunities of various direct participation programs, it's important to have an in-depth understanding of what the program is designed to do. Once a representative understands how the program is designed and the assets the program will invest in, a representative will be in a much better place to make a suitable recommendation to his/her clients. If a representative does not understand the performance risks and operational aspects of a direct participation program, the representative should not recommend the program. In addition to understanding the specific risks and opportunities in a direct participation program, a representative must understand the various stages in the program itself. Virtually all direct participation programs have three distinct stages. The three distinct stages of direct participation programs are:

1. The organization and offering stage
2. The operating stage
3. The liquidation stage

During the organization and offering stage, the sponsor of the program is establishing the legal structure and required documents for the program. Once the legal structure has been selected whether a limited partnership or other entity, the sponsor files required papers with the state and or the SEC. During this time, the sponsor prepares the offering documents to be presented to investors. Contingent upon the type of offering, the offering documents to be prepared may include a prospectus, a private placement memorandum, or other document. During this time, the sponsor prepares the required risk disclosure documents, subscription agreements, and if desired, enters into an underwriting agreement with broker-dealers to offer the interests to investors. Once the registration (if required) is effective, disclosure and purchase documents have been prepared, the program then sells interest to suitable purchasers.

During the operating stage of the program, assets are acquired, business endeavors undertaken, and the business is managed as set forth in the business objectives of the direct participation program. During the operating stage of the program, the management expertise of the sponsor as well as the business environment often dictate if the program will be profitable or will suffer losses. The operating stage of the program is for a finite time as detailed in the offering documents. At the end of this time, the program will cease operations. At the attainment of the partnership's goals or upon a set date, the partnership will enter the liquidation stage. During the liquidation stage, the assets of the partnership are sold, liabilities are paid and final distributions to the partners are made. A partnership could also enter into the liquidation stage if the partnership agreement allows for a voting process by which the partners may elect to liquidate or terminate the partnership's business operations.

AGRICULTURAL PROGRAMS

Agricultural products provide everything from the food we eat to the wood we use to build our houses. Row crops grow staple commodities like corn, wheat, oats, barley and soybeans. These commodities are then refined and are used as key ingredients in much of the food we eat. Direct participation programs designed to invest in row crops tend to provide a relatively predictable rate of return when measured against other types of agricultural programs. These programs would be most suitable for investors seeking an income stream generated by the sale of the cash crops. For successful programs, the returns are generally in the 5 to 10% range on an annualized basis. Agricultural programs that invest in row crops, produce a perishable commodity dependent upon the crop year. The crop year is from the harvest of the current year to the harvest of the following year. Domestically, virtually all of the row crops are planted and harvested at the same time each year. Because the entire year's supply comes to market at the same time, the increased supply tends to depress prices. The crop year for corn is from September 1st until August 31st of the following year. This means that every year, virtually all farmers are going to be selling corn during the month of September. Should the growing conditions produce significant crops, prices may be depressed to the point where the partnership has no choice but to sell the row crop at a loss. Alternatively, when growing conditions are poor and the crop production is low, prices may be substantially higher and allow the partnership to realize a significant return. Some partnerships may use futures or options to hedge the sale price of the crop. Any hedging strategy employed by the partnership will be disclosed in the partnership agreement. In addition to the price risk associated with participating in a row crop agricultural program, other risks include include:

1. Poor weather conditions such as drought

2. Infestation

3. Irrigation issues

4. Poor soil quality

5. Spoilage

6. Overpaying for land

Direct participation programs that are designed to invest in farmland could be geared to those investors who are seeking income or capital appreciation over time. Farmland direct participation programs will often be formed to acquire large plots of farmland with the intention of leasing sections of the land to one or more farmers. The lease payments from the farmers provide a steady stream of income to the partnership. Additionally, the partnership may be able to realize capital gains by selling the farmland to the farmer or to another interested party at an appreciated price. Leasing the farmland from the partnership may allow a farmer to expand or relocate a current farming operation. The lease payments to be received by the partnership will be subject to the credit risk and business risk of the farmer tenant. Should the farmer not be able to make their lease payments on the land, the partnership may sustain significant losses in addition to the lost income.

Timber is created from live trees, once the tree has been cut down the raw product is known as timber. The term timber is used to classify the wood at any point between the time when the tree is cut down and the time the timber is delivered to the lumber mill. The lumber mill will then saw or cut the raw timber into lumber. The lumber is the finished wood products that are used to build the homes we live in and the buildings we work in. Direct participation programs designed to invest in timberland offer several advantages over other types of agricultural programs. Because a tree is not a perishable commodity, the program has a large amount of flexibility as to when to harvest the trees and sell the timber. This flexibility allows the partnership to harvest and sell the timber during periods when prices are the most favorable. Being able to time the market allows the partnership to avoid selling timber at depressed prices. Direct participation programs designed to purchase timber are suitable for investors who are seeking capital appreciation with no need for current income. The returns generated by a direct participation program investing in timberland are the result of:

1.   Biological tree growth
2.   Increase in tree value
3.   Increase in land value

The actual annual growth rate of the trees is estimated to be as much as 8% per year. As the tree grows, the volume of the timber increases. Investors in timberland see the volume of timber grow year-over-year and this is the primary driver of capital appreciation.

The value of timber tends to increase as time passes. Timber has been viewed as an excellent hedge against inflation. The price of timber tends to increase before an increase in the Consumer Price Index. Timber prices are therefore seen as a leading indicator to inflation and the increase in timber prices tends to outpace the increase in inflation (the Consumer Price Index).

The price of timberland also tends to increase as time passes. The appreciation of land prices will also add to the capital appreciation for the partnership. The price appreciation of the land will tend to be driven by the value of timber.

Investors who purchase interests in timber limited partnership should have a long time horizon. It may take many years for the trees to grow to the point where they may be harvested and for the partners to realize a return on their investment. Much like a zero coupon bond that pays no semi-annual interest and appreciates to par at maturity, trees grow on the land producing no income and will only produce a return when the trees mature. The general partner of a timberland program may be a forest management company or may secure the services of a forest management company. The forest management company will help ensure the partnership operates using the best practices and in line with state forestry regulations. The type of services to be provided will depend on the objectives of the partnership. Some of those services include:

1. Land appraisal
2. Timber appraisal
3. Timber management
4. Harvesting and selling
5. Reforesting

Purchasing and selling timberland contains a significant amount of risk. Overpaying for land when the partnership is established could result in the partnership providing substandard returns or even suffering losses. During the termination stage when a partnership may be seeking to sell the timberland, it's important to ensure the partnership receives a fair price. A forest management company can help ensure that the partnership purchases and sells timberland at fair and appropriate prices. The forest management company can also value the timber, ensure that the land is managed appropriately to yield the greatest amount of timber, oversee the harvest and selling process and reforesting the land so new timber grows.

Expenses incurred by a timber partnership include fees to the forest management company, wages, fuel, fertilizer, insurance, repairs to equipment and property taxes. These intangible costs will be passed through to investors creating passive losses.

CATTLE AND LIVESTOCK PROGRAMS

Cattle ranching and growing livestock is a complicated business that can take many forms. For example, a rancher could be in the business of breeding feeder-cattle, growing live cattle, running a feedlot or could be managing a herd of dairy cows. Each of these endeavors has its own risks, rewards and capital requirements. Feeder-cattle breeding is the process of managing a herd of cattle so that they can give birth. These offspring once born and reared, become known as feeder-cattle. The feeder-cattle are then sold to ranchers who will, as the name implies, feed the cattle so that the cattle grow into live cattle. Live cattle are mature full-grown cattle that are ready to go to market. Once live cattle have gone to market, they are sold to meat packers and the meat packers process the cattle and sell the meat to grocery stores and restaurants across the country. A feedlot operator runs a large commercial feedlot which is primarily a storage area for the cattle during the time they are being fed. The feedlot operator usually does not have an interest in the cattle that are being raised on their lot. The feedlot operator merely charges a fee to the cattle owners who place their cattle on the feedlot to be grown into live cattle. The feedlot operator will weigh the cattle, vaccinate the cattle, tag the cattle, and segregate the cattle. The feedlot operator will blend the feed for the cattle depending on their particular requirements and deliver feed to the pens where the cattle are kept. The cattle will arrive on the feedlot generally weighing between 300 and 700 lbs and will remain on the lot until they reach a full grown weight of approximately 1,100 lb. To have an understanding of the costs involved with feeding cattle, it takes approximately 6 to 10 pounds of feed to add 1 pound to the weight of the animal. The cattle will average a weight gain of approximately 2-3 pounds per day for each day the animal is on the feedlot. This means that each head of cattle are fed up to 30 pounds of feed per day. Due to the volatile nature of cattle prices, cattle feeding programs offered to the public must meet specific requirements. Some of the requirements are as follows:

1. The program must ensure that the sponsor of the program is adequately capitalized to meet the requirements of the cattle feeding program.

2. At least one principal of the sponsor must have at least five years of experience in cattle feeding including buying, selling, feeding and maintenance. Three of these five years of experience must be as a feedlot operator managing a lot with a capacity of more than 1,000 head of cattle.

3. The program must have a uniform method for detailing how the specific problems associated with cattle feeding will be managed.

4. The program must provide a uniform plan of business that is fair and reasonable.

5. The program must have fair and equitable plans for distribution and reinvestment of proceeds.

6. The program must be for a specific time of not less than three but no more than 10 years.

7. The sponsor must provide a detailed three-year track record detailing its investment return and disclosing its profit and loss for each head along with the average weight, cost and sex of each head.

FEEDLOT SPONSORS

Sponsors of cattle feeding programs must maintain a minimum participation in the interest of the program. The sponsor of the program must maintain a participation of $100,000 for program offerings that are up to $1 million or more. For programs of less than $1 million, the sponsor must maintain a participation rate of at least 10%. For every $35,000 in net equity possessed by the sponsor, the sponsor may reduce their required participation in the program by 10%. Alternatively, any person or company who owns 50% or more of the voting control of the sponsor may purchase the required participation in the program in lieu of the sponsor to meet the program participation requirements.

Certain feedlot programs allow the sponsor to engage in dealings with affiliates. An affiliate is a person who is controlled directly or indirectly by the sponsor, or who directly or indirectly controls the sponsor. Affiliated transactions or dealings are classified as those where feed is purchased directly or indirectly from the sponsor or an affiliate, or where cattle are fed on a feedlot owned by the sponsor or affiliate. The sale of cattle to the sponsor or an affiliate directly or indirectly is strictly prohibited. Additionally, the program may not purchase cattle directly or indirectly from the sponsor or an affiliate. The feedlot selected by the sponsor must have a minimum capacity of 5,000 and the sponsor must have ready access to feedlots with a capacity of 20,000 or more. It's important to note that the sale of proprietary feed and supplements by an affiliate to independent feedlots will not be seen as affiliate dealing so long as the prices paid are no greater than those prices realized in transactions with independent unrelated parties.

Certain guidelines are in place regarding sponsor compensation for feedlot programs. If the program sponsor is to receive the maximum first-year fee of 12 ½ % of gross receipts, the program sponsor is required to bear the cost of organization and offering expenses. If the organization and offering expenses are to be borne by the program, the total fee including the management fee must not exceed 12 ½ % of the gross receipts.

The amount of compensation that may be charged by the sponsor is impacted when the sponsor is engaged in affiliate dealings. After the first year for programs where the sponsor does not engage in affiliate dealings, the sponsor may charge a monthly management fee of 5/8%. If the sponsor engages in transactions with affiliates, the markups charged on feed are limited to 20%. If the sponsor also charges a per-head handling charge on cattle, the total of the handling and markup charges for feed are limited to 20%. Should a program sponsor who engages in affiliate dealings wish to change the markup policy on feed or the handling charge on cattle, the program sponsor may only do it annually provided that 60 days' prior written notice has been given to investors. In addition to a management fee for sponsors who do not engage in affiliate dealings or in addition to the markups charged by sponsors who do engage in affiliate dealings, the sponsor is allowed to participate in the profits of the program. Once investors have received the return of 100% of their investment, the sponsor may receive a maximum of 25% of the program's profits. The remaining 75% of the profits must be distributed to investors. As it relates to the expenses of the program, the sponsor is required to pay the operating, administrative and overhead expenses. Expenses such as interest, legal, accounting, branding, and feed costs will be charged to the program. The veterinary care including medicines required by the program may be allocated to either the sponsor, the investors or shared as detailed in the offering documents.

Program sponsors are required to provide and maintain reports on behalf of the program. Every program sponsor is required to prepare and deliver an annual audited financial report detailing the:

1. Income
2. Expenses
3. Assets
4. Liabilities
5. Profit and loss

The program sponsor is also required to provide periodic reports to investors containing the current value of the investors' interest in the program and the progress of the program. The frequency of these reports will be provided to investors in line with the reporting procedures detailed in the offering documents.

MORTALITY INSURANCE AND HEDGING

Disease and death are known risks when dealing in livestock. An animal could get injured, stricken with a disease or may simply just die. Because of the special risks associated with raising livestock, program sponsors may elect to purchase mortality insurance on the herd. Unless specifically required by the program, the maintenance of mortality insurance is at the discretion of the sponsor. However, program sponsors must insure against a mortality loss rate of greater than 4%, for the duration of the program. This insurance is specifically required to be provided by the sponsor, and must be provided at no cost to program participants. Further, the program sponsor must indemnify investors against any loss resulting from employee negligence or misconduct. Prices in the cattle and grain markets are especially volatile and pose numerous risks to investors. Program sponsors may use futures to hedge the input costs of grain and feeder-cattle and to hedge the price risk on the sale of live cattle. To hedge against rising input costs, sponsors may elect to purchase or go-long grain futures contracts or purchase or go-long feeder cattle contracts. To hedge against a price decline on the sale of live cattle, the sponsor would sell or go short live cattle contracts. The use of futures contracts to hedge business risk will be detailed in the programs offering documents. It is important to note that the sponsor may never trade futures contracts to speculate on prices.

 TAKENOTE!

Most feeder-cattle programs employ and involve levering program contributions in an effort to maximize returns. However, no program may exceed a leverage ratio greater than 4:1.

CASE STUDY

Kevin Cattlegrower has a ranch in Colorado. Kevin is now seeking to dramatically expand his ranch and acquire the adjacent property to increase the size of his herd. The acquisition of the land, the cost of the feeder-cattle, the additional ranch hands and equipment are estimated to cost Kevin $5 million. Kevin is willing to lay out the money for the land, but he wants to spread the risk associated with the cattle ranching endeavor with other investors. Once Kevin acquires the adjacent property for $1.5 million, Kevin puts together a direct participation program to raise the remaining $3.5 million to expand the ranching operation. Kevin forms KC Cattle Limited Partnership. Kevin will act as the general partner and will manage the ranch. He then raises the money through the sale of limited partnership interests to investors and ranchers Kevin is familiar with. Now that KC Cattle LP has been formed and the money has been raised, Kevin acquires the feeder-cattle and has the cattle delivered to the new ranch property. While the feeder cattle are being raised, the expenses can be passed through to the limited partners. These costs include feed for the cattle, veterinary care and other expenses detailed above. It's interesting to note that all of the feed required to raise the cattle could be purchased upfront and the cost could be used to pass through those expenses to limited partners at the time payment is made. Kevin being a well-seasoned rancher acting on behalf of KC Cattle LP, does an excellent job of raising a world-class herd ready to go to market. Once the cattle are sold, the proceeds could be distributed to the limited partners or reinvested in new feeder-cattle. The limited partnership agreement would detail how the proceeds would be reinvested or distributed to the limited partners.

EXAMPLE:

If Kevin were to pay an average cost of $35 per pound for feeder cattle with an average weight of 550 lb, each head of feeder cattle would cost $192.50. Kevin has calculated that the average cost to grow the cattle into live cattle is $25 per 100 pounds. With the average weight of the live cattle sold being 1,100 lb, the cost to grow the cattle would be $137.50 each. Therefore, the total cost of each live head of cattle would be $330. Later, when the cattle are put up for auction, the average sale price for live cattle is $34 per 100 pounds. As the average weight of each head is 1,100 pounds, the effective sale price for each head is $374. This would provide Kevin and his partners with a profit of $44 per head. Alternatively, if the average selling price for live cattle was $28 per 100 lb the effective selling price per head would be $308 and Kevin and his partners would suffer a loss of $22 per head.

 TAKENOTE!

The test could refer to the process of placing feeder-cattle on a feedlot as a cattle feeding operation or as a cattle growing operation.

DAIRY FARMING

Dairy farms create and sell the milk created from a herd of dairy cows. A dairy cow is a female cow that has given birth. There are a variety of different breeds of cows that can be used on a dairy farm, each have a slightly different milk production. Dairy farming has eight distinct stages, those stages are:

Stage 1 - Rearing. During this stage, the dairy herd largely spend their time eating grass and wandering around on the farm. Or if the dairy farm is operating a confined animal feeding operation, the herd will be kept indoors and fed grain or hay.

Stage 2 - Harvesting. During this stage the cows are milked twice a day. The herd is escorted up to the milking machines and the milk is harvested from the cow. The milking process typically takes approximately five minutes per cow and most dairy farms have machines with capacity to do 20 or more cows simultaneously

Stage 3 - Storing. Once the milk has been harvested from the cow, it is placed in storage silos or vats. The milk is stored for 48 hours at 39 degrees Fahrenheit or colder. The silos also agitate the milk to ensure that the milk fat does not separate from the milk.

Stage 4 - Transportation. Special tanker trucks designed to carry milk collect the milk from the farm every 24 to 48 hours. Prior to pick up, the milk is tested by the driver who is a certified milk grader to ensure quality. Once the milk has been transferred to the tanker, it is brought to factory storage facilities to be stored in refrigerated silos prior to being sent for processing.

Stage 5 - Lab testing. Samples of the milk are tested for antibiotics, temperature, and quality prior to the milk entering the processing facility.

Stage 6 - Processing. During this phase, the raw milk is pasteurized and homogenized and turned into various grades of milk (whole milk, low-fat milk, and skim milk).

Stage 7 - Packaging. Once the milk has been pasteurized and homogenized and turned into various grades of milk, it travels through the packaging machines and is dispensed into paper cartons or plastic jugs. Each container has an expiration date printed on it.

Stage 8 - Selling. The packaged milk is stored in large refrigerated rooms until the milk is delivered to stores to be sold to consumers.

With these three different ranching programs, there are different investment objectives. The cattle breeder who produces feeder-cattle is hoping to sell the young cattle at a price That exceeds their cost to maintain their breeding herd and realize a profit. The cattle grower who purchases the feeder-cattle is hoping that they can maintain and grow the herd until they are ready to go to market and that the price of the live cattle will be sufficient enough to provide a profit. A dairy farmer, on the other hand, is seeking to enjoy a consistent stream of income from the production of milk from the dairy herd. All types of ranching and dairy farming have ongoing costs in the form of:

1.   Equipment

2.   Price of the animal

3.   Feed for the animals

4.   Veterinary care

5.   Ranch hands

6.   Fuel

7.   Utilities

8.   Repairs and maintenance

9.   Property taxes, mortgages, rent

10. Interest on borrowed funds

11. Insurance

To ensure that you are familiar with these terms and to avoid confusion on your exam, we will define the different types of cattle. Some of the terms you're likely to see include:

- A heifer is a female cow younger than 3 years old that has not given birth.
- A dairy cow is a female cow that has given birth.
- A bull is a male cow.
- A steer is a male cow that has been castrated.
- A Holstein cow is a dairy cow known to produce the highest level of milk.
- A calf is a baby cow.

We include these terms not because they are testable concepts, but because the terms will appear on the test. The fact that the test includes these terms in a question doesn't take away from the focus of the question. The focus of the question has to do with the investment objective of the cattle or dairy farming program, it's risks and rewards or the suitability for the investor.

ENTERTAINMENT PROGRAMS

Investing in movies and music can be particularly exciting for investors who have the ability to afford the risks. Few industries offer the glamour of Hollywood or the excitement of a hit record. However, the realities of the entertainment industry are that most movies never make it to the big screen and most albums never make it onto the charts. With this in mind, investing in an entertainment program still may be able to produce a reasonable return for investors with risk capital. Entertainment programs may be established as direct participation programs and distributed through a private placement via a private placement memorandum. Most entertainment programs will be established as limited partnerships with the limited partners contributing the capital and the general partner managing the production of the film or album. In the case of a film program, the capital obtained from the partners may be used to meet a variety of production goals including:

1. The hiring of talent including actors, producers, directors, extras, makeup artists and crew.

2. Script acquisition and editing.

3. The acquisition of equipment such as cameras, film, sets, props and transportation.

4. Location scouting and rental expenses.

5. Production and editing costs.

6. Marketing and distribution expenses.

There are five distinct stages in film development, each having their own unique requirements and risks. The five stages are:

1. **Film development** - During the development-stage, the script is being written, the production being planned, a preliminary budget is established, locations are scouted and actors cast.

2. **Pre-production** - During pre-production, scripts are amended, shooting schedules are set, the crew is employed, sets are built and costumes are made.

3. **Production** - The production is the shortest of the five stages of film production and is the stage which requires the most capital. During the production stage the film is shot.

4. **Post production** - During post-production, the film is edited, the sound is mixed, visual effects are added, titles are created and the soundtrack composed.

5. **Distribution** - The distribution stage is when the partnership seeks to realize a return on its investment. The film may be released in theaters, distributed through a streaming service, sold to a TV network or released straight to DVD.

If the entertainment program is one that is designed to invest in the music industry, the partner's contributions would pay for expenses such as:

1. The acquisition of equipment such as microphones, amplifiers and instruments.

2. The hiring of talent including producers, engineers, backup singers, musicians and crew.

3. Rental of recording studio.

4. Production and editing costs.

5. Marketing and distribution expenses.

For entertainment programs that are organized to develop a film or music project, all of the capital uses listed above will go to create deductions for the limited partners. Oftentimes the partnership's capital is fully consumed and the distribution of the film or album do not generate enough revenue to provide a return to the partners. These programs by their very nature are extremely speculative. As with all programs, the track record of the general partner is extremely important when evaluating the merits of the investment. If a general partner has a successful track record in either the film or music industry, he/she may be able to secure a pre-sale arrangement or other distribution agreement prior to the completion of the film or album. A pre-sale arrangement is one where a distributor pays for the right to distribute a film that has not yet been produced. The general partner would provide the distributor with a copy of the script and the names of the actors attached to the project. Based on the quality of the script and the bankability of the stars, a movie distributor may be willing to pay a significant sum for the right to distribute the finished film.

In the case of a music program, the general partner will seek to obtain a distribution agreement with a record label. A record label like a movie distributor may be willing to pay an upfront fee for the right to distribute the album that is currently in production. The general partner will provide the record label with a demo of the recordings along with relevant information on the artist. Once again, based on the track record of the general partner, the bankability of the artist and the quality of the music, the record label may be willing to pay a significant sum to secure the distribution rights for the album. The offering documents for the partnership should disclose the general partner's track record, detailed information relating to the film or album, and the background of the actors, artists, producers or directors attached to the production. A detailed description of the intended method of distribution should also be included along with any intention to secure a distribution deal with a third party.

A limited partnership that invests in the entertainment industry could also be established to purchase existing titles in order to earn royalty, residual or licensing income from a portfolio of entertainment titles. In this type of program, the partnership will seek to acquire the rights to films or songs in order to generate income for the partners. A portfolio of existing titles such as films, TV shows or music catalogs will have an earnings track record that the partnership can use to predict the future income to be generated by those titles. The cost to acquire these portfolios can be quite significant and is based upon the level of income produced by the titles. While the cost to acquire these assets is significant, this type of income producing program contains significantly less risk than a program designed to produce a movie or an album that may not produce a significant amount of revenue or become popular.

EQUIPMENT LEASING PROGRAMS

Equipment leasing programs are direct participation programs that are designed to acquire and own and either lease or operate heavy equipment. The sponsor of an equipment leasing program is any person or entity that is directly or indirectly in charge of organizing the direct participation program or any part thereof. The sponsor of the program also includes any person or entity that manages or participates in the management of the program. Specifically excluded from the definition of a sponsor for an equipment leasing program is any person or entity who solely acts as an independent equipment manager that is paid a fee for their management of the equipment. Also excluded from the definition of a sponsor are wholly independent third-party such as accountants, attorneys and underwriters who provide services in connection with the sale of partnership interests. In order to qualify as a sponsor of an equipment leasing program, the sponsor or their chief operating officers must have a minimum of three years of equipment leasing experience. This experience must demonstrate that they have the experience in equipment that is identical to the equipment to be acquired by the partnership. If the sponsor is liable for the debts of the program, the sponsor is required to meet a minimum net worth standard. The sponsor must have a minimum net worth equal to the greater of $50,000 or an amount that is at least equal to 5% of the value of all the direct participation offerings sold in the preceding 12 months, plus 5% of any partnership interests currently being offered up to a maximum requirement of $1 million. In the case where the sponsor is deemed to be an individual, the net worth requirement is exclusive of the home, automobile and furnishings. Once the equipment has been acquired and placed into operation, the value of the equipment must be reduced over time through depreciation. Depreciation is a non-cash charge that reduces the value of the asset on the program's balance sheet. Depreciation is an accounting method used to reflect the fact that equipment does not last forever. When the equipment leasing program is calculating its net worth, the program may add the assets' accumulated depreciation back to the value of the equipment on its balance sheet, so long as the depreciation added back to the value of the equipment does not cause the value of the equipment (as reflected in the program's net worth) to exceed the fair market value of the equipment. The ability of the partnership to add the depreciation cost to the value of the asset, allows the partnership to use the estimated current value or estimated fair market value of the equipment when calculating its net worth.

SPONSOR COMPENSATION

The compensation to be paid to the sponsor during the organization and offering stage is not subject to any maximum charge. The expenses charged to the program must be fair and reasonable in line with the costs of formation and services provided by the sponsor and distribution partners for program interests. Generally up to 15% of the gross offering proceeds may be allowed to go towards sponsor compensation during the organization and stage.

During the operational stage, there are several methods available when calculating the compensation for a sponsor in an equipment leasing program. In order to determine the maximum amount of compensation for a sponsor, one must take into consideration the sponsor's investment in the equipment owned by the program. All sponsors are required to maintain a minimum investment in the cost of the equipment owned or acquired by the partnership. The cost of the equipment is defined as the amount of the original investment in the equipment to purchase, manufacture or repair. Included in the cost of the equipment are interest costs, taxes and any funds set aside as working capital reserves up to a maximum of 3%. These working capital reserves are set aside for the operation and maintenance of the program's equipment. The acquisition of equipment often includes front-end fees in the form of leasing fees, acquisition fees and other similar fees to be paid to unaffiliated parties. These front-end fees paid to unaffiliated third parties may be included in the cost of the equipment. However, specifically excluded from the definition of the cost of the equipment are front-end fees paid to the sponsor or affiliated parties and working capital reserves in excess of 3%. While working capital reserves of up to 3% are allowed to be included in the cost of the equipment, working capital reserves of 1% are deemed to be adequate. The sponsor is required to maintain a minimum investment in the cost of the equipment equal to the greater of:

1. 80% of the original investment contributed by the limited partners. This 80% requirement will be reduced by 5/8 of 1% for every 1% borrowed to acquire the equipment provided that such loan is secured by the equipment.

Or;

2.   75% of the original investment

EXAMPLE

Capital contribution	80% investment	Loan-to-value	Required percentage	Required investment
$4,000,000	$3,200,000	0	80%	$3,200,000
$4,000,000	$3,200,000	25%	78.4375% (80-1.5625)	$3,137,500
$4,000,000	$3,200,000	50%	76.875% (80 -3.135)	$3,075,000
$4,000,000	$3,200,000	80%	75% (80-5)	$3,000,000
$4,000,000	$3,200,000	90%	*75% (80-.5625= 74.375)	$3,000,000

* in the final example when the reduction of 5/8 % is taken from the 80% requirement, the result is less than 75% of the total capital contribution. Since the required investment is the greater of the two calculations, a 75% investment is required.

COMMODITY POOLS

A commodity pool is an entity that is organized to invest in commodity futures contracts and other assets by pooling investor capital in one single account. A commodity pool is generally run by an entity that is known as a commodity pool operator. A commodity pool operator (CPO) is an organization which invests money contributed by a group of participants to a single account for the purpose of investing the money in futures contracts, options on futures, retail off-exchange forex contracts or swaps, or to invest in another commodity pool. If the CPO operates more than one commodity pool, each pool must be operated separately. Customer contributions to the pool must be made out in the name of the specific commodity pool. Investors in the commodity pool will own an interest in the specific pool. Registration as a CPO is required for any CPO who:

- Manages a pool or a group of pools with more than $400,000 in total assets in all pools.

Or;

- Manages a pool with more than 15 investors, excluding the operator of the pool and their immediate family.

CASE STUDY

XYZ CPO has two pools, one that invests in metals and one that invests in agricultural products. Each pool has $350,000 invested in it by six investors. XYZ as the operator must register as a CPO because the total amount invested in the two pools is $700,000 and is greater than the $400,000 threshold. Operators are exempt from registering as a CPO if the total amount invested in all pools is less than $400,000 and the total number of investors in any one pool does not exceed 15 investors. Operators of commodity investment clubs are also exempt from registration as a CPO so long as:

- The operator does not receive compensation for operating the club.
- The operator manages only one commodity pool at any one time.
- The operator does not advertise the club.

The operator of the investment club is entitled to be reimbursed for expenses incurred during the course of operating the club. The operator of any commodity pool or club who is exempt from registration must file a notice with the NFA citing the reasons why the pool or club is exempt from registering as a CPO. A copy of this notice must be sent to each of the participants. Participants in commodity pools must get monthly statements if the value of the pool is greater than $500,000. If the value of the pool is $500,000 or less, the participants must get quarterly statements. All statements must show the changes in the net asset value (NAV) of the pool inclusive of all fees and charges. Statements and value computations must be calculated using generally accepted accounting principles (GAAP).

The offering documents for an interest in a commodity pool is required to contain the commodity Futures Trading Commission's risk disclosure statement on the cover page in all capital letters and in boldface type. Immediately following the cover page, a standard risk disclosure statement must also be included. This risk disclosure must appear in the language as prescribed by the cftc and must advise the participant that they may lose all of his/her investment.

STRUCTURED FINANCE PROGRAMS

With a structured finance program, financial assets are pooled and converted into a capital market instrument. These capital market instruments are known as asset-backed securities. The asset-backed security is one that is primarily serviced by the cash flows generated from the pooled assets. The pool of assets could be fixed or it could be revolving and by the nature of the assets they mature or convert into cash at a set time in the future. Assets that are designed to provide a return of the invested capital, plus a distributed rate of interest, generally qualify as assets to secure structured finance programs. Investors' participation in the structured finance program is usually represented by a debt instrument, preferred stock, units or interests of beneficial ownership. Loans, leases, and accounts receivable are all qualifying instruments for structured finance programs. Credit card loans, student loans and car loans may also be pooled to securitize a structured finance program. The entity who creates the structured finance program could be in the business of creating these receivables such as a bank or a finance company, or the receivables could be the product of business operations. Structured finance programs are often created when the originator of the receivable transfers the receivable into a special purpose vehicle or special purpose entity. The special purpose entity then transfers the assets into a trust and sells the interest in the trust to investors. One of the advantages of moving the assets into a special purpose entity and subsequently into a trust created by the entity is that it isolates the assets from the business and credit risk of the originator of these receivables. That is to say that the assets are protected from the liabilities and the potential bankruptcy of the originating party. When an investor is evaluating an investment in structured finance, the investor will evaluate the cash flow of the receivables and will not take into consideration the credit quality of the originator.

CASE STUDY

XYZ manufacturing is a producer of large industrial equipment. Most of the equipment that XYZ sells costs in excess of $5 million. As a result of the high cost of their product, XYZ often extends credit to its clients and allows them to pay for their equipment over time. During a slowdown in the economy, XYZ finds itself in financial difficulty needing additional working capital to pay its current liabilities and to meet its obligations until the economy turns around. As the economy is going through a difficult time, investors are reluctant to lend to manufacturing companies at terms that XYZ feels are reasonable. Looking at its business operations, XYZ realizes that they have approximately 50 million dollars in receivables on their books from customers who have purchased their equipment during the last 24 months. The terms of these receivables are to be paid in full within 60 months and carry an average rate of interest of 7.9%. Since XYZ manufacturing has been cautious with the extension of credit to its customers, the default rate on these receivables historically has been very low. With the above conditions, XYZ manufacturing feels that the best way to obtain the capital it needs is to create a structured finance product by moving the $50 million receivable into a special purpose entity. XYZ manufacturing creates XYZ Finance and moves the receivables into XYZ Finance, the special purpose entity. The sole purpose of XYZ Finance is to create structured finance products or asset-backed securities and to obtain the capital required by XYZ Manufacturing.

VENTURE CAPITAL PROGRAMS

Venture capital programs are designed to raise money from limited partners to invest in early-stage companies. Venture capital funds invest in a portfolio of small companies that show the potential for developing into significant businesses in the future. The general partner of these programs will maintain an investment committee whose role is to identify early-stage and startup companies that meet the investment profile of the fund. Many venture capital programs focus on a particular industry such as technology, biotech or education. This allows the venture capital program to provide business expertise and guidance to the startup company. Once the investment committee determines that the company meets the program's investment requirements, the fund will traditionally take an equity or ownership stake in the early stage business. The size of the ownership stake will vary depending on the amount of the investment made by the fund, relative to:

1. The revenue of the business

2. Profits or losses of the business

3. Outstanding debt obligations

4. Prospects for the business

5. Prospects for the industry

6. Competition in the industry

7. Potential for success or failure

Since many companies fail in the first few years of operation, venture capital funds represent a high-risk, high-reward investment. Adding to the risk of venture capital investing is the fact that many companies will need multiple rounds of financing which could have a dilutive impact to the fund's ownership stake. The initial financing for an early stage company is known as "seed funding" or the "A round" of financing. Many of these companies require additional capital as they grow and will subsequently need B, C and even D rounds of financing. As these capital needs develop, the initial venture capital fund may or may not participate in these rounds depending on the prospects for the business. Should the initial VC not participate in the subsequent rounds, the initial fund may see its ownership stake diluted through the offering of additional shares to new investors. The holding period for these investments is traditionally measured in years. During these years, the company is developing and growing and the VC is most likely not seeing any return on its investment. Once the company has grown to a sufficient level to where the VC believes it can exit its stake in the company profitably, the VC will seek an exit or liquidity event. In this exit or liquidity event, the VC will seek to sell its stake in the company. The largest and most successful exit or liquidity event is for those companies who have grown to the point where the company can be sold to the public through an initial public offering or IPO. Once the company has gone public, there is a ready and liquid market for the shares. The VC may sell part or all of its stake through the IPO or may agree to hold its ownership stake for a stated period of time. The time under which the VC agrees not to sell its stake in the now public company is known as a lock up period. A lock up period is sometimes required in order to reassure investors who are purchasing shares in the newly public company that the VC will not be dropping millions of shares on the market shortly after the public offering. Most companies do not grow to the level where they can justify going public. However, the VC may be able to sell it's interest in a company to another VC firm or to a strategic buyer. This is the more likely scenario for a VC to exit their interest in a company.

Investors considering participating in a venture-capital direct partnership program need to be able to withstand the loss of all of his / her invested capital. In addition to the inherent lack of liquidity in the partnership interest itself, investors must realize that there is also an inherent lack of liquidity in the investments made by the program. As a result, the VC program is unlikely to be making distributions to investors unless or until it realizes a significant gain at the time it enjoys a substantial liquidity event from the sale of its interest in a portfolio company. Further, since most of the investments will be made in companies that are organized as C corporations, little to no deductions will be passed through to the limited partners. Investors who purchase an interest in venture capital programs should have maximum speculative profit as his / her investment objective and their profile should have a high risk tolerance and no need for liquidity.

BUSINESS DEVELOPMENT COMPANIES

In 1980, Congress amended the Investment Company Act of 1940 to allow for the creation of business development companies. A business development company is an unregistered closed-end fund designed to provide capital to small and growing companies. In order to qualify for the classification as a business development company, the fund must invest 70% of its assets in non-public US companies with a market value of less than $250 million. Business development companies are organized under Internal Revenue Code subchapter M. Thus, like an investment company or a REIT, the business development company may pass through its net investment income to investors without paying taxes at the business development company level. This pass through requires the business development company to pay out at least 90% of its net investment income to investors in the form of dividends. Business development companies make loans to these small non-public companies and the interest payments made by the companies are the basis for the portfolio's income. The formula for determining the net investment income is:

Interest income
- expenses
Net investment income

EXAMPLE	LendFast Business Development Company has been investing by making loans to small businesses throughout its region. Its loan portfolio consists of $300 million worth of loans to various private businesses. For the year LendFast's portfolio shows the following information:

Loan portfolio	$300,000,000
Interest income	$28,000,000
Expenses	$3,000,000
Net investment income	$25,000,000

In the above example, LendFast would be required to distribute 90% of the net investment income of $25 million, or in this case $22,500,000. Neither the value of the loan portfolio nor any change in the value of the loan portfolio would impact the required distribution of net investment income. Business development companies are also subject to the diversification requirements of the Investment Company Act of 1940. This diversification requirement is sometimes referred to as a 75 - 5 - 10 rule. 75% of their assets must be invested in the securities (loans) of issuers with no more than 25% being invested in the securities of issuers (businesses) they control. No more than 5% of their assets may be invested in any one issuer and they may not own more than 10% of any issuer's voting assets. Further, the business development company must also receive 90% of their gross income from dividends or interest payments.

The capital raised by the business development company could be raised through a private placement or through a registered public offering. There are numerous business development companies whose shares trade publicly on the New York Stock Exchange and NASDAQ stock markets. Investors in business development companies should have income as their primary objective and should be aware of the risks associated with the investment in a business development company. Specific risks investors should consider include credit risk or the risk of default as well as interest rate risk. Since the business development company is designed to lend money to small companies there is a higher likelihood that the company will default and will not be able to repay the loan. A high level of defaults could result in significant losses to investors. Low liquidity and the negative impact of using leverage add to the risky nature of these investments. Additionally, if interest rates rise investors could see the value of their investment fall as the lower yielding loans in the portfolio become less attractive to investors. Investors who are attracted to the high payouts of business development companies must perform the proper due diligence to ensure they understand the particular risks of the BDC.

 TAKENOTE!

Should interest rates fall, investors in business development companies may see the value of their investment increase as the higher-yielding loans in the portfolio become more attractive to investors. However, while investors in business development companies may see modest gains in the appreciation of the assets, their primary investment objective is interest income.

REAL ESTATE INVESTMENT TRUSTS/REIT

A REIT is an entity designed to own, manage, build or finance real property. A real estate investment trust is organized as a corporation or as a trust and its tax treatment lies between that of a corporation and a direct participation program. Organized under Internal Revenue Code Subchapter M, real estate investment trusts enjoy certain tax benefits not afforded to corporations. A real estate investment trust is allowed to pass through net investment income to its owners. Net investment income is defined as revenue minus expenses. The real estate investment trust is required to distribute at least 90% of its net investment income to maintain its status as a REIT. If the REIT passes through 90% or more of its net investment income, it will only pay taxes on what it retains. If it passes through less than 90% of its net investment income, it will pay taxes on 100% of the income. Further, the REIT must also receive at least 75% of its revenue from real estate investments. While the REIT enjoys the ability to pass through net investment income to investors, it does not pass through gains, losses, expenses, deductions or credits to investors. Many real estate investment trusts have their shares listed on the New York Stock Exchange or on NASDAQ. However, the Series 22 exam does not provide a representative with the ability to transact business in these publicly traded REITs.

NON-TRADED REAL ESTATE INVESTMENT TRUSTS

Non-traded real estate investment trusts or REITs lack liquidity, have high fees, and can be difficult to value. The fees for investing in a non-traded REIT may be as much as 15% of the per share price. These fees include commissions and expenses which cannot exceed 10% of the offering price. Investors are often attracted to the high yields offered by these investments. Firms who conduct business in these products must conduct an ongoing suitability determination on the REITs they recommend. Firms must react to red flags in the financial statements and from the REIT's management and adjust the recommendation process accordingly or stop recommending if material changes take place that would make the REIT unsuitable. Holding periods can be eight years or more and the opportunities to liquidate the investments may be very limited. Furthermore, the distributions from the REITs themselves may be based on the use of borrowed funds and may include a return of principal which may be adversely impacted and cause the distributions to be vulnerable to being significantly reduced or stopped altogether. Distributions may exceed cash flow and the amount of the distributions, if any, are at the discretion of the Board of Directors. Non-traded REITs like exchange traded REITs must distribute 90% of the income to shareholders and must file annual reports (10-Ks) and quarterly reports (10-Qs) with the SEC. Broker dealers who sell non-traded REITs must provide investors with a valuation of the REIT within 18 months of the closing of the offering of shares.

NAV REAL ESTATE INVESTMENT TRUST

In an effort to attract investors who may otherwise not invest in non-traded REITs, many private offerings of REITS are now known as NAV REITs. These NAV REITs are designed to provide liquidity to investors while still paying the high distributions normally associated with non-traded REITs. The NAV REIT allows the investor to redeem their shares at the net asset value that is calculated by the sponsor on a daily, weekly or monthly basis. In addition to the added liquidity, NAV REITs provide additional transparency regarding the value of each share or unit. Many of the same suitability requirements must be met prior to recommending an investor purchase shares in an NAV REIT. However, the ability to lock up their capital for an extended period of time is a much lower consideration when considering an NAV REIT.

Pretest

ADDITIONAL TYPES OF DPPs

1. Which of the following choices accurately reflects the three stages of a direct participation program?

   a. syndication stage, acceleration stage, operational stage.

   b. Organizational stage, distribution stage, operational stage.

   c. Organizational stage, operational stage, liquidation stage.

   d. Operating stage, acceleration stage, liquidation stage.

2. When comparing an investment in a row crop partnership to an investment in a timberland project, which of the following is correct?

   a. The known harvest cycle for row crops provides a substantial advantage over an investment in a timberland project.

   b. A timberland project will provide investors with a more predictable income stream when compared to an investment in a row crop program.

   c. An investment in a timberland project provides investors with little opportunity for appreciation when compared an investment in row crops.

   d. The ability to determine when to harvest the timber provides a substantial benefit to investors in the program when compared to an investment in row crops.

3. ABC direct participation program is organized to operate a feedlot. Grow Big Cattle Inc. is acting as the sponsor of the program. The program will be raising $5 million from partners. Which of the following accurately represents the financial commitment that must be maintained by Grow Big Cattle Inc. ?

    a. Grow Big is required to maintain a financial interest of not less than $350,000.

    b. Grow Big is required to maintain a financial interest of at least $100,000.

    c. Grow Big is required to maintain a financial interest of $35,000 per million dollar investment.

    d. Grow Big must maintain a financial interest a $500,000.

4. Tall Trees Incorporated is a forest management company. Tall Trees provides services to direct participation programs investing in timber. Which of the following would be included in the services provided by Tall Trees?

    a. Land appraisal, timber management, syndication, reforesting.

    b. Timber appraisal, timber management, harvesting, and selling.

    c. Underwriting, appraisal, management, and selling.

    d. Formation, appraisal, management, and selling.

5. Fresh Feed is a feedlot sponsor offering partnership interests to investors. Fresh Feed will be charging a fee for its management services. The maximum fee that may be charged in the first year is:

    a. 12.5 %of the gross receipts.

    b. 12.5% of the value of the land.

    c. 12.5% of the value of the feed to be provided.

    d. 12.5% of the value of the live cattle.

6. Big Rigs direct participation program has been organized to lease cranes and large earth-moving equipment to construction companies. Which of the following would not constitute a sponsor of the direct participation program?

   a. An organization who contracts an affiliated party to organize the program.

   b. An organization who contracts to an unaffiliated party to organize the program.

   c. An individual who contracts to an unaffiliated party to organize the program.

   d. An entity who manages and maintains the equipment for the benefit of the program in exchange for a fee.

7. Which of the following is an advantage of a timber program not found in an investment in a row crop program?

   a. Pass-through tax benefits.

   b. Pass-through of income.

   c. Capital appreciation.

   d. Reasonably predictable demand.

8. Earth Moving limited partnership has been established to lease large equipment to end-users. Construction Management Co. is the sponsor of the program. Jim Walsh is the Chief Operating Officer of Construction Management Co. As it relates to the requirements for equipment leasing programs, which of the following is true?

   a. Construction Management Co. or its Chief Operating Officer need to have at least 5 years of experience.

   b. Construction Management Co. or its Chief Operating Officer need to have at least 2 years of experience.

   c. Construction Management Co. or its Chief Operating Officer must have at least 3 years of experience.

   d. Construction Management Co. or its Chief Operating Officer must have at least 4 years of experience.

9. A feedlot sponsor who charges a markup on the feed supplied to the cattle it grows wishes to increase its revenue by adding a handling charge for each head of cattle. Which of the following is correct?

   a. A feedlot sponsor who charges a markup on feed may not charge a handling charge on the cattle it grows.

   b. A feedlot sponsor who charges a markup on feed may charge a handling charge on the cattle it grows provided the markup and handling charge are limited to 20%.

   c. A feedlot sponsor who charges a markup on feed is limited to charging only a nominal per head fee on the cattle it grows.

   d. A feedlot sponsor who charges a markup on feed may charge a handling charge on the cattle it grows provided the markup and handling charge are limited to 10%.

10. Which of the following programs would be designed specifically to lend money to small business ventures?

   a. Venture capital program.
   b. Business development program.
   c. Structured finance program.
   d. Private equity program.

Issuing Corporate Securities

INTRODUCTION

The Securities Act of 1933 was the first major piece of securities industry regulation that was brought about largely as a result of the stock market crash of 1929. Other major laws were also enacted to help prevent another meltdown of the nation's financial system, such as the Securities Exchange Act of 1934, but we will start our review with the Securities Act of 1933, as it regulates the issuance of corporate securities.

THE SECURITIES ACT OF 1933

The Securities Act of 1933 was the first major piece of securities industry legislation and it regulates the primary market. The primary market consists exclusively of transactions between issuers of securities and investors. In a primary market transaction, the issuer of the securities receives the proceeds from the sale of the securities. The Securities Act of 1933 requires nonexempt issuers (typically corporate issuers) to file a registration statement with the Securities and Exchange Commission (SEC). The registration statement will be under review by the SEC for a minimum of 20 days. During this time, known as the cooling-off period, no sales of securities may take place. If the SEC requires additional information regarding the offering, the SEC may issue a deficiency letter or a stop order that will extend the cooling-off period beyond the original 20 days. The cooling-off period will continue until the SEC has received all of the information it had requested. The registration statement that is formally known as an S1 is the issuer's full disclosure document for the registration of the securities with the SEC.

THE PROSPECTUS

While the SEC is reviewing the security's registration statement, a registered representative is very limited as to what he or she may do with regard to the new issue. During the cooling-off period, the only thing that a registered representative may do is obtain indications of interest from clients by providing them with a preliminary prospectus, also known as a red herring. The term *red herring* originated from the fact that all preliminary prospectuses must have a statement printed in red ink on the front cover stating: "that these securities have not yet become registered with the SEC and therefore may not be sold." An indication of interest is an investor's or broker dealer's statement of interest in purchasing the securities being offered. The preliminary prospectus contains most of the same information that will be contained in the final prospectus, except for the offering price and the proceeds to the issuer. The preliminary prospectus will usually contain a price range for the security to be offered. All information contained in a preliminary prospectus is subject to change or revision.

THE FINAL PROSPECTUS

All purchasers of new issues must be given a final prospectus before any sales may be allowed. The final prospectus serves as the issuer's full disclosure document for the purchaser of the securities. If the issuer has filed a prospectus with the SEC and the prospectus can be viewed on the SEC's website, the prospectus will be deemed to have been provided to the investor through the access equals delivery rule. Once the issuer's registration statement becomes effective, the final prospectus must include:

- Type and description of the securities
- Price of the security
- Use of the proceeds
- Underwriter's discount
- Date of offering
- Type and description of underwriting
- Business history of issuer

 TAKE**NOTE!**

Only the final prospectus may be delivered electronically. The preliminary prospectus must be delivered in hard copy.

- Biographical data for company officers and directors
- Information regarding large stockholders
- Company financial data
- Risks to purchaser
- Legal matters concerning the company
- SEC disclaimer

FREE WRITING PROSPECTUS

A free writing prospectus (FWP) is any form of written communication published or broadcast by an issuer containing information about the securities offered for sale that does not meet the definition of a statutory prospectus. Common examples of a free writing prospectus include:

- Marketing materials
- Graphs
- Term sheets
- Emails
- Press releases

The free writing prospectus should include a legend recommending that the individual read the statutory prospectus to obtain more information relating the securities being offered. A hyperlink will be used in many cases to direct the reader to the statutory prospectus. An issuer who meets the definition of a well-known seasoned issuer may use an FWP at any time before or after the filing of a registration statement. A seasoned issuer may only use an FWP after the filing of the registration statement with the SEC. An unseasoned or non-reporting issuer may use an FWP only after a registration statement is filed with the SEC and must either send a statutory prospectus with FWP or must include a hyperlink to a statutory prospectus. Issuers who use free writing prospectuses will file them with the SEC over the SEC's website.

PROSPECTUS TO BE PROVIDED TO AFTERMARKET PURCHASERS

Certain investors who purchase securities in the secondary market just after a distribution must also be provided with the final prospectus. The term for which a prospectus must be provided depends largely on the type of offering and where the issue will be traded in the aftermarket. If the security has an aftermarket delivery requirement, a prospectus must be provided by all firms that execute a purchase order for the security during the term. The aftermarket prospectus delivery requirements may be met electronically and are as follows:

- For IPOs: 90 days after being issued for securities quoted on the OTCBB or in the pink sheets, 25 days for listed or Nasdaq securities.
- Additional offerings: 40 days for securities quoted on the OTCBB or in the pink sheets. No aftermarket requirement for listed or Nasdaq securities.

SEC DISCLAIMER

The SEC reviews the issuer's registration statement and the prospectus but does not guarantee the accuracy or adequacy of the information contained within them. The SEC disclaimer must appear on the cover of all prospectuses and states: "These securities have not been approved or disapproved by the SEC nor have any representations been made about the accuracy of the adequacy of the information."

MISREPRESENTATIONS

Financial relief for misrepresentations made under the Securities Act of 1933 is available for purchasers of any security that is sold under a prospectus that is found to contain false or misleading statements. Purchasers of the security may be entitled to seek financial relief from any or all of the following:

- The issuer
- The underwriters
- Officers and directors
- All parties who signed the registration statement
- Accountants and attorneys who helped prepare the registration statement

TOMBSTONE ADS

Tombstone ads are the only form of advertising that is allowed during the cooling-off period. A tombstone ad is an announcement and description of the securities to be offered. A tombstone ad lists the names of the underwriters, where a prospectus may be obtained, and a statement that the tombstone ad does not constitute an offer to sell the securities and that the offer may only be made by a prospectus. Tombstone ads are traditionally run to announce the new issue, but they are not required and do not need to be filed with the SEC.

FREE RIDING AND WITHHOLDING/FINRA RULE 5130

FINRA Rule 5130 has replaced the free-riding and withholding rule. FINRA Rule 5130 requires that a broker dealer obtain an eligibility statement from all account owners who purchase a new issue of stock within 12 months prior to the purchase. A broker dealer underwriting a new issue must make a complete and bona fide offering of all securities being issued to the public and may not withhold any of the securities for:

- The account of underwriters.
- The account of another broker dealer.
- The account of a firm employee or the account of those who are financially dependent upon the employee.
- The account of employees of other FINRA members.

An exception to FINRA Rule 5130 applies to employees of limited broker dealers who engage solely in the purchase and sale of investment company products or direct participation programs (DPPs). Employees of limited broker dealers may purchase new issues. This exemption applies only to the employees of the limited broker dealer, not to the firm itself. These rules are in effect for all initial public offerings, but are especially prevalent when dealing with a hot issue. A hot issue is one that trades at an immediate premium to its offering price in the secondary market. A broker dealer may not free ride by withholding securities for its own account or for the accounts of those listed above. There are some people who may purchase hot issues so long as the amount is not substantial and they have a history of purchasing new issues. These conditionally approved people are:

- Officers and employees of financial institutions
- Nonsupported family members
- Accountants, attorneys, and finders associated with the underwriting
- Accounts where the restricted persons interest is limited to 10% or less or where a maximum of 10% of the allocation of new is for the benefit of such persons. This is known as the carve out procedure.

If the demand for the new issue is great, the syndicate may purchase additional shares from the issuer under a greenshoe provision. This will increase the offering by up to 15%. Alternatively, if the demand for the issue is not great, the syndicate may have to support the issue in the aftermarket to ensure that the shares are distributed without a great deal of volatility. The syndicate may enter a single stabilizing bid to support the issue and may only enter the stabilizing bid at or below the offering price. FINRA Rule

5130 covers initial offerings of common stock only. Exempt from the rule are offerings of additional issues, bonds, and preferred shares. These offerings may be purchased by registered persons.

UNDERWRITING CORPORATE SECURITIES

Once a business has decided that it needs to raise capital to meet its organizational objectives, it must determine how to raise the needed capital. Most corporations at this point will hire an investment banker, also known as an underwriter, to advise them. The underwriter works for the issuer, and it is the underwriter's job to advise the client about what type of securities to offer. The issuer and the underwriter together determine whether stocks or bonds should be issued and what the terms will be. The underwriter is responsible for trying to obtain the financing at the best possible terms for the issuer. The underwriter will:

- Market the issue to investors.
- Assist in the determination of the terms of the offering.
- Purchase the securities directly from the issuer to resell to investors.

The issuer is responsible for:

- Filing a registration statement with the SEC.
- Registering the securities in the states in which it will be sold, also known as blue-skying the issue.
- Negotiating the underwriter's compensation and obligations to the issuer.

TYPES OF UNDERWRITING COMMITMENTS

FIRM COMMITMENT

In a firm commitment underwriting, the underwriter guarantees to purchase all of the securities being offered for sale by the issuer regardless of whether they can sell them to investors. A firm commitment underwriting agreement is the most desirable for the issuer because it guarantees all of the money right away. The more in demand the offering is, the more likely it is that it will be done on a firm commitment basis. In a firm commitment, the underwriter puts its own money at risk if it can't sell the securities to investors.

MARKET OUT CLAUSE

An underwriter offering securities for an issuer on a firm commitment basis is assuming a substantial amount of risk. As a result, the underwriter will insist on having a market out clause in the underwriting agreement. A market out clause would free the underwriter from its obligation to purchase all of the securities in the event of a development that impairs the quality of the securities or that adversely affects the issuer. Poor market conditions are not a reason to invoke the market out clause.

BEST EFFORTS

In a best efforts underwriting, the underwriter will do its best to sell all of the securities that are being offered by the issuer, but in no way is the underwriter obligated to purchase the securities for its own account. The lower the demand for an issue, the greater the likelihood that it will be done on a best efforts basis. Any shares or bonds in a best efforts underwriting that have not been sold will be returned to the issuer.

MINI-MAXI

A mini-maxi is a type of best efforts underwriting that does not become effective until a minimum amount of the securities have been sold. Once the minimum has been met, the underwriter may then sell the securities up to the maximum amount specified under the terms of the offering. All funds collected from investors will be held in escrow until the underwriting is completed. If the minimum amount of securities specified by the offering cannot be reached, the offering will be canceled and the investors' funds that were collected will be returned to them.

ALL OR NONE (AON)

With an all-or-none (AON) underwriting, the issuer has determined that it must receive the proceeds from the sale of all of the securities. Investors' funds are held in escrow until all of the securities are sold. If all of the securities are sold, the proceeds will be released to the issuer. If all of the securities are not sold, the issue is canceled, and the investors' funds will be returned. Contingent offerings must have a qualified financial institution QFI to act as an escrow agent for the offering. A general securities broker dealer, bank, or trust company may act as an escrow agent.

STANDBY

A standby underwriting agreement will be used in conjunction with a pre-emptive rights offering. All standby underwritings are done on a firm commitment basis. The standby underwriter agrees to purchase any shares that current shareholders do not purchase. The standby underwriter will purchase the shares at the right's discounted subscription price.

TYPES OF OFFERINGS

INITIAL PUBLIC OFFERING (IPO)/NEW ISSUE

An initial public offering (IPO) is the first time that a company has sold its stock to the public. The issuing company receives the proceeds from the sale minus the underwriter's compensation.

SUBSEQUENT PRIMARY/ADDITIONAL ISSUES

In a subsequent primary offering, the corporation is already publicly owned and the company is selling additional shares to raise new financing.

PRIMARY OFFERING VS. SECONDARY OFFERING

In a primary offering, the issuing company receives the proceeds from the sale minus the underwriter's compensation. In a secondary offering, a group of selling shareholders receives the proceeds from the sale minus the underwriter's compensation. A combined offering has elements of both the primary offering and the secondary offering. Part of the proceeds goes to the company and part of the proceeds goes to a group of selling shareholders.

AWARDING THE ISSUE

There are two ways in which the corporation may select an underwriter. A corporation may elect to have multiple underwriters submit bids and choose the underwriter with the best bid. This is known as a competitive bid underwriting. A company may elect to select one firm to sell the issue and negotiate the terms of the offering with it. This is known as a negotiated underwriting. Most corporate offerings are awarded on a negotiated basis, while municipal bonds offerings are usually awarded through competitive bidding.

THE UNDERWITING SYNDICATE

Because most corporate offerings involve a large number of shares and a very large dollar amount, they will be offered through several underwriters known as the underwriting syndicate. The syndicate is a group of investment banks that have agreed to share the responsibility of marketing the issue. The managing underwriter, also known as the lead underwriter or book running manager, leads the syndicate.

SELLING GROUP

The syndicate may form a selling group in an effort to help market the issue. Members of the selling group have no underwriting responsibility and may only sell the shares to investors for a fee known as the selling concession.

UNDERWRITER'S COMPENSATION

The group of broker dealers that make up the underwriting syndicate will be compensated based upon their role as a syndicate member. The only syndicate member that may earn the entire spread is the lead or managing underwriter.

MANAGEMENT FEE

The lead or managing underwriter will receive a fee known as a management fee for every share that is sold. In most cases, the managing underwriter is the firm that negotiated the terms of the offering with the issuer and formed the syndicate.

UNDERWRITER'S FEE

The underwriter's fee is the cost of bringing the issue to market, and is a fee assessed for each share that is sold by the syndicate. If there is any money remaining after all expenses are paid, the syndicate members will split it based upon their commitment level in the underwriting.

SELLING CONCESSION

The selling concession will be paid to any syndicate member or selling group member who sells the shares to the investors. The selling concession is the only fee that the selling group members may earn.

UNDERWRITING SPREAD

The total amount of the management fee, the underwriting fee, and the selling concession make up the total underwriting spread. This is the difference between the gross proceeds of the offering and the net proceeds to the issuer.

> **PUBLIC OFFERING PRICE: $12**
>
> **SELLING CONCESSION**
> **$1.50**
>
> **UNDERWRITING FEE**
> **$.75**
>
> **MANAGEMENT FEE**
> **$.25**
>
> **PROCEEDS TO ISSUER $9.50 PER SHARE**

In this example, the underwriting spread is $2.50 per share.

FACTORS THAT DETERMINE THE SIZE OF THE UNDERWRITING SPREAD

There are many factors that determine the amount of the underwriter's compensation for offering the securities on behalf of the issuer. Some of the factors are:

- The type of securities to be offered.
- The size of the issue.
- The quality of the securities to be issued.
- The perceived demand for the securities.
- The type of underwriting agreement.
- The quality of the issuer's business.

EXEMPT SECURITIES

Certain securities are exempt from the registration provisions of the Securities Act of 1933 because of the issuer or the nature of the security. Although the securities may be exempt from the registration and prospectus requirements of the act, none are exempt from the antifraud provisions of the act. Examples of exempt securities are:

- Debt securities with maturities of less than 270 days and sold in denominations of $50,000 or more.
- Employee benefit plans.
- Option contracts, both puts and calls, on stocks and indexes.

Examples of exempt issuers are:

- U.S. government
- State and municipal governments
- Foreign national governments
- Canadian federal and municipal governments
- Insurance companies
- Banks and trusts
- Religious and charitable organizations

EXEMPT TRANSACTIONS

Sometimes a security that would otherwise have to register is exempt from the registration requirements of the Securities Act of 1933 because of the type of transaction that is involved. The following are all exempt transactions:

- Private placements/Regulation D offerings
- Rule 144
- Regulation S offerings
- Regulation A offerings
- Rule 145
- Rule 147 intrastate offerings

PRIVATE PLACEMENTS/REGULATION D OFFERINGS

A private placement is a sale of securities that is made to a group of accredited investors and the securities are not offered to the general public. Accredited investors include institutional investors and individuals who:

- Earn at least $200,000 per year if single.

Or

- Earn at least $300,000 jointly with a spouse.

Or

- Have a net worth of at least $1,000,000 without the primary residence.

The SEC has recently added a new category that will allow an individual to qualify as an accredited investor. Individuals who meet certain educational or certification requirements can now meet the definition of an accredited investor. Included in this category are individuals who have an active Series 7, 65 or 82 license. Sales to nonaccredited investors are limited to 35 in any

12-month period. No commission may be paid to representatives who sell a private placement to a nonaccredited investor. All investors in private placements must hold the securities fully paid for at least six months and sign a letter stating that they are purchasing the securities for investment purposes. Stock purchased through a private placement is known as lettered stock, legend stock, or restricted stock, because there is a legend on the stock certificate that limits the ability of the owner to transfer or sell the securities. There is no limit as to how many accredited investors may purchase the securities. Reasonable efforts must be made to ensure purchasers meet the definition of an accredited investor. Brokerage accounts, bank accounts, credit reports and tax documents may be used for verification purposes. An existing partnership which consists of both accredited and non-accredited investors will be seen as one purchaser under regulation D and allowed to purchase the shares. Partnerships formed specifically to purchase shares of the offering would have all of the partners' financial status reviewed independently to determine the eligibility of each partner. The limits on the amount of money that may be raised under the various regulation D offerings are as follows:

> Rule 504 D allows issuers to raise up to $5 million
> Rule 505 D Repealed
> Rule 506 D allows issuers to raise an unlimited amount of capital

The JOBS Act allows investors to view private placement documents online so long as the website requires an investor to submit a questionnaire documenting assets, income, and investment experience. This questionnaire must be reviewed and if qualified for participation the issuer or broker dealer may assign the investor a username and password granting them access to view the details of the offerings.

RULE 144

This rule regulates how control or restricted securities may be sold. Rule 144 designates:

- The holding period for the security.
- The amount of the security that may be sold.
- Filing procedures.
- The method of sale.

Control securities are owned by officers, directors, and owners of 10% or more of the company's outstanding stock. Control stock may be obtained by insiders through open-market purchases or through the exercise of company stock options. There is no holding period for control securities. However, insiders are not allowed to earn a short swing profit through the purchase and sale of control stock in the open market. If the securities were held less than six months, the insider must return any profit to the company.

Restricted securities may be purchased by both insiders and investors though a private placement or be obtained through an offering other than a public sale. Securities obtained through a private placement or other non-public means need to be sold under Rule 144 in order to allow the transfer of ownership. Restricted stock must be held fully paid for six months. After six months, the securities may be sold freely by noninsiders so long as the seller has not been affiliated with the issuer in the last three months. Rule 144 sets the following volume limits for both restricted and control stock during any 90-day period. The seller must file Form 144 at the time the order is entered and is limited to the greater of:

- The average weekly trading volume for the preceding four weeks.

Or

- 1% of the issuer's total outstanding stock.

For orders for 5,000 shares or less and that do not exceed $50,000, Form 144 does not need to be filed. If the owner of restricted stock dies, their estate may sell the shares freely without regard to the holding period or volume limitations of Rule 144.

 TAKE**NOTE!**

Securities may be sold under Rule 144 four times per year. The securities sold under Rule 144 become part of the public float and the seller, not the issuer, receives the proceeds of the sale.

PRIVATE INVESTMENT IN A PUBLIC EQUITY (PIPE)

Public companies that wish to obtain additional financing without selling securities to the general public may sell securities to a group of accredited investors through a private placement. The accredited investors in most cases will be institutional investors who wish to invest a large amount of capital. Common stock, convertible or nonconvertible debt, and rights and warrants may all be sold to investors through a PIPE transaction. Obtaining capital through a PIPE transaction benefits the public company in a number of ways:

- Reduced transaction cost.
- Term disclosure only upon completion of the transaction.
- Increased institutional ownership.
- Quick closing.

Securities sold through a PIPE transaction are subject to Rule 144. If the issuer files a registration statement after the closing of the offering, sales may begin immediately upon the effective date.

REGULATION S OFFERINGS

Domestic issuers who make a distribution of securities exclusively to offshore investors do not have to file a registration statement for the securities under the Securities Act of 1933. In order to qualify for the exemption offered under Regulation S, the issuer may make no offerings of the securities within the United States and may not announce or distribute literature relating to the securities within the United States. Securities distributed under Regulation S are subject to a distribution compliance period, during which the securities may not be resold to domestic investors. The distribution compliance period is 6 months for equities if the issuer is a reporting company and files 10-Qs, 10-Ks and 8-Ks, and one year for non reporting companies. The distribution compliance period is 40 days for debt. Sales of the securities may take place in off-shore markets anytime after the initial sale. Issuers must report the sale of securities under Regulation S by filing form 8K.

REGULATION A OFFERINGS

A Regulation A offering as amended by the Jobs Act of 2012 allows issuers to raise up to $50 million in any 12-month period. A Regulation A offering provides issuers with an exemption from the standard registration process. This exemption from full registration allows smaller companies access to the capital markets without having to go through the expense of filing a full registration statement with the SEC. The issuer will instead file an abbreviated notice of sale or offering circular known as an S 1-A with the SEC and purchasers of the issue will be given a copy of the offering circular rather than a final prospectus. Purchasers of the issue must have the preliminary or final offering circular mailed to them 48 hours before mailing the confirmation. The same 20-day cooling-off period also applies to Regulation A offerings. The JOBS Act further refined Regulation A into two tiers, with Regulation A now sometimes being referred to as Regulation A plus. Tier 1 allows issuers to raise up to $20 million. Of this $20 million, no more than $6 million may be offered by selling shareholders. Tier 2 allows issuers to raise up to $75 million, of which no more than $22.5 million may be offered by selling shareholders.

RULE 145

Rule 145 requires that shareholders approve any merger or reorganization of the company's ownership. Any merger or acquisition will be reported to the SEC on Form S-4. Stockholders must be given full disclosure of the proposed transaction or reclassification and must be sent proxies to vote on the proposal. Rule 145 covers:

- Mergers involving a stock swap or offer of another company's securities in exchange for their current stock.
- Reclassification involving the exchange of one class of the company's securities for another.
- Asset transfers involving the dissolution of the company or the distribution or sale of a major portion of the company's assets.

RULE 147 INTRASTATE OFFERING

Rule 147 pertains to offerings of securities that are limited to one state. Because the offering is being made only in one state, it is exempt from registration with the SEC and is subject to the jurisdiction of the state securities administrator. In order to qualify for an exemption from SEC registration, the issue must be organized and have its principal place of business in the state and meet at least one of the following business criteria:

- 80% of the issuer's income must be received in that state.
- 80% of the offering's proceeds must be used in that state.
- 80% of the issuer's assets must be located in that state.
- A majority of the issuer's employees are based in-state

All purchasers must be located within the state and must agree not to resell the securities to an out-of-state resident for 6 months.

If the issuer is using an underwriter, the broker dealer must have an office in that state.

The SEC has also adopted Rule 147A, which is largely identical to Rule 147. However, Rule 147A allows companies that are incorporated or organized out of state to use the Rule 147 exemption so long as the company's principal place of business is in that state. Rule 147A also allows issuers to use the internet and to advertise securities being offered through Rule 147. Offers may be made to residents while out of state. However, all sales are still limited to investors residing in the state where the offering is being conducted.

CROWDFUNDING

Crowdfunding has become a popular way for issuers to raise capital from small investors. Issuers may offer securities to investors for purchase through a broker dealer or through a registered crowdfunding portal. The portal must be registered with the SEC and must also be a FINRA member firm. Issuers who raise capital through crowdfunding may not engage directly in crowdfunding as a way to sell shares to investors. Issuers who sell shares through crowdfunding must register the securities with the SEC by filing form C. Because most of the securities are speculative in nature, broker dealers and crowdfunding portals must offer educational material to investors who are considering purchasing securities offered through crowdfunding. The material must detail the risks involved in making investments in companies through the crowdfunding process as well as the fact that the securities have a limited amount of liquidity. Investors who purchase shares through crowdfunding may not sell the shares for 12 months. Shares however may be transferred earlier to a relative or to a trust controlled by the investor or as a result of death or divorce. Early transfer will also be allowed if the purchaser is an accredited investor or if the securities are part of an SEC registered offering. Investors who purchase shares are limited to the amount of securities they may purchase through the crowdfunding process in any 12 month period. Investors who have annual income or a net worth of less than $100,000 are limited to purchasing the greater of $2,000 worth of securities or 5% of their annual income or net worth. If the investor uses the 5% calculation to determine their purchase limit the amount the person may purchase will be the lesser of the two amounts. Investors who have an annual income or a net worth greater than $100,000 may invest the lesser of 10% of their annual income or net worth up to a maximum of $100,000.

RULE 415 SHELF REGISTRATION

Rule 415 allows an issuer to register securities that may be sold for its own benefit, for the benefit of a subsidiary, or in connection with business plans in an amount that may be reasonably sold by the issuer within a two-year period. The two-year window starts from the registration date and allows the issuer and the underwriters flexibility in the timing of the offering. Issuers who qualify as well-known seasoned issuers (WKSI) and who qualify for automatic registration may sell securities for up to three years. A well know seasoned issuer has a market capitalization (the value of its common stock) of at least $700 million or has issued at least $1 billion in non-convertible securities. Rule 415 also allows the issuer to register to sell securities on a continuous basis in connection with an employee benefit plan or upon the conversion of other securities.

 TAKE**NOTE!**

An issuer who losses it status as a Well Known Seasoned issuer may continue to sell the securities under Rule 415 until it files its next 10K.

Pretest

ISSUING CORPORATE SECURITIES

1. A syndicate has published a tombstone ad prior to the issue becoming effective. Which of the following must appear in the tombstone?

   I. A statement that the registration has not yet become effective.

   II. A statement that the ad is not an offer to sell the securities.

   III. Contact information.

   IV. No commitment statement.

   a. III and IV

   b. II and III

   c. I and II

   d. I, II, III, and IV

2. During a new issue registration, false information is included in the prospectus to buyers. Which of the following may be held liable to investors?

   I. Officers of the issuer

   II. Accountants

   III. Syndicate members

   IV. People who signed the registration statement

   a. I and III

   b. I, II, and IV

   c. I, II, and III

   d. I, II, III, and IV

3. A syndicate may enter a stabilizing bid:

   a. whenever the price begins to decline.

   b. at or below the offering price.

    c. to ensure an increase from the offering price.

    d. to cover over allotments only.

4. Corporations may do all of the following, EXCEPT:

    a. issue preferred stock only.

    b. issue nonvoting common stock.

    c. sell stock out of the treasury.

    d. repurchase its own shares.

5. Issuance of which of the following would require the approval of existing shareholders?

    a. Mortgage bonds

    b. Collateral trust bonds

    c. Prior lien bonds

    d. Equipment trust certificates

6. During an underwriting of a hot issue, the syndicate exercises its green-shoe provision. This will allow them to buy an additional:

    a. 20% of the offering.

    b. 25% of the offering.

    c. 15% of the offering.

    d. 10% of the offering.

7. Which of the following is NOT a type of offering?

    a. Rule 149 offering

    b. Subsequent primary offering

    c. Secondary offering

    d. Combined offering

8. Once a company decides to raise long-term capital to meet its needs, it will:

    a. approach the money market to determine how much capital can be raised.

    b. hire an underwriter to advise the issuer about the type of securities to issue.

    c. hire a dealer to issue stock for public purchase.

    d. hire a broker to issue stock for public purchase.

9. A firm participating in the offering of a private placement may sell the private placement to:

  a. no more than 12 nonaccredited investors in any 12-month period.

  b. no more than 6 nonaccredited investors in any 12-month period.

  c. no more than 35 nonaccredited investors in any 12-month period.

  d. no more than 15 nonaccredited investors in any 12-month period.

10. A company doing a preemptive right offering would most likely use what type of underwriting agreement?

  a. Best efforts

  b. Firm commitment

  c. All or none

  d. Standby

11. A syndicate distributing a new issue of common stock contains 9 syndicate members and 12 selling group members. The stock will be listed on the Nasdaq. How many bids may be entered for the syndicate?

  a. 9

  b. 1

  c. 21

  d. 0

12. The subscription price of a right is:

  a. the price offered to current stockholders during a subsequent primary offering.

  b. the price of buying shares from a broker.

  c. the price a market maker pays to buy shares.

  d. the price at which the new shareholders can purchase new shares.

13. The SEC has been reviewing a company's registration statement and would like clarification on a few items. It would most likely:

  a. call the company.

  b. issue a stop order.

  c. issue a deficiency letter.

  d. call the lead underwriter.

14. Which of the following is NOT a type of underwriting commitment?

    a. Primary commitment

    b. Standby commitment

    c. Best efforts commitment

    d. Firm commitment

15. XYZ has just gone public and is quoted on the Nasdaq Capital Market. Any investor who buys XYZ must get a prospectus for how long?

    a. 30 days

    b. 90 days

    c. 60 days

    d. 45 days

16. A red herring given to a client during the cooling-off period will contain all of the following, EXCEPT:

    a. proceeds to the company.

    b. use of proceeds.

    c. biographies of officers and directors.

    d. a notice that all the information is subject to change.

17. A member of the selling group assisting in the distribution of securities in an undivided syndicate is:

    a. not liable for a percentage of the unsold securities.

    b. liable for a percentage of the unsold securities.

    c. required to purchase unsold shares for its own account.

    d. responsible for a percentage of the total offering.

DPP Offerings and Suitability

INTRODUCTION

In this chapter, we are going to take a closer look at the registration requirements for public and private offerings, the disclosure requirements and potential conflicts of interest. In order to successfully complete the series 22 exam, you will need to have a full understanding of the various types of offering documents and the information each document is required to disclose.

Specific rules have been enacted by FINRA, the SEC and the states relating to the distribution of a limited partnership. A limited partnership may be distributed directly by the sponsor, through a sponsor managed offering or through a broker-dealer. When a broker-dealer is distributing interests in limited partnerships through a dealer sponsored offering, the broker-dealer will enter into a distribution agreement with the sponsor. The broker-dealer is required to perform due diligence, maintain books and records, solicit and allocate retail participation, and the participation of other broker-dealers. FINRA requires the broker-dealer to adhere to its filing, conduct and underwriting rules. These rules are in place for all offerings regardless of whether the offering of the partnership interests are done on a public basis or through a private offering. In addition to the underwriting agreement as detailed chapter four, the underwriting broker-dealer, must submit the following to FINRA for review:

1. 3 copies of any registration statement, offering circular, or offering memorandum or any other document used to offer securities to investors.

2. 3 copies of any pre- or post-effective amendments to the registration statement or any other offering document. Specifically required to be submitted is one copy showing the changes that have been made.

3. 3 copies of any underwriting agreement, agreement among underwriters, escrow agreements, warrant agreement or letters of intent. In addition, all of the terms and conditions that are the basis of such agreement must be submitted to FINRA along with any other agreements that may be reasonably required by FINRA.

4. 3 copies of the final registration statement or other offering documents along with a list of the members of the underwriting syndicate.

5. Submission of the required filing fee.

PRIVATE PLACEMENT OF SECURITIES

Every member firm that offers private placements to investors must submit a copy of the private placement memorandum, term sheet or other offering document (including any updates or amendments) to FINRA within 15 calendar days of the date of the first sale. In addition, FINRA requires information relating to the participating members, the issuer and offering to be submitted electronically via the private placement questionnaire. If multiple FINRA broker dealers are participating in the offering, the filing member may submit the completed questionnaire with the required information on behalf of all participating members. The filing member will be required to submit responses relating to the issuer to identify if the issuer is a reporting company under the Securities Exchange Act of 1934 and if the participating member or members are in any way affiliated, controlled or under common control of the issuer. The offering information required by FINRA includes:

1. A description of the type of security being offered by the issuer i.e. equity or debt.

2. The minimum investment required by the issuer and any conditions under which that minimum investment may be waived or modified.

3. If the issuer has raised capital within the preceding 12 months from any source other than from affiliates.

4. If the filing member has sold or will sell any of the securities to non-accredited investors.

5. The specific exemption under the Securities Act of 1933 the issuer is relying upon.

6. If the offering is being done on a contingency basis, if the contingency has been met as of the date of the filing.

7. The date when the filing member first offered or sold securities or if sales efforts have not yet begun.

The filing member will only be required to provide a stated or target rate of return if any offering documents provided to investors contain an actual or target rate of return.

Private placements offered exclusively to institutional investors, qualified purchasers, qualified institutional buyers and employees are exempt from this rule. Also exempt from this rule are private placements conducted for the sale of short-term exempt securities. Also exempt are debt obligations sold by the member, so long as the maturity does not exceed 397 days and the securities are issued with a minimum denomination of $150,000.

 TAKE**NOTE!**

On your exam you may see an example of a FINRA member firm trying to raise capital through a subordinated loan. A subordinated loan allows the broker-dealer to raise capital to operate its business. The offering of subordinated loans under the Securities Exchange Act are also exempt from this rule. However, the subordinated loan agreement will be filed with both FINRA and the SEC.

ORGANIZATION AND OFFERING EXPENSES

FINRA closely monitors the costs and expenses associated with the organization and offering of a direct participation program. No FINRA member shall underwrite or participate in an offering of a direct partnership program or REIT if the organization and offering expenses are deemed to be excessive or unfair. FINRA has identified several practices that constitute unreasonable or excessive offering expenses in connection with direct participation programs. FINRA defines the following as unreasonable:

1. Organization and offering expenses that exceed 15% of the gross offering proceeds.

2. Total compensation paid from the offering proceeds including trail commissions paid to underwriters, broker-dealers or affiliates that exceeds 10% of the gross proceeds of the offering.

3. Commissions or compensation paid directly or indirectly to an investment advisor to induce such an advisor to recommend the purchase of interest in a particular direct participation program or REIT. No compensation may be paid to any party other than a registered broker-dealer or to a person registered with a broker-dealer.

4. Any compensation paid in connection with the offering of a direct participation program paid to underwriters, broker-dealers or affiliates prior to the release of the proceeds from escrow.

5. Any compensation structure which provides for payments to be made to members or persons associated with the members in connection with the sale of the program or REIT, that allows the person or the member to share in the management fee, the profits, brokerage commissions, the revenues, or to receive an overriding royalty interest, reversionary interest or a working interest in the program or REIT.

6. Requiring investors who reinvest dividends into the program to pay a sales load on the reinvestment.

7. Reimbursing the member for expenses that are not included in a detailed receipt and are not part of the underwriters non-accountable expense allowance, unless all such non-accountable expenses do not exceed 3% of the offering proceeds.

The organization and offering expenses subject to the limitations detailed above include issuer expenses that are reimbursed or repaid using offering proceeds, along with any of the following:

1. The creation, printing and mailing of offering materials and the processing of subscription agreements.

2. Legal and accounting services provided to the sponsor or issuer.

3. Non-transactional base compensation paid to employees of the sponsor or issuer.

4. Fees paid to escrow depositories, transfer agents, engineers and other experts.

5. Registration expenses paid in connection with federal or state registration of securities.

UNDERWRITING COMPENSATION

Underwriting compensation is the direct cost of distributing an offering. Underwriter compensation includes all items of value to be received by a member, or by a person associated with the member, who are participating in the offering of securities. All forms of underwriting compensation must be disclosed to potential investors in the prospectus, offering circular, private placement memorandum, memo or any other offering document. If the underwriters compensation is to include any form of compensation in addition to the underwriters discount disclosed on the front page of the offering document, a footnote to the offering proceeds table must include a cross reference to the section on underwriting distribution arrangements.

SUITABILITY OF PARTICIPANTS

Each sponsor must establish minimum income and net worth standards for prospective purchasers who wish to invest in the program. The standards that are employed by the sponsor should be sufficiently high in relation to, and reflect the risks associated with the investment. For registered offerings the minimum general guidelines will be annual income of $70,000 and a minimum net worth of $70,000, or a minimum net worth of $250,000. The net worth requirement is exclusive of the home, furnishings and automobiles of the purchaser. For offerings that are being distributed under a private placement, the offering will be limited to accredited investors and higher as defined by Regulation D detailed in chapter 4. Should non accredited investors be allowed to purchase the private placement, the following additional requirements must be met:

1. Non accredited purchasers must be given the same information generally required by registered offerings even if the company did not provide the information to accredited investors and higher.

2. Non-accredited purchasers must be given the same information provided to all other investors.

3. Non-accredited investors must receive financial statement information required under SEC Rule 506.

4. The sponsor, issuer or underwriter must be available to answer questions from prospective purchasers who are not accredited investors.

Should an offer or sale be made to a fiduciary account, such as a trust, the financial requirements may be met by the beneficiaries, the donor or grantor who supplies the funds or by the fiduciary account itself. A suitability determination must be made for each sale made by the sponsor or by any person representing the sponsor. An affirmative determination must be made to ascertain each of the following:

1. That, the investor or participant meets the minimum financial requirements.

2. That, the investor or participant can reasonably expect to benefit from participation in the program.

3. That, the programs business objectives align with the prospective participant's investment objectives.

4. That, the investor or participant can bear the economic risk of the investment.

5. That, the investor or participant can evaluate and understand the risks associated with the investment including the fact that the participant may lose 100% of their invested capital.

6. That, the investor or participant understands and accepts the program's inherent lack of liquidity.

7. That, the investor or participant has no need for liquidity.

8. That, the investor or participant understands the restriction regarding transferability of his/her ownership interest.

9. That, the investor or participant has the ability to evaluate the background and qualifications of the sponsor responsible for managing the program's business.

10. That, the investor or participant understands the unique tax implications associated with their investment in the program.

As part of the subscription agreement, the program sponsor may require that the participant attest to certain financial representations. These representations may include:

1. That, the investor or participant meets certain minimum income and net worth requirements.

2. That, the investor or participant is purchasing the interest for his or her own investment account.

3. That, the investor participant acknowledges, understands and can bear the economic risk.

4. That, the investor or participant acknowledges, understands and can bear the lack of liquidity.

Except in the case of a fiduciary, the investor or participant themselves must sign (or initial) and acknowledge each representation required in the subscription agreement. The investor or participant may not grant a power of attorney to a third party to make representations on their behalf.

No sponsor or person representing the sponsor in the sale of program interest may require a participant to make any acknowledgements that are unreasonable or require any participant to sign away certain rights. Acknowledgements that would be deemed to violate securities laws and conduct rules include:

1. Requiring an investor of participant to sign an acknowledgement that materially misrepresents the investor's financial status or investment objectives.

2. Requiring an investor or participant to sign an acknowledgement that materially misrepresents the investor's risk tolerance.

3. Requiring an investor or participant to sign an acknowledgement that materially misrepresents their understanding of the program's risks.

4. Requiring an investor or participant a sign an acknowledgement that materially misrepresents their need for liquidity.

5. Requiring an investor participant to sign an acknowledgement that materially misrepresents his/her investment experience.

6. Requiring an investor of participant to sign an acknowledgement that shifts the affirmative suitability determination from the sponsor or broker-dealer onto the participant.

7. Requiring an investor or participant to sign an acknowledgement where the investor relinquishes their rights under state or federal law.

These prohibited acknowledgements may not be part of the investor certifications contained in the subscription agreement. However, these prohibited acknowledgements may be placed in the disclosure section of the subscription agreement, so long as the inclusion is designed to inform the participants of their rights.

Restricted securities issued through a private placement under SEC Rule 506, require the company to file a notice with the SEC on Form D. This filing must occur within 15 days of the first sale of securities in the offering. While SEC rule 506 provides for an exemption from state registration for the securities, the states still have the authority to require the issuer to notice file and pay a state fee.

With the implementation of the Dodd-Frank Wall Street Reform and Consumer Protection Act, certain "bad actors" are precluded from participating in offerings under regulation 506. If any covered person has been the subject of a disqualifying event on or after September 23rd 2013, the offering may not rely on an exemption under regulation 506. Covered persons for this rule include:

1. The issuer itself including any predecessors or affiliated issuers.
2. Directors, general partners and managing members of the issuer.
3. Executive officers of the issuer and other officers participating in the offering.
4. Any owner of 20% or more of the issuer's voting stock.
5. Promoters connected to the issuer.
6. Fund investment managers and principals.
7. Any entity compensated for promoting or soliciting investors, including their directors, general partners and managing members.

If any person or entity listed above is subject to a disqualifying event, an offering may not take place under Regulation 506 unless an exemption is available through proper disclosure. A disqualifying event is any of the following:

1. A criminal conviction in relation to the purchase or sale of a security.
2. A criminal conviction in relation to making false statements to the SEC.
3. A criminal conviction in relation to operating as an underwriter, broker, dealer, municipal securities dealer, investment advisor, or paid solicitor.
4. A U.S. Postal Service order relating to false representations within the last 5 years.
5. Final orders barring the individual by state regulators of securities, insurance, banking, savings associations or credit unions.
6. Final orders barring the individual by federal banking agencies, the Commodity Futures Trading Commission, FINRA, or the New York Stock Exchange.
7. SEC orders that suspend, limit or revoke the person's registration as a broker, dealer, municipal securities dealer or investment advisor.
8. A court injunction or restraining order in connection with the sale of a security.

9.   A court injunction or restraining order in connection with making false filings with the SEC.

10.   A court injunction or restraining order regarding the conduct of an underwriter, broker, dealer, municipal securities dealer, investment advisor or paid solicitor of securities.

Only those disqualifying events occurring after September 23rd 2013 impact the offering. If a covered person was subject to a disqualifying event prior to that time, it only needs to be disclosed to potential investors and will not impact the availability of an exemption under regulation 506. The rule provides for a reasonable care exception from disqualification, if the issuer is able to demonstrate that it did not know, and could not have reasonably known, that a covered person with a disqualifying event participated in the offering. Additionally, an issuer who is aware of a disqualifying event impacting a covered person may apply for a waiver to allow the offering to go forward even in light of the disqualifying event impacting the covered person. If a disqualifying event takes place during the offering of securities, the previous sales of securities will not be impacted, but future sales may not take place under Regulation 506 unless the disqualifying event is waived or removed. If the issuer is unaware of the disqualifying event taking place during the offering, the issuer may be able to rely are a reasonable care exception. Should the SEC issue a cease-and-desist order against a covered person that prohibits the covered person from committing a future violation, the order will only serve as a disqualifying event if issued within 5 years of the proposed sale. Further, only orders that remain in effect will be deemed to be disqualifying events. For example, a person who was barred indefinitely has the right to reapply for association after three years have passed. Should that person be permitted to re-associate, in a regulated capacity, the bar will have ended and the individual will no longer be subject to a disqualifying event.

FAILURE TO COMPLY

SEC Rule 508 states that an insignificant deviation from a term or condition required under rule 504 or 506 will not result in the loss of the exemption provided under the rule so long as the person relying on the exemption can demonstrate the following:

1.   That the failure to comply did not relate to any term or condition designed to protect an individual or entity; and

2.   That the failure was insignificant with respect to the offering as a whole; and

3. All parties to the offering made a good-faith attempt to comply with all of the rules of 504 or 506.

FIXED-PRICE OFFERINGS

No FINRA member firm that participates as a syndicate member, selling group member or as sole underwriter in connection with a fixed price offering, may sell the securities to any other entity or account at a discount from the fixed offering price. A discount or reduced price includes without limitation a selling concession, discount, credit, rebate or other allowance. Also included in the definition of a discount or reduced price would be the offering of services or products at a reduced price, in exchange for the purchase of securities covered under the offering. Nothing in this rule will prohibit a member who is part of the syndicate, selling group or a sole underwriter from selling the securities at the public offering price to any affiliated person or any entity or firm that has provided research or will provide research to the member. The requirements of this rule will remain in effect until the offering is completed or until such time as the member having made a bona fide offering of the securities terminates the offering.

 TAKE**NOTE!**

The rules regarding a fixed-price offering apply to all offerings of securities Including registered and unregistered securities. However, these rules do not apply to exempted securities, municipal securities or securities that are offered by a registered investment company or mutual fund.

INSTALLMENT PROCEDURES

Certain private offerings of direct participation programs require the purchasers to make installments or to potentially make payments as a condition of ownership. These installment payments are sometimes referred to as assessments. If the investors have agreed to mandatory installment payments, on a non-contingent basis, the total sum of the mandatory payments must be included in the offering price. Should the terms of ownership potentially require the investor to make additional payments contingent upon a need assessed by the general partner or at the general partner's discretion, the amount of these assessments will not be included in the purchase price. Since these contingent or voluntary assessments are unknown and the assessments may never actually be required, voluntary or contingent assessments do not impact the aggregate offering price.

ESCROW PROCEDURES

Most private placements will have the purchaser's funds placed into escrow prior to be being released to the issuer. This is specifically the case for offerings that are done on a contingency basis such as a minimum / maximum offering or an all-or-none offering. No payments may be made to underwriters as commissions for sales prior to the funds being released from escrow. If funds that have been placed in escrow are part of a blank check offering and an acquisition has not occurred within 18 months of the effective date of the initial registration statement, all funds in the escrow account must be returned to investors. All securities that have been issued by the issuer will be returned to the issuer upon the refund of the investor's purchase price. It's important to note that the issuer is required to file form D not later than 15 days after the first subscription is received into escrow. When determining an investor's holding, under Rule 144, the investor's six-month holding period begins at the time the investor pays for the shares and the money is deposited into the escrow account. Should an investor have shares held in escrow pending future payments, the investor's holding period will commence only to the extent to which payment has been received.

EXAMPLE: An investor has agreed to invest $250,000 into a private placement. The investor agrees to make five $50,000 installments over the next 12 months. The agreed-upon purchase price is $25 per share. The investor's installment schedule is as follows:

Month	Investment	Number of shares	Holding period begins	Shares may be sold
January 1st	$50,000	2,000	January 1st	July 1st
March 1st	$50,000	2,000	March 1st	September 1st
June 1st	$50,000	2,000	June 1st	December 1st
September 1st	$50,000	2,000	September 1st	March 1st
December 1st	$50,000	2,000	December 1st	June 1st

The investor's holding begins only for the shares that have actually been paid for. As the above table details, each of the five purchases will begin the holding period only for the 2,000 shares that were acquired on that date.

PROSPECTUS RELATING TO INTERESTS
IN OIL AND GAS PROGRAMS

Every prospectus used to distribute an interest in an oil and gas program must have a brief description on the cover page of the prospectus detailing the following:

1. The terms of the offering including the title and nature the securities being offered, the maximum aggregate amount, the minimum required to initiate the program, refund procedures if the minimum is not reached, the minimum subscription price, the price of the offering, distribution method including the amount of commissions to be paid and any assessments required to be paid by investors.

2. For offerings that will not use an escrow account or trust, a specific disclosure relating to potential risk of exposure to claims of creditors of the custodian of funds must be included.

3. A general description of all cash or property that will be paid as compensation in connection with the program including underwriting commissions.

4. The general description of the use of proceeds including the minimum amount of net proceeds excluding any potential assessments available to finance the program.

Depending on the type of oil and gas program being offered, the use of proceeds should detail the amount of funds available to pay for the program's principal activity including the acquisition of land, the drilling of exploratory or developmental wells, or the purchase of producing properties.

The risk factors associated with the program should be carefully organized in concise paragraphs in the relevant areas of the offering document and should include a cross reference to where additional information may be found. The offering document must also include a glossary of terms so that the potential investor may have a clear understanding of the language being used in the prospectus or offering document. The glossary must define each of these terms in a manner that is consistent with the term's use in the oil and gas industry. A clear and concise description of all the assessments which may be required to be made by investors must be included in the prospectus for offering document. These additional assessments may be required for drilling of additional wells or for the attainment of other program objectives. If the sponsor or its affiliates have operated similar programs in the past, historical information relating to the amount of additional assessments for past programs should be disclosed in tabular form. The prospectus or offering document must also include the following:

1. A distribution plan regarding how program interests are being offered are to be sold as well as all compensation arrangements.

2. A description of all proposed activities of the program.

3. A detailed description of the application of proceeds including a percentage allocation estimate detailing how the proceeds will be distributed among the principal activities of the program. The purchase of land and drilling, to the extent possible, should be disclosed in tabular form.

4. A detailed description of the cost and revenue sharing arrangement among all parties. To the extent possible this information should be disclosed in tabular form.

5. The sponsor, issuer, or general partner must disclose all potential conflicts of interest that may arise from the formation of the program.

6. A detailed description of all the tax implications regarding oil and gas exploration, drilling and production along with any federal tax legislation that has been proposed which may impact the program.

7. Additional required disclosures should be detailed in a caption, heading or similar style entitled competition, limited partnership agreement, agent agreement, exploration agreement, and operating agreement.

The sponsor or issuer of the program is required to provide detailed performance history showing the results of all relevant programs or operations for the last 10 years. This 10-year performance history must disclose the drilling results, the total investment by investors and the recovery of investment as of the end of the most recent 3 months of the period covered. As part of the tax implications, the sponsor or issuer may include details relating to expense deduction and taxable income in tabular form.

PREPARATION OF REGISTRATION STATEMENT RELATING TO INTERESTS IN REAL ESTATE LIMITED PARTNERSHIPS

Information relating to the general partner, sponsor, promoter, affiliates as well as entities who are controlled or under the common control of aforementioned, must be disclosed in the registration and prospectus prepared in connection with real estate limited partnerships. The SEC details the information to be disclosed as well as the order in which the disclosures are made. The SEC mandates that the following appear on the cover page of the prospectus for a real estate limited partnership:

1. The cover page should disclose the termination date of the offering, any minimum required purchase and any escrow or trust arrangements for subscribers' funds.

2. The cover page should contain tabular presentation of the maximum and minimum size of the offering.

3. The cover page should disclose and tabular format the price to the public, selling commissions and the proceeds to the partnership.

4. The cover page should contain a brief description of the tax aspects of the offering including any material tax risk associated with the offering.

5. The cover page should disclose the risks to the partnership if the proceeds are insufficient to meet the requirement for the partnership's investment objectives.

6. The cover page should disclose any known conflicts of interest, such as if the partnership will be engaging in transactions with the general partner or any of its affiliates.

The suitability standards employed by the real estate limited partnership, if any, to be used to determine acceptance or rejection of a subscription agreement, should appear on the page following the cover page. At a minimum the partnership should use suitability standards established by any self-regulatory agency or state agency having jurisdiction over the offering of the securities. The issuer should develop and disclose the methods it uses to assure that those persons who are selling the securities adhere to the suitability standards being employed. Specifically noteworthy in these disclosures is the inherent lack of liquidity relating to the sale or reassignment of the securities and the potential adverse tax consequences. Further, if suitability standards apply to the resale of the interest to another investor or substitute limited partner, these suitability standards should be disclosed to purchasers.

A two-part concise summary relating to the the partnership and the use of proceeds as described in the tabular summary should immediately follow the suitability section of the prospectus. A summary of the partnership including appropriate cross reference material should include the following:

1. Name address and telephone number of the general partner and names of any persons making investment decisions for the partnership.

2. The intended termination date of the partnership.

3. If applicable that the general partner and its affiliates will receive substantial fees and profits in connection with the sale of partnership interest.

4. For partnerships with current income or distributions as an investment objective, the estimated maximum time between the closing of the offering and the time the investor may have to wait to begin to receive such distributions.

5. A brief description of the properties to be purchased or if a material portion of the net proceeds are not committed to the acquisition of a property a disclosure to that effect.

6. A description of the depreciation method to be used by the partnership.

7. The maximum level of leverage expect to be used by the partnership for the portfolio as a whole and for individual properties.

8. A cross reference and glossary.

USE OF PROCEEDS

The use of proceeds tabular summary may vary depending upon the type of partnership involved. However, if appropriate the following must be disclosed:

1. Estimates of the public offering expenses including organizational and sales expenses.

2. The amount of proceeds available for investment.

3. The non-recurring initial investment fees.

4. The amount of cash down payments.

5. The amount of financing fees.

6. The amount of reserves.

7. The amount of acquisition fees.

8. The amount of acquisition fees paid by the seller.

9. The estimated amount to be paid to the general partner and its affiliates.

This summary should include both dollar amounts and percentages of the maximum and minimum proceeds of the offering. Inclusion of the percentages of the estimated maximum and minimum total assets is optional.

COMPENSATION AND FEES TO THE GENERAL PARTNERS AND AFFILIATES

The information disclosed regarding the compensation and fees to the general partner and its affiliates should include a summary in tabular presentation and detail each item by category, specifying dollar amounts where possible. All items of compensation, fees, profits and other benefits which the general partner and affiliates may earn or receive in connection with the offering or operation of the partnership, including the reimbursement of any out-of-pocket expenses must be disclosed. The disclosure should identify the person who will receive such compensation, fees, profits or benefits along with their affiliation with the general partner and the services to be performed in connection with the receipt of such compensation. Further, the summary should be organized so that it is clear to the reader at which stage of the partnership's life these services will be performed and the resulting compensation paid. The summary should clearly indicate whether the services will be performed during the offering and organizational stage, the development or acquisition stage, the operational stage or the termination and liquidation stage of the partnership. Each stage of the partnership's life and the fees to be earned by those performing services during these stages, should be their own unique line items. The various types of compensation and fees to be disclosed include:

1. Payments related to the purchase and sale of limited partnership interest including sales commissions, reimbursement for expenses, and real estate commissions.

2. Finders fees for property acquisitions, marketing or lease of properties, financing or refinancing, management of properties, insurance and miscellaneous services.

3. Commissions and other fees to be paid upon the sale of partnership properties, any participation interest by the general partner in the cash flow or profits and losses or capital gains and losses arising out of the operation of the partnership's business.

4. Any fees or builder profits, overhead absorption or land mark ups.

5. All profits on the purchase of investments of the partnership from the general partner or its affiliates.

If the partnership limits the losses the general partner and its affiliates can sustain, this should be disclosed. Specific requirements are in place for the disclosures that are made. When calculating the maximum aggregate dollar of front-end fees to be paid during the first fiscal year of operation, the fees to be disclosed should be based upon the assumption that the partnership is operating using its maximum allowed leverage. If any compensation arrangement is based on a formula or percentage, the terms including the underlying dollar figure and calculation should be disclosed and illustrated. For partnerships paying compensation based upon a given return, for example a percentage of contributed investors' capital, the issuer must disclose whether such return is cumulative or non-cumulative. Should a general partner or affiliate of the real estate limited partnership receive a disproportionate interest in the partnership in the form of a carried interest over and above its own contribution, a comparison of the various interest and contributions should be disclosed. The carried interest will sometimes be referred to as an "applicable partnership interest." An applicable partnership interest or a carried interest is a form of payment to the general partner in consideration for the services provided by the general partner. In 2018, the tax treatment for applicable partnership interest changed. In order for a general partner or other party who has received a carried interest or applicable partnership interest to realize a long-term capital gain, the general partner must have held the partnership interest for a period of more than 3 years. Traditionally should the partnership sell an asset and seek to make a distribution to a general partner with a carried interest, the asset that was sold must have been owned by the partnership for greater than 3 years. If a party with a carried-interest liquidates the carried interest or the partnership distributes a capital gain based on an asset held less than 3 years, any gain will be treated as a short-term capital gain for tax purposes.

CONFLICTS OF INTEREST

The prospectus or offering document should include a summary of each transaction that could result in a conflict of interest between program investors and the general partner and its affiliates. This disclosure should include a proposed method for dealing with such conflicts. If applicable, the types of conflicts of interest required to be disclosed include:

1. If the general partner or affiliate of the general partner is the general partner or an affiliate of a general partner in similar investment programs, regardless of whether that program is a public or private offering.

2. If the general partner has the authority to invest partnership funds in other partnerships where the general partner or affiliate of the general partner owns or maintains an interest.

3. If the general partner or its affiliates has an interest in properties sold to the partnership or purchased from the partnership.

4. If an entity where the general partner or its affiliates maintain an interest in properties sold to the partnership or purchased from the partnership.

5. If the general partner or its affiliates have an interest in any properties adjacent to the properties owned and operated by the partnership.

6. If an affiliate of the general partner who acts as an underwriter, real estate broker or manager for the partnership acts in a similar capacity for other partnerships or entities.

7. If an affiliate of the general partner acts as a mortgage broker, finance broker, insurance agent, insurance broker for the partnership and receives commissions for such services.

8. If an affiliate of the general partner acts as an underwriter for the offering or as principal underwriter for the offering due diligence conflicts may exist.

9. That the compensation plan for the general partner may create conflicts of interest between the interest of the partners and the general partner.

The use of an appraiser in connection with any transaction between the partnership and the general partner or an affiliate requires specific disclosures. The general partner must disclose that the appraised value is merely an estimate of value and should not be relied upon as the ultimate measure of realized value. Should the general partner represent that the appraiser is an expert, the appraiser should provide a consent to the general partner to use his / her name as a cited expert. In the case where the registration statement for the partnership includes appraised values for the partnership's properties, the name of the expert appraiser should be disclosed and included in the registration statement. Additionally, a table of appraised values should be furnished as exhibits in a registration statement. In cases where the registration statement merely files a statement indicating that purchase of property does not exceed its appraised value and the specific values are not cited, the appraiser is not required to provide consent to use his / her name. In this case, a copy of the appraisals should be submitted as supplemental material with the registration statement for the partnership.

In the event that the relationship between the general partner, its affiliates and those organizations managed or controlled by the general partner and its affiliates is sufficiently complex, an organizational chart, graph or display should be included to help investors understand the relationship between all relevant parties.

FIDUCIARY RESPONSIBILITIES OF THE GENERAL PARTNER

A specific disclosure regarding the fiduciary obligation of the general partner to perform their duties for the benefit of the partnership must be disclosed. Further, the SEC stipulates the specific language required to be included in the prospectus or offering document. While the SEC allows for modification based on the laws of the state where the partnership is organized, the following disclosure should be included:

"A general partner is accountable to a limited partnership as a fiduciary and consequently must exercise good faith and integrity and handling partnership affairs. This is a rapidly developing and changing area of the law and limited partners who have questions concerning the duties of the general partner should consult with their Counsel."

EXCULPATION

Additional disclosures are required to be made by the partnership when the partnership includes an exculpatory provision and or indemnification for the general partner. In the case of an exculpatory provision, the partnership agrees that the general partner will not be liable to the limited partners for errors resulting in losses to the partnership provide it was not the result of willful misconduct. In the case of an indemnification provision, the partnership agrees to indemnify the general partner for the liabilities incurred in dealings with third parties in furtherance of the partnership's objectives. In the case of an exculpatory clause or indemnification, the SEC requires the following language, which may be modified based on the laws of the state where the partnership is organized.

"The general partner may not be liable to the partnership or the limited partners for errors in judgment or other acts or omissions not amounting to willful misconduct or gross negligence, since provision has been made in the agreement of limited partnership for exculpation of the general partner. Therefore, purchasers of the interest have a more limited right of action than they would have absent the limitation in the partnership agreement."

INDEMNIFICATION

"The partnership agreement provides for indemnification of the general partner by the partnership for liabilities he incurs in dealings with third parties on behalf of the partnership. To the extent of indemnification provision purports to include indemnification for liabilities arising under the Securities Act of 1933, in the opinion of the Securities and Exchange Commission, such indemnification is contrary to the public policy and therefore unenforceable."

RISK FACTORS

The prospectus or offering documents should include a carefully organized risk disclosure section organized in concise subcaption paragraphs and include a cross reference to a more complete disclosure of the related risk. The risk disclosure should be designed to summarize the principal risks relating to the partnership and its particular plan of operations. A summary of the material risk of adverse tax consequences are specifically required to be included in this risk disclosure section. The risks disclosed relating to the tax treatment of the partnership should include:

1. If no Internal Revenue Service ruling has been obtained or applied for, the risk disclosure must include a statement that the IRS may audit and determine that for tax purposes the partnership is taxable as a corporation.

2. If the partnership has obtained the opinion of legal counsel regarding the tax status of the partnership, a statement must be included that the opinion of counsel is not binding on the IRS.

3. If the IRS has advised that it would not rule, not take action or rule adversely as to a ruling applied for by the partnership, that the risk remains that the investors may lose some or all tax benefits associated with the offering.

4. The risk that the investor's tax liability may exceed his / her cash distributions in later years of partnership operation.

5. The risk that upon sale, gift or other disposition of a partnership interest that the investor's tax liability may exceed the cash received resulting in an out-of-pocket expense to the investor.

6. The risk that upon the sale, foreclosure or other disposition of partnership property that the investor's tax liability may exceed the cash received resulting in an out-of-pocket expense to the investor

7. The risk that any gain on the sale or disposition of a partnership interest or any gain on the sale of assets by the partnership could result in the gain being taxed as ordinary income.

8. The risk that an audit of the partnership by the IRS may result in an audit of the investor's personal tax return.

Additional relevant risk disclosures relating to the specific operation of the partnership must also be included in the prospectus or offering documents. These specific disclosures If applicable include:

1. Management's lack of relevant experience or management's lack of success with similar partnerships or other real estate investments.

2. That, if the proceeds of the offering are insufficient to meet the investment requirements of the partnership, a disclosure of the additional sources of capital and that the additional sources for capital may not be sufficient to meet the partnership's objectives.

3. If the partnership plans allow for the use of high leverage, the risks of the leverage needs to be clearly explained.

4. The inherent risk associated with the lack of liquidity in partnership interests, including the fact that no public market exists for partnership interest and that no public market is likely to develop.

5. The legislative risks that could impact the partnership including rent stabilization programs, EPA regulations relating to fuel and energy, construction regulation, environmental regulation, and other federal state or local regulations including those currently enforce as well as any relevant pending regulation.

6. If a substantial portion of the minimum net proceeds of the offering are not committed to specific properties, the partnership must disclose additional risk created by this uncertainty.

7. If a substantial portion of the minimum net proceeds of the offering are not committed to specific properties the risk that there may be a substantial delay to investors in receiving a return on their investment.

If a material portion of the net proceeds is not committed to specific properties, the identity of the individual who will be selecting the properties, along with their appropriate background information must be disclosed to potential investors. Additionally, the risk factors in general relating to the real estate limited partnership should be disclosed immediately after the limited partnership's specific required risk disclosures. These disclosures should include the risk that cash flow to meet fixed and maturing obligations may not be sufficient, adverse local market conditions, leverage and uninsured losses. If a substantial amount of the net proceeds of the minimum offering will be used to acquire a single property, the issuer should provide a detailed description of that property in its registration statement and offering documents. If the probability of the acquisition arises prior to the effectiveness of the registration statement or the offering, the issuer should file an amendment to its registration documents and disclosure documents. Should an issuer identify a property to acquire and subsequently delay the acquisition of that property, to avoid the required disclosure, the issuer will have failed to meet its disclosure obligations regarding material facts relating to the offering.

PRIOR PERFORMANCE OF THE GENERAL PARTNER AND AFFILIATES

The 10-year track record of the prior performance of the general partner and affiliates or sponsors must be disclosed in the prospectus. This prior performance should be disclosed in a narrative summary as well as in prior performance tables included in the prospectus or offering documents. The narrative summary of the sponsors 10-year track record should include the following:

1. The sponsor's experience with all other programs including public and non-public programs that have invested in real estate regardless of the investment objective.
2. The number of programs sponsored.
3. The total amount of money raised from investors in all programs.
4. The total number of investors in all programs.
5. The number of properties purchased and their location by region, including a table of the properties purchased in the last 3 years on the back of the prospectus.
6. The percentage of properties that are commercial or residential as a percentage of dollars invested.
7. A detailed breakdown of commercial properties allocated by type such as shopping centers, office buildings or others.
8. The percentage by price of new, used or construction properties.
9. The number of properties sold.
10. A list of the major adverse business developments or conditions experienced by any program that would be material to investors in the current program.

These disclosures should be broken out separately for public and non-public programs. Additionally, the narrative disclosure should indicate the percentage of the data that represents programs with investment objectives similar to those being currently offered to investors. The sponsor should offer to provide the most recent 10K (annual report) filed with the SEC for any program that has been filed within the last 24 months free of charge to any prospective investor in the current program. Should a prospective investor request the exhibits attached to form 10-K the sponsor may require the investor to pay a reasonable fee. The narrative summary should include a cross reference to the information disclosed in relevant tables and appendix

The table of prior performance must include historical use of proceeds of prior programs, compensation to the sponsors, operations of the programs, and acquisitions and sales of properties by prior programs. Sponsors should not include information in the prospectus about prior performance beyond that required by the SEC except to ensure that the required disclosures are not misleading.

A similar real estate program is deemed to be a program with investment objectives that are similar to those objectives detailed in the prospectus or offering document of the current program. The sponsor of the program is required to determine which previous programs had similar investment objectives when taking into consideration the proposed activities of the current program offered to investors. A sponsor will be deemed to have a "public track record" if it has sponsored at least three reporting programs with investment objectives similar to those of the program currently being offered to investors. At least two of the three programs must have had 3 years of operations with at least 90% of the net proceeds invested. Additionally, at least two of the offerings of the public programs must have closed in the previous three years. A reporting program or public program is one that is registered under the Securities Act of 1933, is one that is required to file reports with the SEC under the Securities Exchange Act of 1934 or one that has least 300 security holders and having an initial capital raise of at least $1 million.

FEES AND COMPENSATION ARRANGEMENTS WITH NON-AFFILIATES

If the sponsor of the program is going to rely on the management of a non-affiliate in connection with the operations of the partnership, this fact must be disclosed to potential investors. If material amounts of compensation or fees are to be paid to non-affiliates a separate disclosure is required and must appear under the heading "fees and compensation arrangements with non-affiliates." A tabular presentation detailing the fees to be paid to these non affiliates should also be provided. An additional disclosure would be required if the general partner or affiliate have any contingent liabilities arising from their management of another program. These contingent liabilities may be disclosed in the financial statements so long as a specific reference to the contingent liabilities appears in the narrative summary.

Should a partnership provide provisions in the partnership agreement or in other documents allowing for a change in the management of the partnership, a detailed description of the conditions and procedures that would allow for such a change should be included.

FEDERAL TAX IMPLICATIONS

Issuers, general partners or sponsors of limited partnership interests should include a summary of all material federal income tax regulations that may potentially impact the offering. This disclosure is required to appear in its own section and must cite the specific Internal Revenue Code, Treasury regulations, case law established by a court or any other source deemed relevant to the tax Implications of the offering. A legal opinion of counsel as to all material tax implications of the offering must also be included and should cite the authority for the opinions and conclusions expressed by counsel. The primary function of the legal opinion is to inform investors of the tax consequences he / she can reasonably expect to realize from an investment in the partnership. If the tax counsel qualifies his / her opinion in relation to any particular tax benefit, due to uncertainty in the law, or for any other reason, the tax counsel must state that there may be a material adverse tax consequence and that the particular benefit could be disallowed based on an audit by the IRS. The potential negative tax implications as well as any material risks of disallowance must be disclosed in a separate heading in the prospectus or offering document. For a registered offering, the opinion of the tax counsel is deemed to have been made at the time of the effective date of the registration statement. Should a material change take place that would impact the counsel's tax opinion, that opinion must be updated to reflect any material changes or events. If the partnership has requested a ruling from the IRS as to the treatment of the partnership for federal income tax purposes, the content of that ruling including any conditions required by the ruling, must appear in the tax section of the prospectus or offering documents. If the classification as a partnership is conditioned upon the maintenance of any standard such as the maintenance of net worth or other standards, an explanation of how the maintenance of those standards will be maintained. If the partnership has not requested an IRS ruling as to the tax status of the partnership a particular summary of the risks that the partnership could be deemed to be a corporation must be included In both the tax section and risk factors section.

The primary function of the tax section is to ensure that each and every investor has a full and complete understanding of the tax implications of an investment in the partnership. Because the partnership is not a taxable entity, the investor must understand that he / she will be required to report his / her distributive share of income, gains, losses, deductions, or credits on his / her own tax return. A specific explanation of the tax treatment of any cash distributions made to partners must also be enclosed. Should the partnership agreement allow for the partnership to make special allocations among partners in the distribution of income, gains, losses, deductions or credits, the partnership's tax counsel must provide an opinion that the purpose of these allocations are not designed to engage in tax avoidance or tax evasion. A specific disclosure that the IRS may disallow special allocations which it deems to be principally designed to avoid or evade taxes must be included. In the event that the partnership allows for retroactive special allocations to new partners the tax implications of those retroactive distributions must also be disclosed. Specific tax implications regarding the impact to potential investors must be detailed including:

1. How the investor's basis in the partnership will be established and the fact that the partner may only deduct his / her share of partnership losses to the extent of his / her adjusted basis.

2. The extent to which any loan taken out by the partnership could impact the investor's basis in the partnership.

3. How a change in the partnership's debt level may impact the limited partner, including how it may change the partner's profit sharing ratio.

4. The potential disallowance of prepaid expenses by the IRS, including the fact that the IRS may disallow large deductions for prepaid interest and require the interest to be deducted over the term of the loan.

5. The method of depreciation as well as the basis for determining the useful life of depreciable property.

6. A disclosure that the IRS may challenge the partnership's estimated useful life for depreciation.

7. If asset depreciation is to be calculated based on first-user, the basis for determining the first-user status must be explained.

8. The potential negative implications of a taxable recapture on the sale of partnership assets should be included along with a cross reference to the section on sale or other disposition of partnership property.

9. A disclosure that if partnership losses offset an investor's earned income buy a rate of at least 50%, partnership income may be subject to higher tax rates in future years.

10. The type and timing of tax information that will be supplied to partners by the partnership.

11. The disclosure that the information return filed by the partnership may be audited and that the audit may result in adjustments to the partnership return as well as to the return of the limited partner.

12. That an audit of the limited partner's return could impact both partnership income and losses as well as income not related to the partnership.

Two particular tax implications relating to the investor are particularly noteworthy. First, should the IRS determine that the investor's sole purpose for purchasing an interest in a limited partnership is merely to generate annual net losses for tax purposes, the investor could be subject to negative consequences by the IRS. If the IRS finds this to be the case, the IRS can take action against the investor even if the partnership is designed for a bona fide profit motive. Secondly, investors should be made aware of the fact that a gift of a limited partnership interest which owns leveraged property may result in a tax liability to the donor or giver.

The information reported by the partnership to the IRS will be included in an informational return to be filed on IRS form 1065. Form 1065 will merely inform the IRS of the result of operations for the partnership. The partnership must include the names and addresses of each partner along with his / her distributive share of taxable income on form 1065. The partnership itself does not pay any income taxes nor take any deductions. All taxable events flow through to the limited partners and the limited partners' proportional interest in the income, expenses, losses, deductions and credits will be detailed on IRS form K-1. The information on a form K-1 will then be reported on the partner's individual return. IRS form K-1 will also provide the investor with a worksheet for adjusting the partner's cost basis for the interest in the partnership. The following are examples of events that can increase the partner's cost basis:

- The partner's additional contributions to the partnership, including an increased share of, or assumption of partnership liabilities.

- The partner's distributive share of taxable and nontaxable partnership income.

- The partner's distributive share of the excess of the deductions for depletion over the basis of the depletable property, unless the property is oil or gas wells whose basis has been allocated to partners.

The following lists a number of items that can decrease the partner's cost basis. However, a partner's basis may never be decreased below zero:

- The money (including a decreased share of partnership liabilities or an assumption of the partner's individual liabilities by the partnership) and adjusted basis of property distributed to the partner by the partnership.
- The partner's distributive share of the partnership losses (including capital losses).
- The partner's distributive share of nondeductible partnership expenses that are not capital expenditures. This includes the partner's share of any Section 179 expenses, even if the partner cannot deduct the entire amount on his or her individual income tax return.
- The partner's deduction for depletion for any partnership oil and gas wells, up to the proportionate share of the adjusted basis of the wells allocated to the partner.
- A partner's distributive share of foreign taxes paid or accrued by the partnership for tax years beginning after 2017.
- A partner's distributive share of the adjusted basis of a partnership's property donation to charity.

For federal tax purposes, specifically excluded from the definition of a partnership are any of the following:

- An organization formed under a federal or state law that refers to it as incorporated or as a corporation, body corporate, or body politic.
- An organization formed under a state law that refers to it as a joint-stock company or joint-stock association.
- An insurance company.
- Certain banks.
- An organization wholly owned by a state, local, or foreign government.
- An organization specifically required to be taxed as a corporation by the Internal Revenue Code (for example, certain publicly traded partnerships).
- Certain foreign organizations identified in section 301.7701-2(b)(8) of the regulations.
- A tax-exempt organization.

- A real estate investment trust.
- An organization classified as a trust under section 301.7701-4 of the regulations or otherwise subject to special treatment under the Internal Revenue Code.
- Any other organization that elects to be classified as a corporation by filing Form 8832.

REDEMPTION, REPURCHASE AND RIGHT OF PRESENTMENT AGREEMENT

This is a partnership agreement that allows limited partners to seek redemption of their interest in the limited partnership, the conditions under which such redemption may be sought as well as the formula used to calculate the redemption price must be disclosed. A limited partnership agreement or other documents should clearly describe the investor's right to redeem, including if the right allows the investor to redeem, require the general partner to repurchase the interest or if the investor's right is simply the right to present the interest for redemption or repurchase without the obligation of the general partner to do so. If the partnership allows the general partner or its affiliates the right to redeem their interest the same disclosure requirements apply.

MEMBER PRIVATE OFFERINGS

FINRA member broker-dealers may from time-to-time wish to raise capital to operate and expand their business. If a member firm is going to raise capital through a member private offering or MPO, the member firm and its associated people must follow specific procedures. If a member private offering is being sold through a private placement and the member has prepared a private placement memorandum or term sheet, the private placement memorandum or term sheet must be given to each and every prospective investor and must disclose the following:

1. The members intended use of the proceeds.
2. The offering expenses including the amount of selling compensation paid to the member and its associated persons.

If the member has not prepared a private placement memorandum or term sheet, the member is required to prepare the offering document that contains the same disclosures. At least 85% of the offering proceeds must be used to operate the member's business. The member shall not use any part of these proceeds for offering costs, commissions, discounts or any non-cash sales incentives in connection with the offering.

DISSOLVING A LIMITED PARTNERSHIP

A limited partnership is designed to end on the occurrence of certain events or on a set date in the future. An example for an oil and gas partnership, may be "this partnership will terminate upon the extraction of all recoverable reserves, but in no event later than June 1st 2075." A partnership may also be dissolved if the partnership agreement establishes voting procedures that allows the partners to vote to dissolve the partnership. These terms will be clearly laid out in the partnership agreement. The specific requirements to dissolve partnerships must also comply with any state regulation where the partnership has been formed. There are a number of steps that must take place in order to dissolve a limited partnership. While state regulations may vary, the following steps should be taken:

Step 1 - A meeting of the partners must be called in line with the meeting procedures laid out in the partnership agreement. Most partnerships require written notice be sent to partners 30 days prior to the date of the meeting.

Step 2 - A vote of all general and limited partners must be conducted, all general partners and a majority of the limited partners must vote to terminate the partnership. A record of the vote must be recorded in the meeting minutes and the minutes must be maintained in the partnership records.

Step 3 - Appoint general partner to oversee the liquidation of the partnership business or hire an outside agency to handle the wind down of a partnership business. If no general partner is available and no agency identified, the partnership may ask a court could supervise the liquidation or to appoint a trustee to oversee the liquidation.

Step 4 - File a certificate of partnership cancellation in the state of formation, stating the date of formation and the effective date of the cancellation.

Step 5 - Liquidate the partnership's assets, settle partnership obligations including taxes and wages, pay off creditors and allocate money to cover any foreseeable liabilities.

Step 6 - Once all liabilities have been satisfied, repay partner capital contributions from remaining assets, distribute any additional money in the form of profits to partners once their capital has been returned, if the remaining funds are insufficient to repay partner capital contributions, distribute the remaining funds proportionally to partners.

Step 7 - In the event any assets remain such as unsold assets, inventory or items that were not liquidated, distribute the assets proportionately to the partners.

Step 8 - Notify all interested parties such as clients and vendors of the dissolution of the business and close all partnership accounts.

Step 9 - File the partnership's final IRS form 1065 and distribute the final K1 to all partners.

The partnership terminates when all of its operations are discontinued and no part of any business, financial, or operational aspect of the partnership continues. The partnership'd final tax year will end on the date of termination of the partnership. Should the termination date of the partnership be any date other than the date of the partnership's fiscal year end, the 1065 will be filed for a short period return. The return will be due on the 15th day of the third month following the date of termination.

CANCELING A LIMITED LIABILITY COMPANY

A limited liability company is a hybrid entity that combines elements of both a partnership and a corporation. Limited liability companies must be cancelled based on the laws of the state of formation. While the steps to cancel a limited liability company are not as complex as those to dissolve a limited partnership, certain steps still must be followed. Those steps include:

Step 1 - Review cancellation procedures in the LLC operating document, if no formal procedures have been established, secure the agreement of a majority of the LLC members to cancel.

Step 2 - Follow cancellation procedures in the operating agreement and wind down operations.

Step 3 - Liquidate assets, settle all debts, pay all liabilities and divide the remaining proceeds under the terms of the operating agreement.

Step 4 - File a certificate of termination or articles of dissolution with the state where the limited liability company was formed.

Pretest

DPP OFFERINGS AND SUITABILITY

1. ABC broker-dealers is a FINRA member firm who regularly represents issuers of direct participation programs who wish to raise money through private placements. As it relates to the filing of the private placement memorandum, which of the following is correct?

   a. The private placement memorandum only needs to be filed with FINRA if the member makes offerings in multiple states.

   b. The private placement memorandum must be filed with FINRA within 48 hours of the first sale.

   c. The private placement memorandum must be filed with FINRA within 15 days of the first sale.

   d. The private placement memorandum must be filed with FINRA 48 hours prior to the first sale.

2. A FINRA member broker-dealer is distributing interests in a real estate direct participation program. The program will be designed to operate and manage large commercial real estate. Which of the following would FINRA consider to be excessive?

   a. ABC real estate limited partnership has gross proceeds of 100 million dollars with organizational and offering expenses of 12 million dollars.

   b. XYZ real estate limited partnership has gross proceeds of 50 million dollars with organizational and offering expenses of 8 million dollars.

    c. TEF real estate limited partnership has gross proceeds of 200 million dollars with organizational and offering expenses of 30 million dollars.

    d. MNO real estate limited partnership has gross proceeds of 40 million dollars with organizational and offering expenses of 5 million dollars.

3. All of the following would be prohibited from signing the acknowledgements in the subscription agreement, except:

    a. An accountant with power of attorney attesting to the income and assets of the purchaser.

    b. An attorney attesting to the fact that the purchaser understands and can afford the risks associated with a partnership.

    c. A purchasing agent who has been granted power of attorney for the purchaser attesting to the purchasers experience.

    d. A trustee attesting to the suitability of the investment on behalf of the beneficiaries of the trust.

4. As it relates to the offering of a limited partnership, which of the following would not be a violation?

    a. Including prohibited acknowledgements in the disclosure section of the subscription agreement in an effort to explain the purchaser's rights.

    b. Having an investor sign an acknowledgement that materially misrepresents his / her understanding of risk.

    c. Requiring an investor to sign an acknowledgement waving state or federal law requirements.

    d. Requiring an investor to sign an acknowledgement regarding liquidity requirements which do not necessarily align with the participants' needs.

5. As it relates to the Dodd-Frank Wall Street Reform Act, which of the following would not be considered a covered person?

    a. Any owner of 10% or more of the issuer's voting stock.

    b. ABC broker-dealers who is acting as a promoter of the issuer.

    c. Fund managers.

    d. XYZ broker-dealers who solicits investors to purchase the issuer's securities.

6. An oil and gas direct participation program is offering units for sale to investors with an initial offering price of $500 per unit. As a condition of ownership each investor will be assessed $2 per unit for the first five years of the partnership's operation. As it relates to this offering, which of the following is correct?

   a. FINRA would deem the assessments to be excessive and would not allow the offering to be made by a FINRA member firm.

   b. As long as the assessments were clearly disclosed, FINRA would allow the offering to be made at an offering price of $500 per unit.

   c. Mandatory assessments as a condition of ownership are a violation of the Securities Act of 1933.

   d. As long as the assessments were clearly disclosed, FINRA would allow the offering to be made at an offering price of $510 per unit.

7. An investor has purchased securities issued as part of an all-or-none offering conducted under Regulation D. As it relates to Rule 144, which of the following is correct?

   a. The investor will be subject to a six-month holding period based on when the funds were released to the issuer.

   b. The investor will be subject to a 12-month holding period based on when the funds were released to the issuer.

   c. The investor will be subject to a 6-month holding period based on when the investor's funds were deposited into the escrow account.

   d. The investor will be subject to a 12-month holding period based when the investor's funds were deposited in the escrow account.

8. As it relates to the offering documents for an oil and gas program, which of the following would not be required to be included?

   a. A glossary providing the definitions of terms as used in the documents.

   b. Details regarding any payments required be made as a condition of ownership.

   c. The total amount of funds available to pay for the program's activities.

    d. The lifetime performance of the sponsor showing results for all similar programs managed by the sponsor.

9. XYZ real estate limited partnership is offering interest to investors through a prospectus. As it relates to the tabular representation detailing the commission's and proceeds, which of the following is correct?

    a. The tabular representation must be contained on the first page of the prospectus.

    b. The tabular representation must be referred to in the footnotes of the prospectus.

    c. The tabular representation must appear on the front cover of the prospectus.

    d. The tabular representation must be highlighted and appear in bold print in the use of proceeds section of the prospectus.

10. ABC property management company is the general partner for a real estate limited partnership. ABC has contributed 10% of the capital and will participate in 15% of the results of the partnership. Which of the following best describes the additional 5% participation to be received by the general partner?

    a. An applicable partnership interest or carried interest.

    b. An overriding interest or a royalty interest.

    c. A participation interest or a carried interest.

    d. A reversionary interest or royalty interest.

Customer Accounts

INTRODUCTION

Prior to executing a customer's order, the firm must open an account for the customer. NYSE rules require that representatives obtain all vital information relating to the customer. Series 7 candidates will see many types of questions dealing with customer accounts on their exam.

Prior to opening an account for any new customer, a registered representative must complete a new account form. Account ownership is divided into five main types:

1. Individual
2. Joint
3. Corporate
4. Trust
5. Partnership

The registered representative should try to obtain as much information about the customer as possible. The representative should obtain the following information about the customer:

- Full name and address
- Home and work phone numbers
- Social security or tax ID number
- Employer, occupation, and employer's address
- Net worth
- Investment objectives
- Estimated annual income

- Bank/brokerage firm reference
- Whether the client is employed by a bank or broker dealer
- Any third-party trading authority
- Citizenship
- Legal age
- How account was obtained
- Whether client is an officer, a director, or a 10% stockholder of a publicly traded company

At the time a registered representative opens a new account for a retail customer, the rep should attempt to obtain the name and contact information for a trusted contact for the client. The trusted contact must be at least 18 years old and the firm may contact this individual if they have been unable to reach the customer after multiple attempts, the account may have been subject to fraud or exploitation or if the customer appears to be suffering from diminished mental capacity. If a new retail customer does not wish to provide a trusted contact, the representative should make note of that fact and the account may still be open by the firm.

All new accounts must be accepted and signed by a principal of the firm. The principal must accept the account in writing for the firm either before or promptly after the first trade is executed. The principal accepts the account by signing the new account card. The representative who introduced the account and the name of the representative who will manage the account should be noted on the new account card as evidence that he or she introduced the account to the firm. While the vast majority of new accounts are opened electronically and approved electronically, the test may still use the older language. Once the account is opened, the firm must send the customer a copy of the new account form within 30 days of the opening of the account and within 30 days of any material change in the customer's information. Firms are also required to verify the account information at least once every 36 months. The customer never has to sign anything to open a new cash account. However, some firms have the customer sign a customer agreement upon opening a new account, but this is not required. The customer agreement will state the policies of the firm and will usually contain a predispute arbitration clause. The predispute clause requires that any potential dispute arising out of the relationship be settled in binding arbitration. The predispute arbitration clause must be presented in a certain format and include:

- A disclosure that arbitration is final and binding.
- A disclosure that the findings of the arbitrators are not based on legal reasoning.
- A statement that the discovery process is generally more limited than the discovery process in a legal proceeding.
- A statement that the parties are waiving their right to a jury trial.
- A statement that the customer must be provided with a copy of the predispute clause and must verify its receipt with a signature.
- A disclosure that a minority of the arbitration panel will be affiliated with the securities industry.

If the predispute clause is contained in the customer agreement, there must be a highlighted disclosure just above the signature line.

If the customer requests a copy of the predispute arbitration agreement the firm must send it to the customer within 10 days. A firm may also have the customer sign a signature card. A signature card will allow the firm to verify the customer's written instructions that are sent in to the firm.

Customers who do not wish to disclose financial information may still open an account if there is reason to believe that the customer can afford to maintain the account. All registered representatives should update the customer's information regularly and note any changes in the following:

- Address
- Phone number
- Employer
- Investment objectives
- Marital status

Registered representatives are also required to maintain an accurate and up-to-date listing of all of their customers' transactions and investment holdings.

Customers are not required to provide their educational background when opening an account.

HOLDING SECURITIES

Upon opening an account, the investor must decide where the securities are to be held. The following methods are available:

- Transfer and ship
- Transfer and hold in safekeeping
- Hold in street name
- Receipt versus payment (RVP)/delivery versus payment (DVP)

TRANSFER AND SHIP

Securities that are to be transferred and shipped will be registered in the customer's name and will be sent to the customer's address of record.

TRANSFER AND HOLD IN SAFEKEEPING

Securities that are to be transferred and held in safekeeping will be registered in the customer's name and will be held by the brokerage firm. The broker dealer may charge a fee for the safekeeping of the securities. Customers may now elect to hold securities registered in their name electronically in the book entry form through the Direct Registration System (DRS). The DRS offered through the depository trust corporation will allow investors to hold their securities on the books of the issuer or the transfer agent. Investors who hold securities with the DRS will receive a statement from the issuer or transfer agent.

HOLD IN STREET NAME

Securities that are held in street name are registered in the name of the brokerage firm as the nominal owner of the securities, and the customer is the beneficial owner. Most securities are held in this manner to make transfer of ownership easier.

RECEIPT VS. PAYMENT (RVP)/
DELIVERY VS. PAYMENT (DVP)

These accounts are normally reserved for trusts and other institutional accounts that require that securities be delivered prior to releasing payment for the securities. These accounts are set up as cash-on-delivery (COD) accounts.

At the time the customer opens the account, the customer will also decide what to do with the distributions from the account. Investors may have the distributions sent directly to them or they may have them reinvested or swept into a money market account.

MAILING INSTRUCTIONS

All confirmations and statements will be sent to the customer's address of record. Statements and confirmations may be sent to an individual with power of attorney if the duplicates are requested in writing. A customer's mail may be held by a brokerage firm for up to two months if the customer is traveling within the United States and for up to three months if the customer is traveling outside the United States. If a customer provides a valid reason and submits a written request, the broker-dealer may hold the customer's mail for up to six months. Customers who are on active duty with the militarily and have no fixed address should be advised to open a military P.O. Box where statements may be sent.

TYPES OF ACCOUNTS

INDIVIDUAL ACCOUNT

An individual account is an account that is owned by one person. That person makes the determination as to what securities are purchased and sold. In addition, that person receives all of the distributions from the account.

JOINT ACCOUNT

A joint account is an account that is owned by two or more adults. Each party to the account may enter orders and request distributions. The registered representative does not need to confirm instructions with both parties. Joint accounts require the owners to sign a joint account agreement prior to the opening of the account. All parties must endorse all securities and all parties must be alive. Checks drawn from the account must be made out in the names of all of the parties.

JOINT TENANTS WITH RIGHTS OF SURVIVORSHIP (JTWROS)

In a joint account with rights of survivorship (JTWROS), all the assets are transferred into the name of the surviving party in the event of one tenant's death. The surviving party becomes the sole owner of all of the assets in the account. Both parties on the account have an equal and undivided interest in the assets in the account.

JOINT TENANTS IN COMMON (JTIC)

In a joint account that is established as tenants in common, if one party dies all the assets of the tenant who has died become the property of the decedent's estate. They do not become the property of the surviving tenant. An account registered as JTIC allows the assets in the account to be divided unequally. One party on the account could own 60% of the account's assets.

 TAKE**NOTE!**

Any securities registered in the names of two or more parties must be signed by all parties and all parties must be alive to be considered good delivery.

TRANSFER ON DEATH (TOD)

An account that has been registered as a transfer-on-death (TOD) account allows the account owner to stipulate to whom the account is to go to in the event of his or her death. Transfer on death accounts are sometimes referred to as pay on death or POD accounts. The party who will become the owner of the account in the event of the account holder's death is known as the beneficiary. The beneficiary may only enter orders for the account if he or she has power of attorney for the account. Unlike an account that is registered as JTWROS, the assets in the account will not be at risk should the beneficiary be the subject of a lawsuit, such as in a divorce proceeding.

DEATH OF A CUSTOMER

If an agent is notified of the death of a customer the agent must immediately cancel all open orders and mark the account deceased. The representative must await instructions from the executor or administrator of the estate. In order to sell or transfer the assets, the agent must receive:

- Letters testamentary
- Inheritance tax waivers
- Certified copy of the death certificate

The death of a customer with a discretionary account automatically terminates the discretionary authority.

CORPORATE ACCOUNTS

Corporations, like individuals, will purchase and sell securities. In order to open a corporate account, the registered representative must obtain a corporate resolution that states which individuals have the power to enter orders for the corporation. If a corporation wants to purchase securities on margin, then the registered representative must obtain a corporate charter and the bylaws that state that the corporation may purchase securities on margin. Finally, a certificate of incumbency must be obtained for the officers who are authorized to transact business for the corporation, within 60 days of the account opening.

TRUST ACCOUNTS

Trusts may be revocable or irrevocable. With a revocable trust, the individual who established the trust and contributes assets to the trust, known as the grantor or settlor, may, as the name suggests, revoke the trust and take the assets back. The income generated by a revocable trust is generally taxed as income to the grantor. If the trust is irrevocable, the grantor may not revoke the trust and take the assets back. With an irrevocable trust, the trust usually pays the taxes as its own entity or the beneficiaries of the trust are taxed on the income they receive. If the trust is established as a simple trust all income generated by the trust must be distributed to the beneficiaries in the year the income is earned. If the trust is established as a complex trust, the trust may retain some or all of the income earned and the trust will pay taxes on the income that is not distributed to the beneficiaries. The grantor of an irrevocable trust is generally not taxed on the income generated by the trust unless the assets in the trust are held for the benefit of the grantor, the grantor's spouse, or if the grantor has an interest in the income of the trust greater than 5 percent. A trust may also be established to hold or to distribute assets after a person's death under the terms of their Will. Trusts that are established under the terms of a Will are known as Testamentary trusts. All assets placed into a Testamentary trust are subject to both estate taxes and probate. A representative who opens a trust account must obtain documentation of the trustees investment powers over the trust's assets.

PARTNERSHIP ACCOUNTS

When a professional organization, such as a law partnership, opens an account, the registered representative must obtain a copy of the partnership agreement. The partnership agreement will state who may enter orders for the account of the partnership. If the partnership wishes to purchase securities on margin, it must not be prohibited by the partnership agreement. A family limited partnership is often used for estate planning. Parents may place significant assets into a family limited partnership as a way to transfer their ownership. Usually, the parents will act as the general partners and will transfer limited partnership interests to their children. As the interests are transferred to the children, the parents may become subject to gift taxes. However, the gift taxes usually will be lower than they would have suffered without the partnership.

TRADING AUTHORIZATION

From time to time, people other than the beneficial owner of the account may be authorized to enter orders for the account. All discretionary authority must be evidenced in writing for the following accounts:

- Discretionary account
- Custodial account
- Fiduciary account

OPERATING A DISCRETIONARY ACCOUNT

A discretionary account allows the registered representative to determine the following, without consulting the client first:

- The asset to be purchased or sold.
- The amount of the securities to be purchased or sold.
- The action to be taken in the account, whether to buy or sell.

The principal of the firm must accept the account and review it more frequently to ensure against abuses. The customer is required to sign a limited power of attorney that awards discretion to the registered representative. The limited power of attorney is good for up to three years; the customer is bound by the decisions of the representative, but may still enter orders. Once discretion is given to the representative, the representative may not, in turn, give discretion to another party. If the representative leaves the firm or stops managing the customer's account, the discretionary authority is automatically terminated. A standard power of attorney will also terminate upon the death or incapacitation of the account owner. A durable power of attorney will continue in full effect in the case of incapacitation and will only terminate upon the account owner's death. A full power of attorney allows an individual to deposit and withdraw cash and securities from the account. A full power of attorney is usually not given to a registered representative. A full power of attorney is more appropriate for fiduciaries such as a trustee, custodian, or a guardian. If a FINRA or MSRB broker dealer has a control relationship with an issuer of securities, the customer must be informed of the relationship and must give specific authorization for the purchase of the securities.

MANAGING DISCRETIONARY ACCOUNTS

All discretionary accounts must have the proper paperwork kept in the account file and must have:

- Every order entered marked discretionary, if discretion was exercised by the representative.
- Every order approved promptly by a principal.
- A designated principal to review the account.
- A record of all transactions.

    Discretion may not be exercised by a representative until the discretionary papers have been received by the firm and approved by the principal.

THIRD-PARTY AND FIDUCIARY ACCOUNTS

A fiduciary account is one that is managed by a third party for the benefit of the account holder. The party managing the account has responsibility for making all of the investments and other decisions relating to the account. The individual with this responsibility must do as a prudent person would do for his or her self and may not speculate. This is known as the prudent man rule. Many states have an approved list of securities, known as the legal list, that may be purchased by fiduciaries. The authority to transact business for the account must be evidenced in writing by a power of attorney. The fiduciary may have full power of attorney, also known as full discretion, under which the fiduciary may purchase and sell securities, as well as withdraw cash and securities from the account. Under a limited power of attorney or limited discretion, the fiduciary may only buy and sell securities; assets may not be withdrawn. The fiduciary has been legally appointed to represent the account holder and may not use the assets in the account for his or her own benefit. The fiduciary may, however, be reimbursed for expenses incurred in connection with the management of the account. Examples of fiduciaries include:

- Administrators
- Custodians
- Receivers

- Trustees
- Conservators
- Executors
- Guardians
- Sheriffs/marshals

When opening a third party or fiduciary account, the registered representative is required to obtain documentation of the individual's appointment and authority to act on behalf of the account holder. Trust accounts require that the representative obtain a copy of the trust agreement. The trust agreement will state who has been appointed as the trustee and any limitations on the trust's operation. Most trusts may only open cash accounts and may not purchase securities on margin, unless specifically authorized to do so in the agreement. When opening an account for a guardian, the representative must obtain a copy of the court order appointing the guardian. The court order must be dated within 60 days of the opening of the account. If the court order is more than 60 days old, the representative may not open the account until a new court order is obtained. Guardians are usually appointed in cases of mentally incompetent adults and orphaned children.

UNIFORM GIFT TO MINORS ACCOUNT (UGMA)

Minors are not allowed to own securities in their own name because they are not old enough to enter into legally binding contracts. The decision to purchase or sell a security creates a legally binding contract between two parties. The Uniform Gift to Minors Act (UGMA) regulates how accounts are operated for the benefit of minors. All UMGA accounts must have:

- One custodian
- One minor
- UGMA and the state in the account title
- Assets registered to the child's name after he or she reaches the age of majority

All securities in a UGMA account will be registered in the custodian's name as the nominal owner for the benefit of the minor who is the beneficial owner of the account. For example, the account should be titled: Mr. Jones as custodian for Billy Jones under New Jersey Uniform Gift to Minors Act.

Only one custodian and one minor are allowed on each account. A husband and wife could not be joint custodians for their minor child. If there is more than one child, a separate account must be opened for each one. The same person may serve as custodian on several accounts for several minors, and the minor may have more than one account established by different custodians. The donor of the security does not have to be the custodian for the account. If the parents are not the custodians of the accounts, they have no authority over the accounts.

RESPONSIBILITIES OF THE CUSTODIAN

The custodian has a fiduciary duty to manage the account prudently for the benefit of the minor child within certain guidelines, such as:

- No margin accounts.
- No high-risk securities (i.e., penny stocks).
- The custodian may not borrow from the account.
- No commodities.
- No speculative option strategies.
- The custodian may not give discretion to a third party.
- All distributions must be reinvested within a reasonable time.
- The custodian may not let rights or warrants expire; they must be exercised or sold.
- The custodian must provide support for all withdrawals from the account.
- Withdrawals may only be made to reimburse the custodian for expenses incurred in connection with the operation of the account or for the benefit of the minor.

CONTRIBUTIONS OF A UGMA ACCOUNT

Gifts of cash and securities or other property may be given to the minor. There is no dollar limit as to the size of the gift that may be given. The limit on the size of the tax-free gift is $15,000 per year. An individual may give gifts valued at up to $15,000 to any number of people each year without incurring a tax liability. Once a gift has been given, it is irrevocable. Gifts to a UGMA account carry an indefeasible title and may not be taken back for any reason whatsoever. The custodian may, however, use the assets for the minor's welfare and educational needs.

 TAKENOTE!

A husband and wife may give up to $30,000 per year per person. The IRS considers half of the gift to be coming from each spouse. The annual gift limit is indexed for inflation.

UGMA TAXATION

The minor is responsible for the taxes on the account. However, any unearned income that exceeds $2,200 per year will be taxed at the parent's marginal tax rate if the child is younger than 14 years old. For gifts that exceed $15,000 per year, the tax liability is on the donor of the gift, not on the minor.

DEATH OF A MINOR OR CUSTODIAN

If the minor dies, the account becomes part of the child's estate. It does not automatically go to the parents. If the custodian dies, a court or the donor may appoint a new custodian.

UNIFORM TRANSFER TO MINORS ACT

Some states have adopted the Uniform Transfer to Minors Act rather than the Uniform Gifts to Minors Act. The main difference is that with a UTMA account the custodian may determine when the assets become the property of the child. The maximum age is 25 years old.

 TAKE**NOTE!**

No evidence of custodial rights is required to open a UGMA or UTMA account.

ACCOUNTS FOR EMPLOYEES OF OTHER BROKER DEALERS

FINRA Rule 3210 governs the opening of accounts for employees of broker-dealers. This rule requires that an employee of a broker dealer who wishes to open an account at another broker dealer to obtain the employer's written permission prior to opening the account. The employee must present written notification to the broker dealer opening the account that he/she is employed by a FINRA member firm at the time the account is opened. This rule is in effect for the employee or any of the employee's immediate family members. This rule will also require the employee to obtain the employer's written permission for accounts that were opened within 30 days of the start of employment. Excluded from this rule are accounts opened by the employee where no transactions may take place in individual securities such as accounts opened to purchase open end mutual funds, variable annuities and UITs.

NUMBERED ACCOUNTS

A broker dealer, at the request of the customer, may open an account that is simply identified by a number or a symbol, so long as there is a statement signed by the customer attesting to the ownership of the account.

ACCOUNT TRANSFER

Clients from time to time will wish to have their accounts transferred from one brokerage firm to another. This is usually accomplished through an Automated Client Account Transfer (ACAT). The ACAT provides transfer and delivery instructions to the firm, which will be required to deliver the account to the client's new firm. The firm that receives the transfer instructions is required to validate the instructions and freeze the account or take exception to them within one business day. No new orders may be accepted and all open orders will be canceled. However, orders may be taken for options positions that expire in 7 days or less. Once the account and positions have been validated, the firm has three additional business days to complete the transfer. A firm may only take exception to the instructions for the following reasons:

- The customer's signature is missing or invalid.
- The account title does not match the carrying firm's account number.
- The social security number does not match.
- The account number is wrong.

From time to time certain investment positions will not be able to be transferred from the old firm to the new firm. A customer is required to give specific instructions as to what should be done with that investment. The customer may elect to:

- Leave the investment at the old firm.
- Have it liquidated.
- Have it shipped.

Any disputes between the two firms must be resolved within 5 business days. A registered rep who changes firms may utilize a bulk account transfer process for his clients' account so long as the clients have provided affirmative consent. FINRA does not allow customer accounts to be transferred or the broker of record to be changed through a negative consent letter.

OPTION ACCOUNTS

A customer wishing to trade options must be given a copy of the OCC's risk disclosure document and sign the firm's option agreement. The customer's account may be initially approved by a branch manager who is not a registered option and security futures principal (ROSFP), so long as the account is approved by a ROSFP within a reasonable amount of time. A branch manager with more than three representatives conducting options business is required to qualify as a registered option and security futures principal.

MARGIN ACCOUNTS

A margin account allows the investor to purchase securities without paying for the securities in full. The investor is required to deposit a portion of the securities' purchase price and may borrow the rest from the broker dealer. The portion of the securities' purchase price that an investor must deposit is called margin. The amount of the required deposit or margin is controlled by the Federal Reserve Board under Regulation T of the Securities Exchange Act of 1934. Regulation T gave the Federal Reserve Board the authority to regulate the extension of credit for securities purchases. The Federal Reserve Board controls:

- Which securities may be purchased on margin.
- The amount of the initial required deposit.
- Payment dates.

Customers who purchase securities on margin must receive a separate margin disclosure statement at the time the account is opened and annually thereafter detailing the risks of purchasing securities on margin. If the broker-dealer allows customers to open accounts online, the margin disclosure statement must be clearly displayed on the firm's website. Unlike when opening a cash account, when a customer opens a margin account he or she will be required to sign certain account documents. The customer will be asked to sign the following:

- Credit agreement
- Hypothecation agreement
- Loan consent

THE CREDIT AGREEMENT

The credit agreement states the terms and conditions under which credit will be extended to the customer. It will include information about how interest is charged as well as information about the rates that will be charged. A margin loan does not amortize, meaning that the principal is not paid down on a regular schedule. The brokerage firm simply charges interest to the account.

THE HYPOTHECATION AGREEMENT

The hypothecation agreement pledges the customer's securities that were purchased on margin as collateral for the loan. It also allows the brokerage firm to take the same securities and repledge or rehypothecate them as collateral for a loan at a bank to obtain a loan for the customer.

LOAN CONSENT

By signing a loan consent agreement, the customer allows the brokerage firm to lend out the securities to customers who wish to sell the securities short. This is the only part of the margin agreement that the customer is not required to sign. The credit and hypothecation agreement must be signed prior to the account being approved to purchase securities on margin.

All securities purchased in a margin account will be held in street name, the name of the brokerage firm, so that the broker dealer may sell the securities to protect itself if the value of the securities falls significantly. Day trading is an investment strategy defined by the entering of round-trip orders, consisting of both a buy and sell order, on the same day for the same security. Firms that promote the use of day trading strategies to individual investors must adhere to special account opening requirements. A broker dealer will be considered to be promoting day trading strategies if it holds seminars, advertises, or uses another company to promote its services. If the firm promotes day trading, it must provide the customer with a risk disclosure document and approve the account for day trading. If the customer is not approved for day trading, the customer may still open an account so long as the firm obtains a written statement from the customer stating that he or she will not be engaging in day trading strategies. A firm will be considered to be promoting day trading if the registered representatives promote day trading strategies with the knowledge of the firm's principal.

COMMINGLING CUSTOMERS' PLEDGED SECURITIES

A broker dealer may not commingle a customer's pledged securities with another customer's pledged securities as joint collateral to obtain a loan from a bank without both customers' written authorization. This authorization is required by SEC Rule 15c2-1 and is part of most margin agreements. A customer's securities may never be commingled with the firm's securities.

WRAP ACCOUNTS

A wrap account is an account that charges the customer a set annual fee for both advice and execution costs. The fee is based on the assets in the account. Wrap account holders must be given Schedule H, which details how fees are to be charged, prior to opening the account. A firm that offers wrap accounts to its clients must be registered as investment advisers. Agents who service wrap accounts must have passed the Series 65 or Series 66 exams. Wrap accounts and other asset based fee accounts are usually not appropriate for clients who trade infrequently and use a buy and hold strategy. The practice of placing these types of accounts into fee based programs constitutes a violation known as reverse churning.

REGULATION S-P

Regulation S-P requires that the firm maintain adequate procedures to protect the financial information of its customers. Firms must guard against unauthorized access to customer financial information and must employ policies to ensure its safety. Special concerns arise over the ability for a person to "hack" into a firm's customer data based by gaining unauthorized access. Firms must develop and maintain specific safeguards for its computer systems and WiFi access. Regulation S-P was derived from the privacy rules of the Gramm-Leach-Bliley Act. A firm must deliver:

- An initial privacy notice to customers, no later than when the account was opened.
- An annual privacy notice to all customers.

The annual privacy notice may be delivered electronically via the firm's website, so long as the customer has agreed to receive it in writing and it is clearly displayed. Regulation S-P also states that a firm may not disclose nonpublic personal information to nonaffiliated companies for clients who have opted out of the list.

The method by which a client may opt out may not be unreasonable. It is considered unreasonable to require a customer to write a letter to opt out. Reasonable methods are emails or a toll-free number. The rule also differentiates between who is a customer and who is a consumer. A customer is anyone who has an ongoing relationship with the firm (i.e., has an account). A consumer is someone who is providing information to the firm and is considering becoming a customer or who has purchased a product from the firms and has no other contact with the firm. The firm must give the privacy notice to consumers prior to sharing any nonpublic information with a non-affiliated company.

 TAKE**NOTE!**

A client of a brokerage firm may not opt out of the sharing of information with an affiliated company.

Regulation S-AM prohibits broker dealers from soliciting business based on information received from affiliated third parties unless the potential marketing had been clearly disclosed to the potential customer, the potential customer was provided an opportunity to opt out, but did not opt out.

IDENTITY THEFT

The fraudulent practice of identity theft may be used by criminals in an attempt to obtain access to the assets or credit of another person. The Federal Trade Commission (FTC) requires banks and broker dealers to establish and maintain written identity theft prevention programs. A broker dealer's written supervisory procedures manual must reference its identity theft program. The program must be designed to detect red flags relating to the known suspicious activity employed during an attempt at identity theft. The identity theft prevention program should be designed to allow the firm to respond quickly to any attempted identity theft to mitigate any potential damage.

DAY TRADING ACCOUNTS

Day trading is an investment strategy defined by the entering of round-trip orders, consisting of both a buy and sell order, on the same day for the same security.

Firms that promote the use of day trading strategies to individual investors must adhere to special account opening requirements. A broker dealer will be considered to be promoting day trading strategies if it holds seminars, advertises, or uses another company to promote its services. If the firm promotes day trading, it must provide the customer with a risk disclosure document and approve the account for day trading. If the customer is not approved for day trading, the customer may still open an account so long as the firm obtains a written statement from the customer stating that he or she will not be engaging in day trading strategies. A firm will be considered to be promoting day trading if the registered representatives promote day trading strategies with the knowledge of the firm's principal. A pattern day trader is defined as anyone who enters 4 or more round trip orders in a 5 day period. The minimum equity for a day trading account is $25,000.

ABLE ACCOUNTS

An ABLE account, sometimes referred to as a 529 ABLE account, may be established as a tax-advantaged savings account to provide for the care of individuals with disabilities. The Achieving a Better Life Experience (ABLE) account regulations were passed in order to recognize the unique financial burdens inherent in caring for a disabled person. Individuals with disabilities may have only one ABLE account at a time and the individual with the disability is deemed to be both the account owner and the designated beneficiary. ABLE accounts may be transferred or rolled over into new ABLE accounts for the same beneficiary. Contributions to the account are made with after-tax dollars and are allowed to grow tax deferred. The contributions and the growth may be used tax free by the beneficiary for qualified care and quality-of-life expenses. Tax-free withdrawals may be made by the beneficiary to cover qualified expenses incurred or in anticipation of paying expenses to be incurred. Qualified expenses would include things such as:

- Medical care
- Wellness care
- Transportation
- Housing expenses (including mortgage, tax, rent, insurance, and utility payments)
- Transportation
- Assistive technology
- Education
- Job training

Withdrawals from an ABLE account for expenses that do not meet the definition of qualified expenses will be seen as part of the beneficiary's resources if retained past the month the distribution occurred. In order to qualify for an ABLE account, the individual must have been disabled by the time he or she reached their 26th birthday. The maximum annual contribution to an ABLE account is equal to the annual tax-free gift limit of $15,000 and is subject to change each year. Anyone may make contributions to an ABLE account and the account may be rolled over to another family member if that person meets the eligibility guidelines. The assets in the ABLE account will not impact the disabled person's eligibility for many assistance programs. When calculating eligibility for assistance, the first $100,000 in assets in the ABLE account are excluded when estimating the amount of resources available. However, ABLE account balances which exceed $100,000 can cause the beneficiary of the account to be placed in a suspended status for receiving supplemental security income (SSI) until all resources in the ABLE and other accounts owned by the individual fall to $100,000 or lower. Upon the death of the beneficiary of an ABLE account, the remaining assets will be used to repay Medicaid for any payments made to the beneficiary.

FINRA RULES ON FINANCIAL EXPLOITATION OF SENIORS

While many people are living active and productive lives well into their eighties and beyond, FINRA has enacted rules designed to protect the financial interests of seniors who are 65 or older. FINRA is particularly concerned about clients being taken advantage of by unscrupulous or otherwise self-serving people. Registered representatives should have a clear understanding of the financial needs, resources, and behavior of their clients. This is specifically important when dealing with older clients who may require the assets to meet their current financial needs, and who can fall victim to bad actors. Registered representatives should be particularly concerned with any requests to withdraw money from an account that is outside the normal actions of the client.

EXAMPLE

Sally is a retired school administrator who is 83 years old and is living on her assets. Sally and her late husband had planned well for their retirement. She has the proceeds from her husband's life insurance policy, and a significant savings and retirement account, as well as her social security. Sally has been a client of your firm for 10 years and generally moves $1,800 to $2,000 per month from her brokerage account to her checking account. Twice per year she travels and moves $5,000 to her checking account to pay her travel expenses. One day Sally calls up and says she needs $35,000 wired to an out-of-state bank account. When the agent inquires what this is for, Sally says her friend has told her of an investment opportunity in real estate that she would like to take advantage of. When the agent inquiries about the opportunity, the details Sally provides do not sound right to the agent.

ANALYSIS

This is a serious red flag, and in this situation the agent has a significant conflict. On the one hand, the agent is required to do as the client requests. On the other, the agent feels a duty to protect the client and senses that their client may be the victim of senior exploitation. Even discussing the matter with a principal of the firm is not enough to determine if the client is being taken advantage of.

FINRA's rules allow broker dealers to withhold distributions to senior clients for 15 business days in cases of suspected financial exploitation. The firm should notify the trusted contact as well as any individuals who are authorized to transact business in the account within two business days of placing the hold on the transfer. During this time, the broker dealer should investigate the client's request and obtain as much information regarding the receiving party as they can. To further protect seniors, broker dealers should obtain the name and contact information of a "trusted contact" for senior clients. The firm in very limited circumstances may contact the trusted contact to inquire about requests to withdraw money when financial exploitation is suspected. The firm may also contact the person to inquire as to the welfare of the client and to inquire as to the identity of any individual who may hold power of attorney or who may be named as executor of the client's Will. If the firm at the end of 15 business days has gathered information relating to the request that indicates that this is a case of financial exploitation, the firm may withhold the funds for another 10 business days. The firm should share their findings with the National Center for Elder Abuse as well as with law enforcement.

REGULATION BEST INTEREST

Regulation Best Interest (Reg BI) was adopted by the SEC in June of 2019 as an amendment to the Securities Exchange Act of 1934. All broker dealers, investment advisers, and agents are subject to standards of conduct that require the firm and its agents to act in the best interest of retail customers. Regulation BI covers all recommendations to effect securities transactions as well as all recommendations regarding account establishment. That is to say, when recommending that a client open a joint, transfer on death, trust, or fee-based account, the type of account established must be in the client's best interest. In June of 2020, as part of Regulation BI, all broker dealers and investment advisers will be required to provide retail clients with a client relationship summary (CRS) and will be required to post the CRS on their publicly available website. The CRS may be provided in hardcopy or electronically. If the CRS is provided in hardcopy, the CRS may not be more than two pages long and the CRS must be the first page among any documents sent in the same package. The following rules are in place relating to the CRS:

- The CRS must be written in plain English using everyday terms.
- The CRS should be written using "active voice" with a strong, direct, and clear meaning.
- The CRS must follow the standard format and order as detailed by the SEC.
- The CRS should be written as if speaking to the retail investor directly.
- The CRS must be factual and avoid boilerplate, vague, or exaggerated language.
- The CRS may not include disclosures other than those required under Regulation BI.
- Electronic CRSs should use graphs and charts, specifically dual column charts to compare services.
- Electronic CRSs may use videos and popups and must provide access to any referenced information via hyperlink or other means.
- Electronic CRSs may be delivered via email provided that the email contains a direct link to the CRS.

Some of the required disclosures are referred to as "conversation starters." These conversation starters should be in bold or in other text to ensure that they are more noticeable than other disclosures. These conversation starters include questions such as:

1. Who is my primary contact and does he or she represent a broker dealer or an investment adviser?
2. Who can I speak to about how the person is treating me?
3. Given my financial situation, should I choose a brokerage service? Why or why not?
4. Given my financial situation, should I choose an investment advisory service? Why or why not?
5. How will you choose investments to recommend to me?
6. What is your relevant experience, including licenses, education, and qualifications? What do these qualifications mean?
7. What fees will I pay?
8. How will these fees affect my investments? If I give you $10,000, how much will go toward fees and expenses and how much will be invested for me?

9. What are your legal obligations to me when providing recommendations (broker dealer)?

10. What are your legal obligations to me when acting as my investment adviser?

11. How else does your firm make money?

12. How do your financial professionals make money?

13. What conflicts of interest do you have?

14. Does the firm or its financial professionals have legal or disciplinary history?

Both broker dealers and investment advisers are required to adhere to the standards of conduct under Regulation BI. As such, both must disclose that they must put the interests of the client ahead of theirs when making a recommendation and that the way the firm makes money for providing the services causes a conflict of interest. These conflicts include recommending proprietary products, receiving payments from third parties, principal trading, or revenue sharing.

Online broker dealers who only provide access to trading, as well as investment advisers who only offer automated services and who do not offer access to specific registered individuals, must disclose this fact in the CRS and must provide a section on their website that answers questions relating to the conversation starters. If a broker dealer or investment adviser provides both online services and access to registered personnel, a registered person must be made available to discuss the conversation starters.

Broker dealers are required to provide the CRS to customers before or upon the earlier of recommending the type of account to establish or an investment strategy or upon opening an account or placing an order. Investment advisers must provide the CRS to clients prior to or at the time the contract is entered into even if the contract is oral. The CRS is now known as ADV part 3. For entities who are registered as both a broker dealer and as an investment adviser, the CRS must be delivered upon the earliest requirement for either registration. Any changes required to be made to the CRS must be completed within 30 days and an updated CRS clearly reflecting the changes must be sent to existing customers within 60 days. All broker dealers and investment advisers are required to file the CRS along with any changes with the SEC. Broker dealers will file through the Central Registration Depository (CRD) system and investment advisers will file through the Investment Adviser Registration Database (IARD). The relationship summary must be provided to a client upon request within 30 days.

Pretest

CUSTOMER ACCOUNTS

1. A registered representative may accept orders for a client's account from which of the following?

   I. Client
   II. Client's spouse
   III. Client's attorney
   IV. Client's investment adviser

   a. I and II
   b. I, II, and III
   c. I only
   d. I, II, III, and IV

2. In which type of account does the nominal owner of the account enter all orders for the beneficial owner of the account?

   a. Custodial account
   b. Fiduciary account
   c. Authorized account
   d. Discretionary account

3. Which of the following is NOT allowed as a joint account?

   a. A registered representative and a customer
   b. A registered representative and a spouse
   c. A registered representative and a friend
   d. A registered representative and his 16-year-old child

4. A customer and his spouse have an account registered as joint tenants in common. If the customer dies, what would happen to the account?

   a. The decedent's assets will be distributed according to his will.

   b. The executor of the estate will determine how all of the assets are to be distributed.

   c. All of the assets in the account will be distributed according to the trustee.

   d. The spouse would get the assets in the account.

5. To open a guardian account, the firm must obtain:

   a. trust papers.

   b. power of attorney.

   c. declaration papers.

   d. affidavit of domicile.

6. In which type of account does a trustee enter all orders for the owners of the account?

   a. Custodial account

   b. Fiduciary account

   c. Authorized account

   d. Discretionary account

7. The maximum allowable gift to a minor under UGMA is:

   a. $15,000.

   b. $1,500.

   c. $30,000.

   d. There is no limit.

8. The nominal owner of a UGMA account is the:

   a. custodian.

   b. minor.

   c. trustee.

   d. parent.

9. A representative may borrow money from a client:

   a. if the client is the issuer of securities.

   b. if the client is a credit union.

   c. if the client is a wealthy individual who regularly makes private loans.

   d. under no circumstances.

10. Which of the following may be able to purchase shares of a hot issue?
    a. Registered representative
    b. Minor child of a firm employee
    c. Registered representative's spouse
    d. Registered representative's father-in-law

11. Which of the following is NOT required in the account title for a custodial account?
    a. The state
    b. The minor's social security number
    c. The name of the custodian
    d. UGMA

12. You have just opened up a new account for a customer. You are required to have all of the following, EXCEPT the:
    a. Agent's name noted.
    b. principal's signature.
    c. customer's signature.
    d. customer's social security number.

13. A customer calls in asking about how to put money aside for his children. He wants to open a custodial account for his two children, Bobby and Sue. What should you recommend?
    a. Open two accounts for both children, with him and his wife as custodian.
    b. Open two accounts for the two children, with him being the custodian on one and his wife being custodian on the other, as one parent may only be custodian for one child.
    c. Open one account immediately for both children.
    d. Open two accounts, one for each child with he or his wife as custodians for both or for either.

14. Which of the following is true?
    a. Representatives and broker dealers may not disclose any information regarding a client to a third party without the client's expressed consent or a court order.
    b. A representative may not obtain outside employment because of the potential conflict of interest.
    c. A client may not have a numbered account for his investment account.
    d. Broker dealers may not give gifts to the employees of other broker dealers.

15. A potential customer that you have been trying to get to open an account with you for some time has agreed to put some money in a mutual fund you have recommended. Which of the following customer information is NOT required on the new account form?
    a. Address
    b. Social security number
    c. Educational information
    d. Investment objective

16. Two brothers, both married with children, have opened an account with your firm as JTWROS. One brother has passed away. All of the following will happen with regard to the account, EXCEPT:
    a. all assets will become the property of the surviving party.
    b. the account will be retitled in the name of the surviving party.
    c. the portion of the assets belonging to the deceased will go to his estate.
    d. the original account will become an individual account.

17. Before opening a new account for any customer, a registered representative must:
    a. fill out and sign a new account form.
    b. send a declaration of investor intent (DII) to the IRS.
    c. fill out a new account form and present it to the investor for his signature.
    d. fill out and sign a full financial declaration.

18. A client died in testate. The client's assets will be liquidated by the:
    a. heirs.
    b. administrator.
    c. executor.
    d. spouse.

CHAPTER **7**

Retirement Plans

INTRODUCTION

For most people, saving for retirement has become an important investment objective for at least part of their portfolio. Investors may participate in retirement plans that have been established by their employers, as well as those they have established for themselves. Both corporate and individual plans may be qualified or nonqualified, and it is important for an investor to understand the difference before deciding to participate. Series 7 candidates will see a fair number of questions on the exam dealing with retirement plans. The following table compares the key features of qualified and nonqualified plans.

Feature	Qualified	Nonqualified
Contributions	Pretax	After tax
Growth	Tax deferred	Tax deferred
Participation must be allowed	For everyone	The corporation may choose who gets to participate
IRS approval	Required	Not required
Withdrawals	100% taxed as ordinary income	Growth in excess of cost base is taxed as ordinary income

INDIVIDUAL PLANS

Individuals may set up a qualified retirement plan for themselves and allow contributions to the plan to be made with pre-tax dollars. Individuals may also purchase investment products such as annuities that allow their money to grow tax deferred. The money used to purchase an annuity has already been taxed, making an annuity a nonqualified product.

INDIVIDUAL RETIREMENT ACCOUNTS (IRAs)

All individuals with earned income may establish an Individual Retirement Account (IRA) for themselves. Contributions to traditional IRAs may or may not be tax deductible, depending on the individual's level of adjusted gross income and whether the individual is eligible to participate in an employer-sponsored plan. Individuals who do not qualify to participate in an employer-sponsored plan may deduct their IRA contributions regardless of their income level. The level of adjusted gross income that allows an investor to deduct their IRA contributions has been increasing since 1998. These tax law changes occur too frequently to make them a practical test question. Our review of IRAs will focus on the four main types, which are:

1. Traditional
2. Roth
3. SEP
4. Educational

TRADITIONAL IRAS

Currently, a traditional IRA allows an individual to contribute a maximum of 100% of earned income or $6,000 per year or up to $12,000 per couple. If only one spouse works, the working spouse may contribute $6,000 to an IRA for themselves and $6,000 to a separate IRA for their spouse, under the nonworking spousal option. Investors over 50 may contribute up to $7,000 of earned income to their IRA. Regardless of whether the IRA contribution was made with pre- or after-tax dollars, the money is allowed to grow tax deferred. All withdrawals from an IRA are taxed as ordinary income regardless of how the growth was generated in the account. Withdrawals from an IRA prior to age 59-1/2 are subject to a 10% penalty tax as well as ordinary income taxes. The 10% penalty will be waived for first-time homebuyers or educational expenses for the taxpayer's child, grandchildren, or spouse. The 10% penalty will also be waived if the payments are part of a series of substantially equal payments. Withdrawals from an IRA must begin by April 1st of the year following the year in which the taxpayer reaches 72. If an individual fails to make withdrawals that are sufficient in size and frequency, the individual will be subject to a 50% penalty on the insufficient amount. An individual who makes a contribution to an IRA that exceeds 100% of earned income or

$6,000, whichever is less, will be subject to a penalty of 6% per year on the excess amount for as long as the excess contribution remains in the account.

ROTH IRAs

A Roth IRA is a nonqualified account. All contributions made to a Roth IRA, are made with after-tax dollars. The same contribution limits apply for Roth IRAs. An individual may contribute the lesser of 100% of earned income to a maximum of $6,000 per person or $12,000 per couple. Any contribution made to a Roth IRA reduces the amount that may be deposited into a traditional IRA, and vice versa. All contributions deposited in a Roth IRA are allowed to grow tax deferred, and all of the growth may be taken out of the account tax-free provided that the individual has reached age 59-1/2 and the assets have been in the account for at least five years. A 10% penalty tax will be charged on any withdrawal of earnings prior to age 59-1/2 unless the owner is purchasing a home, has become disabled, or has died. There are no requirements for an individual to take distributions from a Roth IRA by a certain age.

 TAKENOTE!

Individuals and couples who are eligible to open a Roth IRA may convert their traditional IRA to a Roth IRA. The investor will have to pay income taxes on the amount converted, but it will not be subject to the 10% penalty.

SIMPLIFIED EMPLOYEE PENSION IRA (SEP IRA)

A SEP IRA is used by small corporations and self-employed individuals to plan for retirement. A SEP IRA is attractive to small employers because it allows them to set up a retirement plan for their employees rather quickly and inexpensively. The contribution limit for a SEP IRA far exceeds that of traditional IRAs. The contribution limit is the lesser of 25% of the employee's compensation or $61,000 per year. Employees may make their annual IRA contribution to their SEP IRA or they may make their standard contribution to a traditional or Roth IRA.

PARTICIPATION

All eligible employees must open an IRA to receive the employer's contribution to the SEP. If the employee does not open an IRA account, the employer must open one for the employee. The employee must be at least 21 years old and have worked during three of the last five years for the employer and have earned at least $550. All eligible employees must participate, as well as the employer.

EMPLOYER CONTRIBUTIONS

The employer may contribute between 0 and 25% of the employee's total compensation to a maximum of $61,000. Contributions to all SEP IRAs, including the employer's SEP IRA, must be made at the same rate. An employee who is over 72 must also participate and receive a contribution. All eligible employees are immediately vested in the employer's contributions to the plan.

SEP IRA TAXATION

The employer's contributions to a SEP IRA are immediately tax deductible by the employer. Contributions are not taxed at the employee's rate until the employee withdraws the funds. Employees may begin to withdraw money from the plan at age 59-1/2. All withdrawals are taxed as ordinary income, and withdrawals prior to age 59-1/2 are subject to a 10% penalty tax.

IRA CONTRIBUTIONS

All contributions to an IRA must be made by April 15th of the following calendar year, regardless of whether an extension has been filed by the taxpayer. Contributions may be made between January 1 and April 15 for the previous year, the current year, or both. All IRA contributions must be made in cash.

IRA ACCOUNTS

All IRA accounts are held in the name of the custodian for the benefit of the account holder. Traditional custodians include banks, broker dealers, and mutual fund companies.

IRA INVESTMENTS

Individuals who establish IRAs have a wide variety of investments to choose from when deciding how to invest the funds. Investors should always choose investments that fit their investment objectives. The following is a comparison of allowable and nonallowable investments:

Allowable	Nonallowable
Stocks	Margin accounts
Bonds	Short sales
Mutual funds	Tangibles/collectibles/art
Annuities	Speculative option trading
UITs	Term life insurance
Limited partnerships	Rare coins
U.S. minted coins ETFs	Real estate

IT IS NOT WISE TO PUT A MUNICIPAL BOND IN AN IRA

Municipal bonds or municipal bond funds should never be placed in an IRA because the advantage of those investments is that the interest income is free from federal taxes. Because their interest is free from federal taxes, the interest rate that is offered will be less than the rates offered by other alternatives. The advantage of an IRA is that money is allowed to grow tax deferred, therefore an individual would be better off with a higher yielding taxable bond of the same quality.

ROLLOVER VS. TRANSFER

An individual may want or need to move an IRA from one custodian to another. There are two ways by which this can be accomplished. Individuals may rollover their IRA or they may transfer their IRA.

ROLLOVER

With an IRA rollover, the individual may take possession of the funds for a maximum of 60 calendar days prior to depositing the funds into another qualified account. Investors may only rollover their IRA once every 12 months. Investors have 60 days from the date of the distribution to deposit 100% of the funds into another qualified account or they must pay ordinary income taxes on the distribution and a 10% penalty tax, if the investor is under 59-1/2.

TRANSFER

An investor may transfer an IRA directly from one custodian to another by simply signing an account transfer form. The investor never takes possession of the assets in the account, and the investor may directly transfer an IRA as often as he or she would like.

THE SECURE ACT OF 2019

The Secure Act of 2019 made substantial changes to retirement planning. Many investors who have other assets saved for retirement or who are still actively working may want to continue to enjoy the tax benefits offered by traditional IRAs. The secure Act increased the age at which investors must take required minimum distributions (RMDs) from IRA accounts. The Secure Act raised the age for RMDs to 72 and removed the age limits for contributions for older workers. The Secure Act also made substantial changes to the rules regarding inherited IRAs. Most individuals who inherit an IRA will be required to withdraw all of the assets within 10 years of the death of the original account owner. Exempt from the 10-year distribution requirement are surviving spouses, disabled or chronically ill individuals, a minor child and individuals who are less than 10 years younger than the decedent. Additionally, The Secure Act modified the rules regarding the use of assets in 529 plans. Individuals who have established 529 plans may withdraw up to $10,000 tax free each year to repay student loans. The Secure Act also had a substantial impact on retirement plans established by both large and small employers. The Secure Act includes the following provisions:

- Increased the contribution limits for small employers who set up 401K plans from 10% to 15% of wages

- Provide small employers with a tax credit of up to $500 per year to create 401K plans or simple IRA plans with automatic enrollment for employees

- Allow employers to offer retirement plans to part-time employees who work either 1,000 hours per year or who have worked at least 500 hours per year for 3 consecutive years

- Allow individuals to withdraw up to $5,000 tax free from their 401k to offset the cost of having or adopting a child

- Require define contribution plans to disclose the lifetime income that could be generated from a lump sum in a retirement account

- Encourage the inclusion of annuities inside retirement plans

EDUCATIONAL IRA/COVERDELL IRA

An educational IRA allows individuals to contribute up to $2,000 in after-tax dollars to an educational IRA for each student who is under age 18. The money is allowed to grow tax deferred, and the growth may be withdrawn tax free, as long as the money is used for educational purposes. If all of the funds have not been used for educational purposes by the time the student reaches 30 years of age, the account must be rolled over to another family member who is under 30 years of age or distributed to the original student, at which point it is subject to a 10% penalty tax as well as ordinary income taxes.

529 PLANS

Qualified tuition plans more frequently referred to as 529 plans may be set up either as a prepaid tuition plan or as a college savings plan. With the prepaid tuition plan, the plan locks in a current tuition rate at a specific school.

The prepaid tuition plan can be set up as an installment plan or one where the contributor funds the plan with a lump sum deposit. Many states will guarantee the plans but may require that either the contributor or the beneficiary to be a state resident. The plan covers only tuition and mandatory fees. A room and board option is available for some plans. A college cost-savings account may be opened by any adult and the donor does not have to be related to the child. The assets in the college savings plan can be used to cover all costs of qualified higher education including tuition, room and board, books, computers, and mandatory fees. These plans generally have no age limit when assets must be used. College savings accounts are not guaranteed by the state and the value of the account may decline based on the investment results of the account. College savings accounts are not state specific and do not lock in a tuition rate. Contributions to a 529 plan are made with after-tax dollars and are allowed to grow tax deferred. The assets in the account remain under the control of the donor, even after the student reaches the age of majority. The funds may be used to meet the student's educational needs and the growth may be withdrawn federally tax-free. Most states also allow the assets to be withdrawn tax free. Any funds used for non-qualified education expenses will be subject to income tax and a 10% penalty tax. If funds remain or if the student does not attend or complete qualified higher education the funds may be rolled over to another family member within 60 days without incurring taxes and penalties.

There are no income limits for the donors and contribution limits vary from state to state. 529 plans have an impact on a student's ability to obtain need based financial aid. However, because the 529 plans are treated as parental assets and not as assets of the student, the plans are assessed at the expected family contribution (EFC) rate of 5.64%. This will have a significantly lower impact than plans and assets that are considered to be assets of the student. Student assets will be assessed at a 20% contribution rate. It's important to note that the assets in a 529 plan can be used for educational expenses incurred for private K through 12 schooling

LOCAL GOVERNMENT INVESTMENT POOLS (LGIPS)

Local government investment pools (LGIPs) allow states and local governments to manage their cash reserves and to receive money market rates on the funds. LGIPs may also be created to invest the proceeds of a bond offering if the proceeds of the offering are intended to be used to call in an existing bond issue. If the LGIP was created to prerefund an existing issue, additional restrictions will apply as to the type of investments that may be purchased by the pool. LGIPs that are created to manage cash reserves must only invest in securities on the state's legal or approved list. The legal list usually includes investments such as:

- Commercial paper rated in the two highest categories.
- U.S. government and agency debt
- Bankers' acceptances
- Repurchase agreement
- Municipal debt issues within the state
- Investment company securities
- Certificates of deposit
- Savings accounts

Each state has an investment advisory board that works with the state treasury office to administer the pools. The main objective of these pools is safety of principal, with liquidity and interest income as secondary objectives. The pools require that the following be detailed in writing:

- Delegation of authority to make investments
- Annual investment activity reports

- Statement of safekeeping of securities

Municipal fund securities are not considered to be investment companies and are not required to register under the Investment Company Act of 1940. Additionally, prepaid tuition plans are not considered to be municipal fund securities. LGIP employees who market the plans directly to investors are exempt from MSRB rules; however, if the LGIP is marketed to investors by employees of a broker dealer, the broker dealer and all of its employees are subject to MSRB rules.

KEOGH PLANS (HR-10)

A Keogh is a qualified retirement plan set up by self-employed individuals, sole proprietors, and unincorporated businesses. If the business is set up as a corporation, a Keogh may not be used.

CONTRIBUTIONS

A Keogh may only be funded with earned income during a period when the business shows a gross profit. If the business realizes a loss, no Keogh contributions are allowed. A self-employed person may contribute the lesser of 25% of postcontribution income or $61,000. If the business has eligible employees, the employer must make a contribution for the employees at the same rate as his or her own contribution. Employee contributions are based on the employee's gross income and are limited to $61,000 per year. All money placed in a Keogh plan is allowed to grow tax deferred and is taxed as ordinary income when distributions are made to retiring employees and plan participants. From time to time, a self-employed person may make a nonqualified contribution to a Keogh plan; however, the total of the qualified and nonqualified contributions may not exceed the maximum contribution limit. Any excess contribution may be subject to a 10% penalty tax.

An eligible employee is defined as one that:

- Works full time (at least 1,000 hours per year) or 500 hours per year for 3 years
- Is at least 21 years old.
- Has worked at least one year for the employer.

Employees who participate in a Keogh plan must be vested after five years. Withdrawals from a Keogh may begin when the participant reaches 59-1/2. Any premature withdrawals are subject to a 10% penalty tax. Keoghs, like IRAs, may be rolled over every 12 months. In the event of a participant's death, the assets will go to the individual's beneficiaries.

TAX-SHELTERED ANNUITIES (TSAS)/TAX-DEFERRED ACCOUNTS (TDAS)

Tax-sheltered annuities (TSAs) and tax-deferred accounts (TDAs) are established as retirement plans for employees of nonprofit and public organizations such as:

- Public schools (403B)
- Nonprofit organizations (IRC 501C3)
- Religious organizations
- Nonprofit hospitals

TSAs/TDAs are qualified plans, and contributions are made with pre-tax dollars. The money in the plan is allowed to grow tax deferred until it is withdrawn. TSAs/TDAs offer a variety of investment vehicles for participants to choose from, such as:

- Stocks
- Bonds
- Mutual funds
- CDs

PUBLIC EDUCATIONAL INSTITUTIONS (403B)

In order for a school to be considered a public school and qualify to establish a TSA/TDA for its employees, the school must be supported by the state, the local government, or by a state agency. State-supported schools include:

- Elementary schools
- High schools
- State colleges and universities
- Medical schools

Any individual who works for a public school, regardless of the position held, may participate in the school's TSA or TDA.

NONPROFIT ORGANIZATIONS/TAX-EXEMPT ORGANIZATIONS (501C3)

Organizations that qualify under Internal Revenue Code 501C3 as a nonprofit or tax-exempt entity may set up a TSA or TDA for their employees. Examples of nonprofit organizations are:

- Private hospitals
- Charitable organizations
- Trade schools
- Private colleges
- Parochial schools
- Museums
- Scientific foundations
- Zoos

All employees of organizations that qualify under Internal Revenue Code 501C3 or 403B are eligible to participate as long as they are at least 21 years old and have worked full time for at least one year.

CONTRIBUTIONS

In order to participate in a TSA or TDA, the employees must enter into a contract with their employer agreeing to make elective deferrals into the plan. The salary reduction agreement will state the amount and frequency of the elective deferral to be contributed to the TSA. The agreement is binding on both parties and covers only one year of contributions. Each year a new salary reduction agreement must be signed to set forth the contributions for the new year. The employee's elective deferral is limited to a maximum of $22,500 per year. Employer contributions are limited to the lesser of 25% of the employee's earnings or $61,000.

TAX TREATMENT OF DISTRIBUTIONS

All distributions for TSAs/TDAs are taxed as ordinary income in the year in which the distribution is made. Distributions from a TSA/TDA prior to age 59-1/2 are subject to a 10% penalty tax, as well as ordinary income taxes.

Distributions from a TSA/TDA must begin by age 72 or be subject to an excess accumulation tax.

CORPORATE PLANS

Corporations may establish a variety of retirement plans for their employees. The type of plan that is established will be based on the type of entity and the employment of the participant. A corporate retirement plan can be qualified or nonqualified. We will first review the nonqualified plans.

NONQUALIFIED CORPORATE RETIREMENT PLANS

Nonqualified corporate plans are funded with after-tax dollars, and the money is allowed to grow tax deferred. If the corporation makes a contribution to the plan, it may not deduct the contribution from its corporate earnings until the plan participant receives the money. Distributions from a nonqualified plan that exceed the investor's cost base are taxed as ordinary income. All nonqualified plans must be in writing, and the employer may discriminate as to who may participate.

PAYROLL DEDUCTIONS

The employee may set up a payroll deduction plan by having the employer make systematic deductions from the employee's paycheck. The money that has been deducted from the employee's check may be invested in a variety of ways. Mutual funds, annuities, and savings bonds are all usually available for the employee to choose from. Contributions to a payroll deduction plan are made with after-tax dollars.

DEFERRED COMPENSATION PLANS

A deferred compensation plan is a contract between an employee and an employer. Under the contract, the employee agrees to defer the receipt of money owed to the employee from the employer until after the employee retires. After retirement, the employee will traditionally be in a lower tax bracket and will be able to keep a larger percentage of the money. Deferred compensation plans are traditionally unfunded and, if the corporation goes out of business, the employee becomes a creditor of the corporation and may lose all of the money due under the contract. The employee may only claim the assets if he or she retires or becomes disabled. In the case of death, the employee's beneficiaries may claim the money owed. Money due under a deferred compensation plan is paid out of the corporation's working funds when the employee or the employee's estate claims the assets. Should the employee leave the corporation and go to work for a competing company, the employee may lose the money owed under a noncompete clause. Money owed to the employee under a deferred compensation agreement is traditionally not invested for the benefit of the employee and, as a result, does not increase in value over time. The only product that traditionally is placed in a deferred compensation plan is a term life policy. In the case of the employee's death, the term life policy will pay the employee's estate the money owed under the contract.

QUALIFIED PLANS

All qualified corporate plans must be in writing and be established as a trust. A trustee or plan administrator will be appointed for the benefit of all plan holders.

TYPES OF PLANS

There are two main types of qualified corporate plans: defined benefit plans and defined contribution plans.

DEFINED BENEFIT PLANS

A defined benefit plan is designed to offer the participant a retirement benefit that is known or "defined." Most defined benefit plans are set up to provide employees with a fixed percentage of their salary during their retirement, such as 74% of their average earnings during their five highest paid years. Other defined benefit plans are structured to pay participants a fixed sum of money for life. Defined benefit plans require the services of an actuary to determine the employer's contribution to the plan based upon the participant's life expectancy and benefits promised.

DEFINED CONTRIBUTION PLAN

With a defined contribution plan, only the amount of money that is deposited into the account is known, such as 6% of the employee's salary. Both the employee and the employer may contribute a percentage of the employee's earnings into the plan. The money is allowed to grow tax deferred until the participant withdraws it at retirement. The ultimate benefit under a defined contribution plan is the result of the contributions into the plan, along with the investment results of the plan. The employee's maximum contribution to a defined contribution plan is $21,500 per year. Some types of defined contribution plans are:

- 401K
- Money purchase plan
- Profit sharing
- Thrift plans
- Stock bonus plans

All withdrawals from pension plans are taxed as ordinary income in the year in which the distribution is made.

PROFIT SHARING PLANS

Profit sharing plans let the employer reward the employees by letting them "share" in a percentage of the corporation's profits. Profit sharing plans are based on a preset formula, and the money may be paid directly to the employee or placed in a retirement account. In order for a profit sharing plan to be qualified, the corporation must have substantial and recurring profits. The maximum contribution to a profit sharing plan is the lesser of 100% of the employee's compensation or $61,000.

401K THRIFT PLANS

401K and thrift plans allow employees to contribute a fixed percentage of their salary to their retirement account and have the employer match some or all of their contributions.

ROLLING OVER A PENSION PLAN

An employee who leaves an employer may move his or her pension plan to another company's plan or to another qualified account. This may be accomplished by a direct transfer or by rolling over the plan. With a direct transfer, the assets in the plan go directly to another plan administrator, and the employee never has physical possession of the assets. When the employee rolls over a pension plan, the employee takes physical possession of the assets. The plan administrator is required to withhold 20% of the total amount to be distributed, and the employee has 60 calendar days to deposit 100% of the assets into another qualified plan. The employee must file with the federal government at tax time to receive a return of the 20% of the assets that were withheld by the plan administrator.

HEALTH SAVINGS ACCOUNTS

A tax advantaged health savings account may be established to help offset the potential impact of medical expenses incurred by individuals who maintain a high deductible health insurance plan. Many individuals select a health insurance plan with a high deductible to lower the monthly premium expenses. A high deductible health plan is often used to insure against catastrophic illness. Individuals covered by these plans may elect to establish a health savings account. The individual, their employer, or both may make contributions to the health savings account. The contribution limit varies and is based on the person's age and the type of health insurance coverage. If a person is eligible on the first day of the last month of the year, the person may make a full contribution for that year. This is known as the "last month rule". Contributions to the health savings account may be made with pretax dollars. The money in the account grows tax free and can be used tax free for qualified medical expenses. The individual may use the money to pay the expense directly to the health care provider to reimburse themselves for payments they have made for qualified medical expenses incurred for themselves, their spouse or any dependent claimed on their tax return. Prescription drugs are considered to be qualified medical expenses. If the person requires a nonprescription drug to be covered the person still must get a prescription from their doctor. If money is used for non-qualified medical expenses the money will be subject to income taxes and could be subject to a 20% penalty tax. The money is allowed to accumulate over time and any unused amounts may be carried over to future years. If the owner of an HSA dies the account will pass to the owner's spouse and will be treated as the spouse's HSA. If the beneficiary is not the spouse the account will cease to be an HSA and the amount will be taxable to the beneficiary in the year in which the owner dies.

EMPLOYEE RETIREMENT INCOME SECURITY ACT OF 1974 (ERISA)

The Employee Retirement Income Security Act of 1974 (ERISA) is a federal law that establishes legal and operational guidelines for private pension and employee benefit plans. Not all decisions directly involving a plan, even when made by a fiduciary, are subject to ERISA's fiduciary rules. These decisions are business judgment type decisions and are commonly called "settlor" functions. This caveat is sometimes referred to as the "business decision" exception to ERISA's fiduciary rules. Under this concept, even though the employer is the plan sponsor and administrator, it will not be considered as acting in a fiduciary capacity when creating, amending or terminating a plan. Among the decisions which would be considered settlor functions are:

- Choosing the type of plan, or options in the plan.
- Amending a plan, including changing or eliminating plan options.
- Requiring employee contributions or changing the level of employee contributions.
- Terminating a plan, or part of a plan, including terminating or amending as part of a bankruptcy process.

ERISA also regulates all of the following:

- Pension plan participation
- Funding
- Vesting
- Communication
- Beneficiaries

PLAN PARTICIPATION

All plans governed by ERISA may not discriminate among who may participate in the plan. All employees must be allowed to participate if:

- They are at least 21 years old.
- They have worked at least one year full time (1,000 hours).

FUNDING

Plan funding requirements set forth guidelines on how the money is deposited into the plan and how the employer and employee may contribute to the plan.

VESTING

Vesting refers to the process of how the employer's contribution becomes the property of the employee. An employer may be as generous as it would like, but it may not be more restrictive than either one of the following vesting schedules:

- Three- to six-year gradual vesting schedule.
- Three-year cliff (the employee is not vested at all until three years, at which point the employee becomes 100% vested).

COMMUNICATION

All corporate plans must be in writing at inception, and the employee must be given annual updates.

BENEFICIARIES

All plan participants must be allowed to select a beneficiary who may claim the assets in case of the plan participant's death.

ERISA 404C SAFE HARBOR

All individuals and entities acting in a fiduciary capacity must act solely in the interest of the plan participants. Investment advisers, trustees and all individuals who exercise discretion over the plan including those who select the administrative personnel or committee are considered to be fiduciaries. ERISA Rule 404C provides an exemption from liability or a "safe harbor" for plan fiduciaries and protects them from liabilities that may arise from investment losses that result from the participant's own actions. This safe harbor is available so long as:

- The participant exercises control over the assets in their account.
- Participants have ample opportunity to enter orders for their account and to provide instructions regarding their account.
- A broad range of investment options is available for the participant to choose from and the options offer suitable investments for a variety or investment objectives and risk profiles.
- Information regarding the risks and objective of the investment options is readily available to plan participants.

DEPARTMENT OF LABOR FIDUCIARY RULES

The Department of Labor has been trying to enact significant new legislation for financial professionals who service and maintain retirement accounts for clients. These new rules subject financial professionals to higher fiduciary standards. These standards require financial professionals to place the interest of the client ahead of the interest of the broker dealer or investment advisory firm. Professionals who service retirement accounts are still permitted to earn commissions and/or a fee based on the assets in the account and may still offer proprietary products to investors. However the rule requires that the client receive significant disclosures relating to the fees and costs associated with the servicing of the account. Simply charging the lowest fee will not ensure compliance with the fiduciary standard. Both the firm and the individual servicing the account must put the interests of the client ahead of their own. Broker dealers and advisory firms must establish written supervisory procedures and training programs designed to supervise and educate their personnel on the new requirements for retirement accounts. Many representatives will now be required to obtain the Series 65 or Series 66 license to comply with the new Department of Labor rules.

These rules have been hotly debated for the last several years, and as a result the exam may not test the application of these rules.

Pretest

RETIREMENT PLANS

1. Which of the following are features of a 401K plan?

   I. A 401K may be easily rolled over.

   II. Employees' contributions are excluded from their gross income.

   III. Employees are 100% vested in all contributions immediately.

   IV. The employer may match a certain percentage of the employee's contributions.

   a. I and II

   b. II and IV

   c. I, II, III, and IV

   d. I and III

2. Which of the following are funded with pre-tax dollars?

   I. Keogh

   II. Variable annuity

   III. Fixed annuity

   IV. TDA

   a. I and II

   b. I and IV

   c. II and IV

   d. II and III

3. You have been working for the local school system for 15 years and have been contributing to a payroll deduction plan for 9 years. You have deposited $11,000 during the period, and it has grown to $16,200. What is

your tax liability upon a lump sum withdrawal, if you are in the 30% tax bracket when you retire?

a. $4,840

b. $0

c. $3,300

d. $1,560

4. The penalty for an excess contribution to a Keogh plan is:

a. 8%.

b. 6%.

c. 20%.

d. 10%.

5. A 45-year-old investor has rolled over $10,000 from an IRA to buy a car. How much time does he have to deposit the money into another qualified plan?

a. 45 days

b. 60 days

c. 30 days

d. 90 days

6. Which of the following is true of Keoghs?

a. They are usually set up by individuals, sole proprietors, or unincorporated businesses.

b. They are a type of qualified retirement plan.

c. They may be funded only with earned income during a period when the business showed a gross profit.

d. All of the above.

7. A qualified retirement plan differs from a nonqualified retirement plan in all of the following ways, EXCEPT:

a. IRS approval is required for both plans.

b. withdrawals from a qualified plan are 100% taxed as ordinary income, whereas growth in excess of the cost base is taxed as ordinary income in a nonqualified plan.

c. contributions for the qualified plan are made pre-tax, whereas contributions for the nonqualified plan are made after tax.

    d. participation must be allowed for everyone in the qualified plan, whereas the corporation may choose who participates in the non-qualified plan.

8. An investor has deposited $100,000 into a qualified retirement account over a 10-year period. The value of the account has grown to $175,000, and the investor plans to retire and take a lump sum withdrawal. He will pay:

    a. ordinary income taxes on the $75,000 only.

    b. ordinary income taxes on the $100,000 and capital gains on the $75,000.

    c. ordinary income taxes on the whole $175,000.

    d. capital gains tax on $75,000 only.

9. Which of the following plans is nonfunded?

    a. Keogh

    b. TSA

    c. TDA

    d. Deferred compensation plan

Customer Recommendations, Professional Conduct, and Taxation

INTRODUCTION

All recommendations to customers must be suitable based on the customers' investment objectives, financial profile, and attitudes towards investing. Representatives usually make verbal recommendations to customers. The representative will review the customer's investment objective and offer facts to support the basis for his or her recommendations, as well as an explanation as to how the recommendations will help the customer meet the desired objective. Any predictions about the performance of an investment should be stated strictly as an opinion or belief, not as a fact. If the firm uses reports that cite past performance of the firm's previous recommendations, the report must contain:

- The prices and dates when the recommendations were made.
- General market conditions.
- The recommendations in all similar securities for 12 months.
- A statement disclosing that the firm is a market maker (if applicable).
- A statement regarding whether the firm or its officers or directors own any of the securities being recommended or options or warrants for the same security.
- If the firm managed or comanaged an underwriting of any of the issuer's securities in the last three years.

- A statement regarding the availability of supporting documentation for the recommendations.

   While making a recommendation, a representative may not:

- Guarantee or promise a profit or promise no loss.
- Make false, misleading, or fraudulent statements.
- Make unfair comparisons to dissimilar products.

PROFESSIONAL CONDUCT IN THE SECURITIES INDUSTRY

The securities industry is a highly regulated industry. All broker dealers are required to regulate their employees. A broker dealer must designate a principal to supervise all of the actions of the firm and its employees. The broker dealer and all of its employees are also regulated by a self-regulatory organization (SRO), such as FINRA or the NYSE. The SROs and all industry participants answer to the SEC. The SEC is the ultimate securities industry authority. Additionally, each state has adopted its own rules and regulations regarding securities transactions that occur within the state. Violations of industry regulations may lead to fines and expulsion from the industry. Violations of state and federal laws may result in fines, expulsion from the state or industry, or a jail term. Industry participants are expected to adhere to all of the industry's rules and regulations, as well as all state and federal laws.

FAIR DEALINGS WITH CUSTOMERS

All broker dealers are required to act in good faith in all of their dealings with customers and are required to uphold just and equitable trade practices. FINRA's rules of fair practice, also known as the rules of conduct, regulate how business is conducted with members of the general public. The rules of conduct prohibit all of the following:

- Churning.
- Manipulative and deceptive practices.
- Unauthorized trading.
- Fraudulent acts.
- Blanket recommendations.
- Misrepresentations.
- Omitting material facts.

- Making guarantees.
- Selling dividends.
- Recommending speculative securities without knowing the customer can afford the risk.
- Short-term trading in mutual funds.
- Switching fund families.

CHURNING

Most representatives are compensated when the customer makes a transaction based on their recommendation. Churning is a practice of making transactions that are excessive in size or frequency, with the intention to generate higher commissions for the representative. When determining if an account has been churned, regulators will look at the frequency of the transactions, the size of the transactions, and the amount of commission earned by the representative. Customer profitability is not an issue when determining if an account has been churned.

In addition to churning where the agent or firm executes too many transactions to increase revenue, a practice known as reverse churning is also a violation. Reverse churning is the practice of placing inactive accounts or accounts that do not trade frequently into fee based programs that charge an annual fee based on the assets in the account. This fee covers all advice and execution charges. Since these inactive accounts do not trade frequently it will cause the total fees charged to the account to increase and makes a fee based account unsuitable for inactive accounts and for accounts that simply buy and hold securities for a long period of time. These accounts will generally be charged an annual fee in the range of 1%–2% of the total value of the assets in lieu of commissions when orders are executed.

MANIPULATIVE AND DECEPTIVE DEVICES

It is a violation for a firm or representative to engage in or employ any artifice or scheme that is designed to gain an unfair advantage over another party. Some examples of manipulative or deceptive devices are:

- Capping
- Pegging
- Front running
- Trading ahead
- Painting the tape/matched purchases/matches sales

Capping: A manipulative act designed to keep a stock price from rising or to keep the price down.

Pegging: A manipulative act designed to keep a stock price up or to keep the price from falling.

Front running: The entering of an order for the account of an agent or firm prior to entering a large customer order. The firm or agent is using the customer's order to profit on the order it entered for its own account.

Trading ahead: The entering of an order for a security based on prior knowledge from a soon to be released research report.

Painting the tape: A manipulative act by two or more parties designed to create false activity in the security without any beneficial change in ownership. The increased activity is used to attract new buyers.

UNAUTHORIZED TRADING

An unauthorized transaction is one that is made for the benefit of a customer's account at a time when the customer has no knowledge of the trade and the representative does not have discretionary power over the account.

FRAUD

Fraud is defined as any act that is employed to obtain an unfair advantage over another party. Fraudulent acts include:

- False statements
- Deliberate omissions of material facts
- Concealment of material facts
- Manipulative and deceptive practices
- Forgery
- Material omission
- Lying

BLANKET RECOMMENDATIONS

It is inappropriate for a firm or a representative to make blanket recommendations in any security, especially low-priced speculative securities. No matter what type of investment is involved, a blanket recommendation to a large group of people will always be wrong for some investors. Different investors have different objectives, and the same recommendation will not be suitable for everyone.

EXAMPLE   Mr. Jones, an agent with XYZ brokers, has a large customer base that ranges from young investors who are just starting to save to institutions and retirees.

Mr. Jones has been doing a significant amount of research on WSIA industries, a mining and materials company. Mr. Jones strongly believes that WSIA is significantly undervalued based on its assets and earning potential. Mr. Jones recommends WSIA to all his clients. In the next six months the share price of WSIA increases significantly as new production dramatically increases sales, just as Mr. Jones's research suggested. The clients then sell WSIA at Mr. Jones's suggestion and realize a significant profit.

ANALYSIS

Even though the clients who purchased WSIA based on Mr. Jones's recommendation made a significant profit, Mr. Jones has still committed a violation because he recommended it to all of his clients. Mr. Jones's clients have a wide variety of investment objectives, and the risk or income potential associated with an investment in WSIA would not be suitable for every client. Even if an investment is profitable for the client it does not mean it was suitable for the client. Blanket recommendations are never suitable.

SELLING DIVIDENDS

Selling dividends is a violation that occurs when a registered representative uses a pending dividend payment as the sole basis of a recommendation to purchase the stock or mutual fund. Additionally, using the pending dividend as a means to create urgency on the part of the investor to purchase the stock is a prime example of this type of violation. If the investor was to purchase the shares just prior to the ex dividend date simply to receive the dividend, the investor in many cases will end up worse off. The dividend in this case will actually be a return of the money that the investor used to purchase the stock, and then the investor will have a tax liability when the dividend is received.

MISREPRESENTATIONS

A representative or a firm may not knowingly make any misrepresentations regarding:

- A client's account status
- The representative
- The firm
- An investment
- Fees to be charged

OMITTING MATERIAL FACTS

A representative of a firm may not omit any material fact, either good or bad, when recommending a security. A material fact is one that an investor would need to know in order to make a well-informed investment decision. The representative may, however, omit an immaterial fact.

GUARANTEES

No representative, broker dealer, or investment adviser may make any guarantees of any kind. A profit may not be guaranteed, and a promise of no loss may not be made.

RECOMMENDATIONS TO AN INSTITUTIONAL CUSTOMER

FINRA recognizes an institutional customer as one that has at least $10,000,000 in assets. The agent's or member's suitability determination can be met if the customer:

- Can independently evaluate the investment risks and merits.
- Can independently make its own investment decisions.

If the customer meets the above criteria, the member or agent may recommend almost any investment to the customer and allow the customer to determine if it is suitable.

INFORMATION OBTAINED FROM AN ISSUER

If a broker dealer obtains information during the performance of duties to an issuer of securities, it may not use that information to solicit business. A broker dealer may obtain information from an issuer while acting as:

- An underwriter
- Transfer agent
- Paying agent
- Investment banker

DISCLOSURE OF CLIENT INFORMATION

Registered representatives and broker dealers may not disclose any information regarding clients to a third party without the client's expressed consent or without a court order. If the client is an issuer of securities and the broker dealer is an underwriter, transfer agent, or paying agent for the issuer, then the broker dealer is precluded from using the information it obtains regarding the issuer's security holders for its own benefit.

BORROWING AND LENDING MONEY

Borrowing and lending of money between registered persons and customers is strictly regulated. If the member firm allows borrowing and lending between representatives and customers the firm must have policies in place that will allow for the loans to be made. Loans may be made between an agent and a customer if the customer is a bank or other lending institution, where there is a personal or outside business relationship and that relationship is the basis for the loan, or between two agents registered with the same firm. The firm must provide the agent with written preapproval for the loan unless the loan is being made between the agent and an immediate family member or a bank. The approval documentation must be maintained for three years from the date when the loan was repaid or three years from the rep's termination from the firm.

GIFT RULE

Broker dealers may not pay compensation to employees of other broker dealers. If a broker dealer wants to give a gift to an employee of another broker dealer, it must:

- Be valued at less than $100 per person per year.
- Be given directly to the employing member firm for distribution to the employee.
- Have the employing member's prior approval for the gift.

The employing member must obtain a record of the gift, including the name of the giver, the name of the recipient, and the nature of the gift. These rules have been established to ensure that broker dealers do not try to influence the employees of other broker dealers. An exception to this rule would be in cases where an employee of one broker dealer performs services for another broker dealer under an employment contract. Occasional meals, tickets to sporting events, and lucite plaques and prospectuses are all acceptable. The key to determine if tickets to events are entertainment is if the person providing the tickets attends the event. If this is the case the tickets are not deemed to be a gift.

OUTSIDE EMPLOYMENT

If a registered representative wants to obtain employment outside of his or her position with a member firm, the registered representative must first notify the employing member prior engaging in the activity. Prior approval is not required but the employer has the right to refuse or limit the outside business activity. Exceptions to this rule are if the registered representative is a passive investor in a business or if the representative owns rental property. All other outside business activities must be disclosed to the member firm.

PRIVATE SECURITIES TRANSACTIONS

A registered representative may not engage in any private securities transactions without first obtaining the broker dealer's prior approval. The registered representative must provide the employing firm with all documentation regarding the investment and the proposed transaction. An example of a private securities transaction would be if a representative helped a startup business raise money through a private placement. If the representative is going to receive compensation, the employing member firm must supervise the transaction and the transaction must be run though the books of the broker dealer. If a representative sells investment products that the employing member does not conduct business in without the member's knowledge, then the representative has committed a violation known as selling away.

CUSTOMER COMPLAINTS

All written complaints received from a customer or from an individual acting on behalf of the customer must be reported promptly to the principal of the firm. The firm is required to:

- Maintain a copy of the complaint in a supervising office of supervisory jurisdiction for 4 years.
- Electronically report all complaints to FINRA within 15 days of the end of each calendar quarter.
- Report complaints within 10 days to FINRA if the complaint alleges misappropriation of funds or securities or forgery.

INVESTOR INFORMATION

All broker dealers that carry customer accounts must send their customers information detailing FINRA's BrokerCheck public disclosure program at least once per calendar year. The BrokerCheck program, accessible via the FINRA website, provides detailed registration and disciplinary history for firms and agents maintained at the Central Registration Depository (CRD). The information must contain the program's 800 number, FINRA's website address, and a statement that an investor brochure includes the same information and is available.

NYSE/FINRA KNOW YOUR CUSTOMER

The NYSE and FINRA both require that any recommendation to a customer be suitable for the customer. The representative has an affirmative obligation to determine the suitability of the recommendations made to customers. The suitability obligation is triggered at the time the investment is discussed with the client not based on if the customer makes the investment. The rules require that the agent obtain enough information about the customer to ensure that all recommendations are suitable based on a review of the client's:

- Investment objectives
- Financial status
- Income
- Investment holdings
- Retirement needs
- College and other major expenses
- Tax bracket
- Attitude towards investing

The more you know about a customer's financial position, the better you will be able to help the customer meet his or her objectives. You should always ask questions like:

- How long have you been making these types of investments?
- Do you have any major expenses coming up?
- How long do you usually hold investments?
- How much risk do you normally take?
- What tax bracket are you in?
- How much money do you have invested in the market?
- Have you done any retirement planning?

Of course there are other questions that you should ask, but these are examples of the style of questions that all representatives should ask.

Other questions a representative should ask the customer include:

- How old are you?
- Are you married?
- Do you have any children?
- How long have you been employed at your current job?

Registered representatives must make sure that their recommendations meet their customers' objectives. Should a client have a primary and a secondary objective, a representative must make sure that the recommendation meets the investor's primary objective first and the secondary objective second.

INVESTMENT OBJECTIVES

All investors want to make or preserve money. However, these objectives can be met in different ways. Some of the different investment objectives are:

- Income
- Growth
- Preservation of capital
- Tax benefits
- Liquidity
- Speculation

INCOME

Many investors are looking to have their investments generate additional income to help meet their monthly expenses. Some investments that will help to meet this objective are:
- Corporate bonds
- Municipal bonds
- Government bonds
- Preferred stocks
- Money market funds
- Bond funds
- Bond ladder

GROWTH

Investors who seek capital appreciation over time want their money to grow in value and are not seeking any current income. The only investments that will achieve this goal are:

- Common stocks
- Common stock funds

PRESERVATION OF CAPITAL

Investors who have preservation of capital as an investment objective are very conservative and are more concerned with keeping the money they have saved. For these investors, high-quality debt will be an appropriate recommendation. The following are good investments for preserving capital:

- Money market funds
- Government bonds
- Municipal bonds
- High-grade corporate bonds

TAX BENEFITS

For investors seeking tax advantages, the only two possible recommendations are:

- Municipal bonds
- Municipal bond funds

LIQUIDITY

Investors who need immediate access to their money need to own liquid investments that will not fluctuate wildly in value in case they need to use the money. The following investments are listed from most liquid to least liquid:

- Money market funds
- Stocks/bonds/mutual funds
- Annuities
- Collateralized mortgage obligations (CMOs)
- Direct participation programs
- Real estate

SPECULATION

A customer investing in a speculative manner is willing to take a high degree of risk in order to earn a high rate of return. Some of the more speculative investments are:

- Penny stocks
- Small cap stocks
- Some growth stocks
- Junk bonds

RISK VS. REWARD

Risk is the reciprocal of reward. An investor must be offered a higher rate of return for each unit of additional risk the investor is willing to assume. There are many types of risk involved with investing money. They are as follows:

- Capital risk
- Market risk
- Nonsystematic risk
- Legislative risk
- Timing risk
- Credit risk
- Reinvestment risk
- Call risk
- Liquidity risk

CAPITAL RISK

Capital risk is the risk that an investor may lose all or part of the capital that has been invested.

MARKET RISK

Market risk is also known as a systematic risk, and it is the risk that is inherent in any investment in the markets. For example, you could own stock in the greatest company in the world and you could still lose money because the value of your stock is going down, simply because the market as a whole is going down.

NONSYSTEMATIC RISK

Nonsystematic risk is the risk that pertains to one company or industry. For example, the problems that the tobacco industry faced a few years ago would not have affected a computer company.

LEGISLATIVE RISK

Legislative risk is the risk that the government will do something that adversely affects an investment. For example, beer manufacturers probably did not fare too well when the government enacted prohibition.

TIMING RISK

Timing risk is simply the risk that an investor will buy and sell at the wrong time and will lose money as a result.

CREDIT RISK

Credit risk is the risk of default inherent in debt securities. An investor may lose all or part of an investment because the issuer has defaulted and cannot pay the interest or principal payments owed to the investor.

REINVESTMENT RISK

When interest rates decline and higher yielding bonds have been called or have matured, investors will not be able to receive the same return given the same amount of risk. This is reinvestment risk, and the investor is forced to either accept the lower rate or must take more risk to obtain the same rate.

CALL RISK

Call risk is the risk that, as interest rates decline, higher yielding bonds and preferred stocks will be called and investors will be forced to reinvest the proceeds at a lower rate of return or at a higher rate of risk to achieve the same return. Call risk only applies to preferred stocks and bonds with a call feature.

LIQUIDITY RISK

Liquidity risk is the risk that an investor will not be able to liquidate an investment when needed or will not be able to liquidate the investment without adversely affecting the price.

ALPHA

A stock's or portfolio's alpha is its projected independent rate of return, or the difference between an investment's expected (benchmark) return and its actual return. Portfolio managers whose portfolios have positive alphas are adding value through their asset selection. The outperformance as measured by alpha indicates that the portfolio manager is adding additional return for each unit of risk taken on in the portfolio.

BETA

A stock's beta is its projected rate of change relative to the market as a whole. If the market was up 10% for the year, a stock with a beta of 1.5 could reasonably be expected to be up 15%. A stock with a beta greater than one has a higher level of volatility than the market as a whole and is considered to be more risky than the overall market. A stock with a beta of less than one is less volatile than prices in the overall market and is considered to be less risky. An example of a low beta stock would be a utility stock. The price of utility stocks does not tend to move dramatically.

CAPITAL ASSET PRICING MODEL (CAPM)

The capital asset pricing model (also known as CAPM) operates under the assumption that investors are risk averse. Investors who take on risk through the purchase of an investment must be compensated for that risk through a higher expected rate of return known as the risk premium. A security's risk is measured by its beta. Therefore, securities with higher betas must offer investors a higher expected return in order for the investor to be compensated for taking on the additional risk associated with that investment. As such CAPM states that securities with higher risk will have lower market prices than securities with less risk. Proponents of CAPM have developed the capital market line or CML to evaluate and measure the expected returns of a diversified portfolio relative to the expected returns of the market and the expected risk-free return. The CML also measures the standard deviation of the portfolio relative to the standard deviation of the market. A further derivative measure known as the security market line or SML is used to measure the expected return of a single security based on its beta relative to the expectations of the market and risk-free rate of return. The CML is not based on alpha or beta, while the SML is partially computed based on the beta of the single security in question.

PRODUCTS MADE AVAILABLE THROUGH MEMBER FIRMS

All products offered through member firms must meet a reasonable basis suitability requirement. The reasonable basis suitability requirement has two parts. The member must understand the risks and performance characteristics of the investment and the agents offering the products for sale must understand the risks and performance characteristics of the investment. The member is required to educate agents about the risks and rewards of the products it allows agents to recommend to clients. If a member maintains a new product committee to review potential investments offered to clients the committee must believe that the products are suitable for at least some of the firm's clients. FINRA member firms should train representatives about the characteristics relating to specific products including product features, risks, and pricing. Members should also provide representatives with suitability guidance for recommending products and product related risk assessments and reviews. It is the responsibility of the representative to meet the client specific suitability requirement. The representative's principal will review the transaction promptly to ensure client specific suitability.

 TAKE**NOTE!**

If the firm's product committee understands the risks and allows agents to offer the securities to clients, but the representative does not, neither the firm nor the representative has met their obligations under suitability standards.

Members must track ongoing changes that impact suitability such as changes in interest rates, and oil prices that can impact the suitability of an investment. Specifically members should discus, and disclose how changing interest rates may impact a portfolio of fixed income securities such as high yield bonds, CMOs, and other mortgaged-backed products.

RECOMMENDATIONS THROUGH SOCIAL MEDIA

The use of social media such as Linkedin, Facebook, and Twitter all need to be closely supervised by the member firm, specifically in cases where the communication posted by the firm or its agents could be deemed to be a recommendation. Being able to determine when communication reaches the level of a recommendation is a key element on the exam and for supervisors in general. When communication is deemed to be a recommendation it becomes subject to the suitability requirements of FINRA Rule 2111. Certain types of communications that are deemed to be recommendations are as follows:

- Targeted email distributions and tweets that advise the reader to buy or sell a security or securities within a sector
- Targeted pop up, redirect, and mouse-over messages displayed to website visitors that advise the visitor to buy or sell a security or securities within a sector.

If the firm maintains a website that allows access to a library of research containing pervious buy and sell recommendations the ability to access the library will not constitute a recommendation.

Due to the complex compliance issues social media present, member firms are within their rights to limit or restrict employees' use of social media. Should a member firm allow its representatives to communicate over social media the level of supervision required will depend on the type of social media used and the content of the communication. Member firms must properly train its employees on the use of social media and maintain written policies and procedures regarding its use and supervision. Static content that may be accessed by any visitor at any time requires prior approval from a principal before the static post is made. Static content includes Facebook walls, LinkedIn profiles, blogs, and Twitter posts. Aggressively tweeting positive or negative messages about an investment is a cause for concern and may result in sanctions being imposed on both the agent and the firm. Only agents who have the approval of their firm to tweet about investments should do so. Interactive blogs and chatroom conversations are deemed to be public appearances. These public appearances do not require prior principal approval but are subject to FINRA rules. Statements made must be factual and not exaggerated and no statements should be made about a security during a quiet period. It is important to note that most blogs are static and require prior approval for posts, merely updating a blog on a regular basis does not constitute an interactive blog. FINRA members must carefully supervise the use of social media by its agents and must have systems in place designed to detect potential violations. These systems should be designed to detect red flag words such as "guarantee" and "can't lose." Agents who have a history of questionable sales practices or who have been sanctioned should be prohibited from using social media for business purposes. A post on social media from a client of the firm or from an unrelated third party will not be deemed to have been made by the firm and is not subject to supervision unless the firm assisted in preparing such post or approved the content.

TAKE**NOTE!**

One way for a firm to keep close supervision for representatives who make recommendations using social media is to have a preapproved catalog of research available for the representatives to use.

TAX STRUCTURE

There are two types of taxes: progressive and regressive. A progressive tax levies a larger tax on higher income earners. Examples of progressive taxes are:

- Income taxes
- Estate taxes

Regressive taxes level the same tax rate on everyone, regardless of their income. As a result, a larger portion of the lower income earner's earnings will go toward the tax. Examples of regressive taxes are:

- Sales taxes
- Property taxes
- Gasoline taxes
- Excise taxes

INVESTMENT TAXATION

Investors must be aware of the impact that federal and state taxes will have on their investment results. A taxable event will occur in most cases when an investor:

- Sells a security at a profit.
- Sells a security at a loss.
- Receives interest or dividend income.

CALCULATING GAINS AND LOSSES

When investors sell their shares, in most cases they will have a capital gain or loss. In order to determine if there is a gain or loss, the investor must first calculate the cost basis, or cost base. An investor's cost base, in most cases, is equal to the price the investor paid for the shares plus any commissions or fees. Once an investor knows the cost base, calculating any gain or loss becomes easy. A capital gain is realized when the investor sells the shares at a price that is greater than the cost base. Any gain on an asset held more than one year is considered a long-term capital gain and is taxed at a maximum rate of 15%. Any gain on an asset held for less than one year is considered a short-term capital gain and is taxed at the investor's ordinary income tax rate. The investor's holding period begins the day after the purchase and ends on the sale date.

EXAMPLE

An investor who purchased a stock at $10 per share three years ago and receives $14 per share when he sells the shares has a $4 capital gain. This was found by subtracting the cost base from the sales proceeds: $14 − $10 = $4. If the investor had 1,000 shares, he would have a capital gain of $4,000.

An investor's cost base is always returned to the investor tax-free. A capital loss is realized when investors sell shares at a price that is less than their cost base. If the investor in the previous example were to have sold the shares at $8 instead of $14, the investor would have a $2 capital loss, or a total capital loss of $2,000 for the entire position.

Again this is found by subtracting the cost base from the sales proceeds: $8 − $10 = −$2. Capital gains, like dividends, are taxed at a 15% rate for ordinary income earners and at a 20% rate for high income earners.

COST BASE OF MULTIPLE PURCHASES

Investors who have been accumulating shares through multiple purchases must determine their cost base at the time of sale through one of the following methods:

- FIFO (first in, first out)
- Share identification
- Average cost

FIFO (FIRST IN, FIRST OUT)

If the investor does not identify which shares are being sold at the time of sale, the IRS will assume that the first shares that were purchased are the first shares that are sold under the FIFO method. In many cases, this will result in the largest capital gain, and, as a result, the investor will have the largest tax liability.

SHARE IDENTIFICATION

An investor may at the time of the sale specify which shares are being sold. By keeping a record of the purchase prices and the dates that the shares were purchased, the investor may elect to sell the shares that create the most favorable tax consequences.

AVERAGE COST

An investor may decide to sell shares based on their average cost. An investor must determine the shares' average cost by using the following formula:

$$\text{average cost} = \frac{\textbf{total dollars invested}}{\textbf{total \# of shares purchased}}$$

Once an investor has elected to use the average cost method to calculate gains and losses, another method may not be used without IRS approval.

DEDUCTING CAPITAL LOSSES

An investor may use capital losses to offset capital gains dollar for dollar in the year in which they are realized. A net capital loss may be used to reduce the investor's taxable ordinary income by up to $3,000 in the year in which it is realized. Any net capital losses that exceed $3,000 may be carried forward into future years and may be deducted at a rate of $3,000 from ordinary income every year until the loss is used up. If the investor has a capital gain in subsequent years, the investor may use the entire amount of the net capital loss remaining to offset the gain up to the amount of the gain.

WASH SALES

Investors may not sell a security at a loss and shortly after repurchase the security, or a security that is substantially the same, to reestablish the position if they intend to claim the loss for tax purposes and deduct the loss from their ordinary income. This is known as a wash sale, and the IRS will disallow the loss. In order to claim the loss, the investor has to have held the securities for 30 days and must wait at least 30 days before repurchasing the securities or securities that are substantially the same. The total number of days in the wash sale rule is 61.

- Holding period   30 days
- Sale date   1 day

- Waiting period   30 days
- Total   61 days

Securities that are substantially the same are call options, rights, warrants, and convertibles.

TAXATION OF INTEREST INCOME

Interest earned by investors may or may not be subject to taxes. The following table illustrates the tax consequences of various interest payment received by investors:

Resident	Investment	Taxation
New Jersey	Corporate bond	All taxes
New Jersey	CMO	All taxes
New Jersey	GNMA	All taxes
New Jersey	T-bond	Federal taxes only
New Jersey	New York muni bond	New Jersey taxes only
New Jersey	New Jersey muni bond	No taxes
New Jersey	Puerto Rico/Guam muni bond	No taxes

 TAKE**NOTE!**

Investors may deduct margin interest only to the extent of their investment income. Investors may not deduct margin expenses from municipal bonds.

INHERITED SECURITIES

If an investor dies and leaves securities to another person, that person's cost base for those securities is the fair market value of the securities on the day the decedent died. The cost base of the original investor does not transfer to the person who inherited the securities.

TAKE**NOTE!**

If a person gives a gift of securities during his or her lifetime, that person's cost base is used for calculating the recipient's capital gain. If, however, there is a loss on the sale, the lower of the giver's cost base or the fair market value at the time of the gift is used to calculate the loss.

DONATING SECURITIES TO CHARITY

An investor who donates securities to a charity will receive a tax deduction equal to the value of the securities. If the investor has an unrealized gain and has held the securities for more than 12 months, the investor will not owe any taxes on the appreciation. If the securities were held less than 12 months, the investor will be responsible for taxes on the appreciation. The recipient's cost base will be equal to the value of the securities on the day the gift was received.

GIFT TAXES

When gifts are made to family members or others individuals, the donor does not receive any tax deduction. The donor's cost base will transfer to the recipient for tax purposes. Individuals may give gifts of up to $15,000 per person per year without incurring any tax liability. If a gift in excess of $15,000 is given to an individual, the donor owes the gift tax.

  TAKE**NOTE!**

A husband and wife may give up to $30,000 per year per person. The IRS considers half of the gift to be coming from each spouse.

ESTATE TAXES

Individuals are allowed to leave an estate worth just over $5,000,000 without subjecting the beneficiaries to estate taxes. This rule is subject to continuous debate and change and the number is unlikely to be tested. This amount is increased periodically. There is an unlimited marital deduction or unified credit that allows surviving spouses to inherit the entire estate tax-free.

WITHHOLDING TAX

All broker dealers are required to withhold 31% of all sales proceeds if the investor has not provided a social security number or a tax identification number. In addition, 31% of all distributions from a mutual fund will also be withheld without a social security number or a tax identification number.

 TAKE**NOTE!**

Individuals who receive dividends from common stock and mutual funds will be subject to a 15% tax rate. High income earners are subjected to a 20% tax.

ALTERNATIVE MINIMUM TAX (AMT)

Certain items that receive beneficial tax treatment must be added back into the taxable income for some high-income earners. These items include:

- Interest on some industrial revenue bonds.
- Some stock options.
- Accelerated depreciation.
- Personal property tax on investments that do not generate income.
- Certain tax deductions passed through from DPPs.

TAXES ON FOREIGN SECURITIES

U.S. investors who own securities issued in a foreign country will owe federal taxes on any gains or income realized. In the event that the foreign country withholds taxes from the investor, the investor may file for a credit with the IRS at tax time. Most foreign governments that withhold taxes will withhold 15%.

FINRA RULE 3241

FINRA Rule 3241 is designed to address the potential conflicts of interest that can arise when a registered person is named as a beneficiary, Trustee, or executor of a client's estate. The intent of this rule is to ensure that registered individuals act appropriately and that the employing member carefully supervises the actions of registered individuals. A multitude of conflicts can arise when a registered person is named as a beneficiary or is placed in a position of trust over a client's estate. One of the greatest concerns are cases where a registered person subjects an elderly client to undo or inappropriate influence. In these instances the representative may use this influence to be named as a beneficiary or to be placed in a position of trust upon the death of the client. The impact of this undue influence may not be known or realized by the client's family for years. FINRA Rule 3241 establishes a National Standard to protect individuals and to provide a consistent policy for member firms to follow. A registered person should decline being named as a beneficiary of, or placed in a position of trust over a client's estate. If the registered person does not decline, the registered person must provide written notification to his / her employer and receive his / her employer's written approval to receive the bequest or to accept the appointment as trustee or executor. Upon being notified that a registered person is going to be named to a position of trust or is being named as a beneficiary, the member firm the member firm is required to:

Perform an assessment of the risks created by the registered person being named as a beneficiary or to a position of trust. Specific emphasis should be placed upon evaluating whether such a scenario will interfere with or compromise the registered person's responsibilities to the customer.

Make a determination to approve or disapprove the representative's acceptance or to limit the registered persons activities by placing conditions upon the acceptance.

FINRA further States that That the following factors should be carefully evaluated:

- The customer's age
- The length and type of relationship between the customer and the registered person
- The size of the bequest relative to the size of the customers estate
- If the representative has been named as a beneficiary or has received bequests from other customer accounts or estates

- An evaluation of the customer's mental capacity and ability to protect their own interests. specific weight should be given to any observations the member has made during the course of the relationship with a customer
- Any red flags observed in the management of the customer's account such as excessive trading
- Any red flags observed relating to instances of undue influence on the part of the registered rep

Member firms are well within their right to prohibit representatives from accepting bequests or appointments from clients. However, if the member firm allows representatives to receive bequests or appointments, the member firm must have clear policy and procedures designed to meet the national standards and to supervise such matters. When evaluating the potential risks associated with the acceptance of a bequest or an appointment, the relationship between the representative and the client is a significant matter. For example, the risk associated with the acceptance or appointment being made by a client who has no other relationship with a representative other than that of a client is far greater than that being made by someone who is a lifelong friend of the representative who also happens to be a client.

Should the member firm allow the representative to accept the appointment or bequest, the firm must carefully supervise the registered person's activities and compliance with any limitations placed on the representative's acceptance.. An interesting situation may arise if a registered person is allowed to serve in a position of trust over a client's estate for which the registered person is being compensated. The registered representative is now engaging in an outside business activity and as a result, the activity would be required to be disclosed and supervised by the member firm. The member firm is required to maintain all documents relating to notifications, approvals, denials, bequests and appointments for 3 years from the date of the bequest or the termination of the position of trust or termination of the registered rep by the member firm, whichever occurs first.

All estate matters of the registered person's immediate family are specifically excluded from this rule. Further, this rule does not apply to registered persons who do not manage customer accounts. A registered representative may not circumvent the rules by resigning from managing the customer's account or transferring the customer's account to another associated person. Other attempts to circumvent the rules, such as having the client name the registered representative's spouse or child as a beneficiary are also prohibited. If the registered person is unaware that he / she has been named as a beneficiary or appointed to a position of trust for a client's estate, the registered person will not have violated the disclosure rules. However, once the registered representative becomes aware of the bequest or appointment the knowledge of such triggers the disclosure and compliance requirements.

Pretest

CUSTOMER RECOMMENDATIONS, PROFESSIONAL CONDUCT, AND TAXATION

1. Creating false activity in a security to attract new purchases is a fraudulent practice known as:

    a. trading ahead.

    b. painting the tape.

    c. active concealment.

    d. front running.

2. A client has phoned in concerned about what will happen to his investment in a waste management company if the new EPA laws are enacted requiring disposal companies to reduce pollution. What type of risk is he concerned with?

    a. Call risk

    b. Environmental risk

    c. Investment risk

    d. Legislative risk

3. A customer has a large position in GJH, a thinly traded stock whose share price has remained flat for some time. The customer contacts the agent and wants to sell his entire position. The customer is most subject to which of the following?

    a. Liquidity risk

    b. Credit risk

    c. Conversion risk

    d. Execution risk

4. An investor who is most concerned with changes in interest rates would least likely purchase which of the following?

  a. Long-term warrants

  b. Long-term corporate bonds

  c. Long-term equity

  d. Call options

5. Which of the following is true?

  a. If an investor buys shares just prior to the ex date, he will have his investment money returned.

  b. After an investor's money is returned, the investor is still liable for taxes on the dividend amount.

  c. A registered representative may not use the pending dividend payment as the sole basis for recommending stock purchase.

  d. All of the above.

6. An investor gets advance notice of a research report being issued and enters an order to purchase the security that is the subject of the research report. This is known as:

  a. front running.

  b. trading ahead.

  c. insider trading.

  d. advance trading.

7. Which of the following is not a violation of the rules of conduct?

  a. Recommending a security because of its future price appreciation

  b. Recommending a mutual fund based on a pending dividend to an investor seeking income

  c. Implying that FINRA has approved the firm

  d. Showing a client the past performance of a mutual fund for the last three years since its inception

8. An investor who may lose part or all of his investment is subject to which of the following?

  a. Capital risk

  b. Market risk

  c. Reinvestment risk

  d. Credit risk

Securities Industry Rules and Regulations

INTRODUCTION

Federal and state securities laws, as well as industry regulations, have been enacted to ensure that all industry participants adhere to a high standard of just and equitable trade practices. In this chapter, we will review the rules and regulations, as well as the registration requirements, for firms, agents, and securities.

THE SECURITIES EXCHANGE ACT OF 1934

The Securities Exchange Act of 1934 was the second major piece of legislation that resulted from the market crash of 1929. The Securities Exchange Act of 1934 regulates the secondary market that consists of investor-to-investor transactions. All transactions between two investors that are executed on any of the exchanges or in the over-the-counter (OTC) market are secondary market transactions. In a secondary market transaction, the selling security holder, not the issuing corporation, receives the money. The Securities Exchange Act of 1934 also regulates all individuals and firms that conduct business in the securities industry. The Securities Exchange Act of 1934:

- Created the Securities and Exchange Commission (SEC).
- Requires registration of broker dealers and agents.
- Regulates the exchanges and the NASD (now part of FINRA).

- Requires net capital for broker dealers.
- Regulates short sales.
- Regulates insider transactions.
- Requires public companies to solicit proxies.
- Requires segregation of customer and firm assets.
- Authorized the Federal Reserve Board to regulate the extension of credit for securities purchases under Regulation T.
- Regulates the handling of client accounts.

The Securities Exchange Act of 1934 also regulates the issuers of publicly owned securities and requires issuers of these securities to file annual reports (10-Ks) and quarterly reports (10-Qs). Issuers are also required to report material information to the public by filing form 8-K with the SEC. Issuers who file 10-K and 10-Qs are known as reporting issuers. All publicly traded corporations must solicit proxies from investors to vote on major issues relating to the corporation.

THE SECURITIES AND EXCHANGE COMMISSION (SEC)

One of the biggest components of the Securities Exchange Act of 1934 was the creation of the SEC. The SEC is the ultimate securities industry authority and is a direct government body. Five commissioners are appointed to five-year terms by the President of the United States, and each must be approved by the Senate. The SEC is not a self-regulatory organization (SRO) or a designated examining authority (DEA). An SRO is an entity that regulates its own members, such as the NYSE or FINRA. A DEA is an entity that inspects a broker dealer's books and records, and it can also be the NYSE or FINRA. All broker dealers, exchanges, agents, and securities must register with the SEC. All exchanges are required to file a registration statement with the SEC that includes the articles of incorporation, bylaws, and constitution. All new rules and regulations adopted by the exchanges must be disclosed to the SEC as soon as they are enacted. Issuers of securities with more than 500 shareholders and with assets exceeding $5,000,000 must register with the SEC, file quarterly and annual reports, and solicit proxies from stockholders. A broker dealer that conducts business with the public must register with the SEC and maintain a certain level of financial solvency known as net capital. All broker dealers are required to forward a financial statement to all customers of the firm. Additionally, all employees of the broker dealer who are involved in securities sales, have access to cash and securities, or who supervise employees must be fingerprinted.

EXTENSION OF CREDIT

The Securities Act of 1934 gave the authority to the Federal Reserve Board (FRB) to regulate the extension of credit by broker dealers for the purchase of securities by their customers. The following is a list of the regulations of the different lenders and the regulation that gave the FRB the authority to govern their activities:

- Regulation T: Broker dealers
- Regulation U: Banks
- Regulation G: All other financial institutions

THE NATIONAL ASSOCIATION OF SECURITIES DEALERS (NASD)

The Maloney Act of 1938 was an amendment to the Securities Exchange Act of 1934 that allowed for the creation of the NASD. The NASD was the SRO for OTC market, and its purpose was to regulate the broker dealers who conduct business in the OTC market. The NASD is now part of FINRA and has four major bylaws. They are:

1. The rules of fair practice
2. The uniform practice code
3. The code of procedure
4. The code of arbitration

THE RULES OF FAIR PRACTICE/ RULES OF CONDUCT

The rules of fair practice are designed to ensure just and equitable trade practices among members in their dealings with the public. In short, the rules of fair practice require members to deal fairly with the public. The rules of fair practice may also be called the conduct rules or the rules of conduct. Among other things, they govern:

- Commissions and markups
- Retail and institutional communication
- Customer recommendations
- Claims made by representatives

THE UNIFORM PRACTICE CODE

The uniform practice code sets forth guidelines for how FINRA members transact business with other members. The uniform practice code sets standards of business practices among its members and regulates:

- Settlement dates
- Ex dividend dates
- Rules of good delivery
- Confirmations
- Don't know (DK) procedures

THE CODE OF PROCEDURE

The code of procedure regulates how FINRA investigates complaints and violations. The code of procedure regulates the discovery phase of alleged violations of rules of fair practice. The code of procedure is not concerned with money; it is only concerned with rule violations.

THE CODE OF ARBITRATION

The code of arbitration provides a forum to resolve disputes. Arbitration provides a final and binding resolution to disputes involving a member and:

- Another member
- A registered agent
- A bank
- A customer

FINRA is divided into districts based on geography. Each district elects a committee to administer the association's rules. The committee is composed of up to 12 members who serve up to a three-year term. The committee appoints the Department of Enforcement to handle all trade practice complaints within the district and has the power to assess penalties against members who have violated one or more of the association's rules. FINRA's executive committee, which consists of the Board of Governors, oversees the national business of FINRA.

BECOMING A MEMBER OF FINRA

FINRA sets forth strict qualification standards that all prospective members must meet, prior to being granted membership with FINRA. Any firm that engages in interstate securities transactions with public customers is required to become a FINRA member. Additionally, any broker dealer that wishes to participate as a selling group member in the distribution of mutual fund shares must also be a FINRA member.

In order to become a FINRA member, a firm must:

- Meet net capital requirements (solvency).
- Have at least two principals to supervise the firm.
- Have an acceptable business plan detailing its proposed business activities.
- Attend a premembership interview.

Members must also agree to:

- Abide by all of the association's rules.
- Abide by all federal and state laws.
- Pay dues, fees, and membership assessments as required by the association.

FINRA members must pay the following fees:

- Basic membership fee
- Fee for each representative and principal
- Fee based on the gross income of the firm
- Fee for all branch offices

HIRING NEW EMPLOYEES

A registered principal of a firm will be the individual who interviews and screens potential new employees. The principal will be required to make a thorough investigation into the candidate's professional and personal backgrounds. With few exceptions, other than clerical personnel, all new employees will be required to become registered as an associated person with the firm. The new employee will begin the registration process by filling out and submitting a Uniform Application for Securities Industry Registration, also known as Form U4. Form U4 is used to collect the applicant's personal and professional history, including:

- 10-year employment history
- Five-year resident history
- Legal name and any aliases used
- Any legal or regulatory actions

The principal of the firm is required to verify the employment information for the last three years and must attest to the character of the applicant by signing Form U4 prior to its submission to FINRA. All U4 forms will be sent to the Central Registration Depository (CRD) along with a fingerprint card for processing and recording. Any applicant who has answered yes to any of the questions on the form regarding his or her background must give a detailed explanation in the DRP pages attached to the form. The applicant is not required to provide information regarding:

- Marital status
- Educational background
- Income or net worth

The only information regarding the employee's finances that is disclosed on Form U4 is if the associated person has ever declared bankruptcy and if the employee has any unsatisfied judgments, liens, or entered into a compromise with creditors. For example, if a registered person entered into a short sale in a real estate transaction, and the bank forgave any portion of the loan, this must be reported on the employee's form U4. Interestingly, if the representative is in the process of being foreclosed upon for their primary residence, this action need not be reported by the employee.. Any development that would cause an answer on the associated person's U4 to change requires that the member update the U4 within 30 days of when the member becomes informed of the event. In the case of an event that could cause the individual to become statutorily disqualified, such as a felony conviction or misdemeanor involving cash or securities, the member must update the associated person's U4 within 10 business days of learning of the event. If a member firm conducts employee drug testing, and a registered person fails the drug test, this is neither reportable on form U4 nor a reason for statutory disqualification.

 TAKENOTE!

Broker dealers are required to perform background checks on its employees every 5 years to ensure that no judgements, liens or disclosable events have gone unreported by the registered person. Registered persons who fail to disclose an unsatisfied judgements or liens are subject to significant regulatory action that could result in the person being barred from the industry in extreme cases.

DISCIPLINARY ACTIONS AGAINST A REGISTERED REPRESENTATIVE

If another industry regulator takes disciplinary action against a representative, the employing member firm must notify FINRA. Actions by any of the following should be immediately disclosed to the association:

- The SEC
- An exchange or association
- A state regulator
- A clearing firm
- A commodity regulatory body

Also immediately reportable to FINRA are any of the following:

- A customer compliant alleging theft, forgery, or misappropriation of customer assets
- Indictment, conviction, or plea of guilty or no contest to a criminal matter
- If the agent becomes a respondent or defendant in a matter in excess of $15,000 or if the firm becomes a respondent or defendant in a matter in excess of $25,000
- An agent is disciplined by the employing member firm or commissions are withheld from an agent or the agent is fined in either case in amounts in excess of $2,500.

FINRA defines immediate notification for the previously listed matters as being within 10 days. All disclosures must include the type of action brought as well as the name of the party bringing the actions and the name of the representative involved. The firm will make the disclosure on Form U4. FINRA will submit disciplinary actions that are taken by FINRA on Form U6 and they will be recorded on the employee's record. All disciplinary actions, along with a record of the agent's registrations and employment history, are available through FINRA's BrokerCheck program. FINRA members are required to regulate the activities of its associated people and must disclose to the association any action that the member takes against a registered representative. Should a registered representative feel that the information disclosed through the BrokerCheck program is inaccurate the representative may request an amendment to the disclosure by filling out and submitting a BrokerCheck comment form.

RESIGNATION OF A REGISTERED REPRESENTATIVE

If a registered representative voluntarily terminates his or her association with a member firm, the member must fill out and submit a uniform termination notice known as a U-5 to FINRA within 30 days. An associated person's registration is nontransferable. A representative may not simply move the registration from one firm to another. The employing firm that the representative is leaving must fill out and submit a U-5 to FINRA, which terminates the representative's registration. The new employing firm must fill out and submit a new U-4 to begin a new registration for the associated person with the new employer. A representative who leaves the industry for more than 24 months is required to requalify by exam.

During a period of absence from the industry of two years or less, FINRA retains jurisdiction over the representative in cases involving customer complaints and violations. Agents who volunteer or who are called to active duty with the military have their registrations and continuing education requirements "tolled" and their registrations are placed in "special inactive" status. During this time, the 24-month requirement is not in effect and the agent may continue to receive compensation from transactions but may not contact customers during their time of active military duty. Once active duty ends the agent has 90 days to reenter the business. If the person is not associated with a member at that time the 24-month window will begin. An agent who had already left the industry and subsequently joined the military will have his or her 24-month window tolled as of the date active-duty begins. The individual will have 90 days to re-enter the industry upon return. If the individual has not become employed by a broker-dealer on the 91st day, the 24 month window will restart from the date at which it was tolled.

CONTINUING EDUCATION

Most registered agents and principals are required to participate in industry-mandated continuing education programs. The continuing education program consists of a firm element, which is administered by the broker dealer, and a regulatory element, which is administered by the regulators.

FIRM ELEMENT

Every FINRA member firm at least annually must identify the training needs of its covered employees and develop a written training plan based on their employees' needs. A covered employee is a registered person who engages in sales of securities to customers, trading, investment banking, and their immediate supervisors. The firm, at a minimum, should institute a plan that increases the covered employees' securities knowledge and should focus on the products offered by the firm. The plan should also highlight the risks and suitability requirements associated with the firm's investment products and strategies. The firm is not required to file its continuing education plan with FINRA unless it is specifically requested to do so. However, firms that fail to adequately document their continuing education program, including their covered agents' compliance with the program, may be subject to disciplinary action.

REGULATORY ELEMENT

All registered agents who were not registered on or before July 1, 1988, must participate in the regulatory element of the continuing education requirement. Agents subject to the requirement must complete the computer-based training at an approved facility on the second anniversary of their initial registration and every three years thereafter. The content of the exam is developed by The Securities Industry Regulatory Council on Continuing Education and is not the responsibility of the broker dealer. FINRA will notify the agent 30 days prior to their anniversary date. This notification provides the agent with a 120 day window to complete the regulatory continuing education requirement. An agent who fails to complete the requirement within that period will have their registration become inactive. Agents whose registrations have become inactive may not engage in any securities business that requires a license and may not receive commissions until their registration is reactivated. Registered representatives are subject to Series 101 of the regulatory element, while registered principals are subject to Series 201 of the requirement. Agents who were exempt from the regulatory element as a result of having been registered for 10 years or more with a clean disciplinary history on July 1, 1998, who become the subject of a significant disciplinary action, will now be required to participate in the regulatory element of the continuing education requirement. Additionally, if an agent who was exempt from the regulatory element subsequently becomes registered as a principal, they will become subject to the Series 201 requirement. The one-time exemption is only for the regulatory element; there is no exemption from the firm element of the continuing education program. An agent who leaves the industry for more than 24 months will have to requalify by exam and will have a regulatory education requirement based on the date of reassociation (the date they passed the exam for the second time). An agent who temporarily leaves the industry (less than 24 months) who is not required to requalify by exam will have a regulatory continuing education requirement based on the original sate of association.

TERMINATION FOR CAUSE

A member may terminate a registered representative for cause if the representative has:

- Violated firm policy.
- Violated the rules of the NYSE, FINRA, SEC, or any other industry regulator.
- Violated state or federal securities laws.

A firm may not terminate a representative who is the subject of investigation by any securities industry regulator until the investigation is completed.

RETIRING REPRESENTATIVES/CONTINUING COMMISSIONS

Retiring representatives may continue to receive commissions from the business that they have built over their career provided that a contract is in place prior to the representative's retirement. A retiring representative may continue to receive commissions on old business only. The retiring representation may not receive commissions on any new business and may not receive finder's fees. If the retired representative dies, the representative's beneficiary may continue to receive the commissions that were due the representative.

STATE REGISTRATION

In addition to registering with FINRA, all broker dealers and agents must register in their home state as well as in any state in which they transact business.

REGISTRATION EXEMPTIONS

The following individuals are exempt from registration:

- Clerical
- Nonsupervising officers and managers not dealing with customers
- Non-U.S. citizens working abroad
- Floor personnel

PERSONS INELIGIBLE TO REGISTER

Individuals applying for registration must meet the association's requirements in the following areas:

- Training
- Competence
- Experience
- Character

Anyone who fails to meet the association's requirements in any of the above listed areas may not become registered. An individual may also be disqualified by statute or through rules for any of the following:

- Expulsion, suspension, or disciplinary actions by the SEC or any foreign or domestic SRO.
- The individual caused the expulsion or suspension of a broker dealer or principal.
- The individual made false or misleading statements on the application for registration on form U-4 or form B-D.
- Felony conviction or misdemeanor involving securities within the last 10 years.
- Court injunction or order barring the individual.

COMMUNICATIONS WITH THE PUBLIC

Member firms will seek to increase their business and exposure through the use of both retail and institutional communications. There are strict regulations in place in order to ensure all communications with the public adhere to industry guidelines. Some communications with the public are available to a general audience and include:

- Television/radio
- Publicly accessible websites
- Motion pictures
- Newspapers/magazines
- Telephone directory listings
- Signs/billboards
- Computer/internet postings
- Video tape displays

- Other public media
- Recorded telemarketing messages

Other types of communications are offered to a targeted audience. These communications include:

- Market reports
- Password-protected websites
- Telemarketing scripts
- Form letters or emails (sent to more than 25 people)
- Circulars
- Research reports
- Printed materials for seminars
- Option worksheets
- Performance reports
- Prepared scripts for TV or radio
- Reprints of ads

FINRA RULE 2210 COMMUNICATIONS WITH THE PUBLIC

FINRA Rule 2210 regulates how FINRA member firms communicate with the public. FINRA Rule 2210 classifies communication into three main categories. The three categories of member communication are:

1. Retail communication
2. Institutional communication
3. Correspondence

RETAIL COMMUNICATION

Retail communication is defined as any written communication distributed or made available to more than 25 retail investors in a 30-day period. The communication may be distributed in hard copy or in electronic formats. The definition of a retail investor is any investor who does not meet the definition of an institutional investor. Retail communications contain all components of advertising and sales literature. All retail communications must be approved by a registered principal prior to first use. All retail communications must be maintained for three years from the date of the last use. A copy should be readily accessible for the first two years and the file should contain the name of the principal who approved communication as well as the date it was first and last used. If the member firm is a new member firm which has been in existence for less than 12 months based on the firm's approval date in the Central Registration Depository or CRD the member must file all retail communications with FINRA 10 days prior to its first use unless the communication has been previously filed and contains no material changes or has been filed by another member such as investment company or ETF sponsor. Member firms who have been established for more than 12 months may file retail communications with FINRA 10 days after the communication is first used. Knowing what communications are filed with FINRA and when they are filed with FINRA can present challenges for many test takers. The information that is contained in the communication and its intended recipients dictate when or if the communication is filed with FINRA. Exempt from FINRA's filing requirements are:

- Recruiting and generic advertisements
- Retail Communications created from a template previously filed with FINRA
- Retail Communications that do not promote a product or service
- Retail Communications that merely contain a list of products the member offers
- Retail Communications that do not contain investment advice
- Mutual fund profiles
- Reprints and excerpts of articles published by non-affiliated third parties
- Press releases issued only to media outlets
- Institutional communications
- Correspondence
- Internal communications
- Tombstone ads, preliminary and statutory / final prospectus filed with the SEC

It is important to note that while preliminary and statutory prospectus that are filed with the SEC are exempt from being filed with FINRA, free writing prospectus prepared by the broker-dealer are required to be filed with FINRA as part of retail communication. The following types of retail communication must be filed with FINRA within 10 days of first being used:

- Storyboards for television or video Communications
- mutual fund communications that do not include raking information

- Communications containing information relating to publicly traded direct participation programs and sec-registered collateralized mortgage obligations
- SEC registered securities whose value is based on an index, a basket of securities, commodities, debt securities, or currencies. This includes ETFs, ETNs and other publicly offered structured products
- Free writing prospectus prepared by the broker-dealer
- Report templates created from an investment analysis tool

Investment analysis tools allow individuals to input a set of criteria and have a computer software program model portfolios, potential outcomes or hypothetical returns using statistical analysis. If a member firm allows retail investors to access investment analysis tools, the firm must provide access to that tool to FINRA's advertising department within 10 days of its first use.

FINRA members are required to pre file the following retail communications 10 days prior to use:

- Communications containing single stock and other security futures
- Communications containing mutual fund ranking or comparisons created by the investment company
- Communications containing volatility ranking information concerning bond funds
- Communications prepared by member firms less than 1 year old
- Communications prepared by sanctioned firms or firms directed to pre-file by FINRA

For most retail communications, the term first use means when it is first published, broadcast, distributed or made available by the member.

 TAKE**NOTE!**

Research reports concerning only securities listed on a national securities exchange are excluded from Rule 2210's filing requirements.

INSTITUTIONAL COMMUNICATIONS

Intuitional communication is defined as any written communication distributed or made available exclusively to institutional investors. The communication may be distributed in hard copy or in electronic formats. Institutional communications do not have to be approved by a principal prior to first use so long as the member has established policies and procedures regarding the use of institutional communications and has trained its employees on the proper use of institutional communication. Institutional communication is also exempt from FINRA's filing requirement but like retail communications it must be maintained by a member for three years. If the member believes that the institutional communication or any part thereof may be seen by even a single retail investor the communication must be handled as all other retail communication and is subject to the approval and filing requirements as if it was retail communication. An institutional investor is a person or firm that trades securities for his or her own account or for the account of others. Institutional investors are generally limited to large financial companies. Because of their size and sophistication, fewer protective laws cover institutional investors. It is important to note that there is no minimum size for an institutional account. Institutional investors include:

- Broker dealers
- Investment advisers
- Investment companies
- Insurance companies
- Banks
- Trusts
- Savings and loans
- Government agencies
- Employment benefit plans with more than 100 participants
- Any non-natural person with more than $50,000,000 in assets

CORRESPONDENCE

Correspondence consists of electronic and written communications between the member and up to 25 retail investors in a 30-calendar-day period. With the increase in acceptance of email as business communication, it would be impractical for a member to review all correspondence between the member and a customer. The member instead may set up procedures to review a sample of all correspondence, both electronic and hard copy. If the member reviews only a sample of the correspondence, the member must train their associated people on their firm's procedures relating to correspondence and must document the training and ensure the procedures are followed. Even though the member is not required to review all correspondence, the member must still retain all correspondence. The member should, where practical, review all incoming hard copy correspondence. Letters received by the firm could contain cash, checks, securities, or complaints.

BROKER DEALER WEBSITES

A broker dealer will not be deemed to have a place of business in a state where it does not maintain an office simply by virtue of the fact that the publicly available website established by the firm or one of its agents is accessible from that state so long as the following conditions are met:

- The website clearly states that the firm may only conduct business in states where it is properly registered to do so.
- The website only provides general information about the firm and does not provide specific investment advice.
- The firm or its agent may not respond to Internet inquiries with the intent to solicit business without first meeting the registration requirements in the state of the prospective customer.

The content of any website must be reviewed and approved by a principal prior to its first use and must be filed with FINRA within 10 days of use. If the firm or its agent updates the website and the update materially changes the information contained on the website, the updates must be reapproved by a principal and refiled with FINRA. Registered representations may never post to the firm's website without prior principal approval. The website may use the FINRA logo so long as the use is only to demonstrate that the firm is a FINRA member and a hyperlink to the FINRA website is included in close proximity to the logo. Member firms are not required to display the FINRA logo.

BLIND RECRUITING ADS

A blind recruiting ad is an ad placed by the member firm for the specific purpose of finding job applicants. Blind recruiting ads are the only form of advertising that does not require the member's name to appear in the ad. The ads may not distort the opportunities or salaries of the advertised position. All other ads are required to disclose the name of the member firm, as well as the relationship of the member to any other entities that appear in the ad.

GENERIC ADVERTISING

Generic advertising is generally designed to promote firm awareness and to advertise the products and services generally offered through the firm. Generic ads will generally include:

- Securities products offered (i.e., stocks, bonds, mutual funds)
- Contact name, number, and address
- Types of accounts offered (i.e., individual, IRA, 401K)

TOMBSTONE ADS

A tombstone ad is an announcement of a new security offering coming to market. Tombstone ads may be run while the securities are still in registration with the SEC and may only include:

- Description of securities.
- Description of business.
- Description of transaction.
- Required disclaimers.
- Time and place of any stockholders meetings regarding the sale of the securities.

All tombstone ads must include the following:

- A statement that the securities registration has not yet become effective.
- A statement that responding to the ad does not obligate the prospect.
- A statement as to where a prospectus may be obtained.
- A statement that the ad does not constitute an offer to sell the securities and that an offer may only be made by the prospectus.

All retail communication is required to be approved by a principal of the firm prior to its first use. A general security principal (Series 24) may approve most retail communication. Any retail communication relating to options must be approved by a registered option principal or the compliance registered options principal. Research reports must be approved by a supervisory analyst.

TESTIMONIALS

From time to time, firms will use testimonials made by people of national or local recognition in an effort to generate new business for the firm. If the individual giving the testimonial is quoting past performance relating to the firm's recommendations, it must be accompanied by a disclaimer that past performance is not indicative of future performance. If the individual giving the testimony was compensated in any way, the fact that the person received compensation must also be disclosed. Should the individual's testimony imply that the person making the testimony is an expert, a statement regarding the person's qualifications as an expert must also be contained in the ad or sales literature. Research prepared by outside parties must disclose the name of the preparer.

FREE SERVICES

If a member firm advertises free services to customers or to people who respond to an ad, the services must actually be free to everyone with no strings attached.

MISLEADING COMMUNICATION WITH THE PUBLIC

The following are some examples of misleading statements, which are not allowed to appear in communication with the public:

- Excessive hedge clauses.
- Implying an endorsement by FINRA, the NYSE, or the SEC.
- Printing the FINRA logo in type that is larger than the type of the member's name.
- Implying that the member has larger research facilities than it actually has.
- Implying that an individual has higher qualifications than he or she actually has.

SECURITIES INVESTOR PROTECTION CORPORATION ACT OF 1970

The Securities Investor Protection Corporation (SIPC) is a government-sponsored corporation that provides protection to customers in the event of a broker dealer's failure. All broker dealers that are registered with the SEC are required to be SIPC members. All broker dealers are required to pay annual dues to SIPC's insurance fund to cover losses due to broker dealer failure. If a broker dealer fails to pay its SIPC assessment, it may not transact business until the assessment is paid.

NET CAPITAL REQUIREMENT

All broker dealers are required to maintain a certain level of net capital in order to ensure that they are financially solvent. A broker dealer's capital requirement is contingent upon the type of business that it conducts. The larger and more complex the firm's business is, the greater the net capital requirement. Should a firm fall below its net capital requirement, it is deemed to be insolvent, and SIPC will petition in court to have a trustee appointed to liquidate the firm and protect the customers. The trustee must be a disinterested party and, once the trustee is appointed, the firm may not conduct business or try to conceal any assets.

CUSTOMER COVERAGE

SIPC protects customers of a brokerage firm in much the same way that the FDIC protects customers of banks. SIPC covers customer losses that result from broker dealer failure, not for market losses. SIPC covers customers for up to $500,000 per separate customer. Of the $500,000, up to $250,000 may be in cash. Most broker dealers carry additional private insurance to cover larger accounts, but SIPC is the industry-funded insurance and is required by all broker dealers. The following are examples of separate customers:

Customer	Securities Market Value	Cash	SIPC Coverage
Mr. Jones	$320,000	$75,000	All
Mr. & Mrs. Jones	$290,000	$90,000	All
Mrs. Jones	$397,000	$82,000	All

All of the accounts shown would be considered separate customers, and SIPC would cover the entire value of all of the accounts. If an account has in excess of $250,000 in cash, the individual would not be covered for any amount exceeding $250,000 in cash and would become a general creditor for the rest. SIPC does not consider a margin account and a cash account as separate customers and the customer would be covered for the maximum of $500,000. SIPC does not offer coverage for commodities contracts, and all member firms must display the SIPC sign in the lobby of the firm. Many firms purchase excess insurance for customers that go above and beyond

SIPC coverage. If the firm reduces or eliminates this excess coverage it must inform customers 30 days prior to the effective date of the change.

FIDELITY BOND

All SIPC members are required to obtain a fidelity bond to protect customers in the event of employee dishonesty. Some things that a fidelity bond will insure against are check forgery and fraudulent trading. The minimum amount of the fidelity bond is $25,000; however, large firms are often required to carry a higher amount.

THE SECURITIES ACTS AMENDMENTS OF 1975

The Securities Acts Amendments of 1975 gave the authority to the MSRB to regulate the issuance and trading of municipal bonds. The MSRB has no enforcement division. Its rules are enforced by other regulators.

THE INSIDER TRADING & SECURITIES FRAUD ENFORCEMENT ACT OF 1988

The Insider Trading & Securities Fraud Enforcement Act of 1988 sets forth guidelines and controls for the use and dissemination of nonpublic material information. Nonpublic information is information that is not known by people outside of the company. Material information is information regarding a situation or development that will materially affect the company in the present or in the future. It is not only just for insiders to have this type of information, but it is required in order for them to do their jobs effectively. It is, however, unlawful for an insider to use this information to profit from a forthcoming move in the stock price. An insider is defined as any officer, director, 10% stockholder, or anyone who is in possession of nonpublic material information, as well as the spouse of any such person. Additionally, it is unlawful for the insider to divulge any of this information to any outside party. Trading on inside information has always been a violation of the Securities Exchange Act of 1934, and the Insider Trading Act prescribed penalties for violators, which include:

- A fine up to 300% of the amount of the gain or 300% of the amount of the loss avoided for the person who acts on the information.
- A civil or criminal fine for the person who divulges the information.
- Insider traders may be sued by the affected parties.

- Criminal prosecutions and a criminal fine of up to $1,000,000 and 20 years in prison.

Information becomes public information once it has been disseminated over public media. The SEC will pay a reward of up to 10% to informants who turn in individuals who trade on inside information. In addition to the insiders already listed, the following are also considered insiders:

- Accountants
- Attorneys
- Investment bankers

FIREWALL

Broker dealers who act as underwriters and investment bankers for corporate clients must have access to information regarding the company in order to advise the company properly. The broker dealer must ensure that no inside information is passed between its investment banking department and its retail trading departments. The broker dealer is required to physically separate these divisions by a firewall. The broker dealer must maintain written supervisory procedures to adequately guard against the wrongful use or dissemination of inside information.

TELEMARKETING RULES

FINRA Rule 3230 regulates how telemarketing calls are made by businesses. On your exam you may see the telemarketing rule tested under the telephone Consumer Protection Act of 1991, FINRA Rule 3230 or as telemarketing rules. Telemarketing calls that are designed to have consumers invest in or purchase goods, services, or property must adhere to the strict guidelines. All firms must:

- Call only between the hours of 8 a.m. and 9 p.m. in the customer's time zone.
- Maintain a do not call list. Individuals placed on the do not call list may not be contacted by anyone at the firm for 5 years.
- Solicitors must give the prospect the firm's name, address, and phone number. Caller ID must display firm name and phone number caller ID blocking may not be used.
- Must maintain adequate policies and procedures to maintain a firm specific do not call list.
- Maintain adequate policies and procedures to ensure numbers called do not appear on the national do not call list.

- Must train representatives on calling policies and use of the do not call list.
- Ensure that any fax solicitations have the firm's name, address, and phone number.

 TAKE**NOTE!**

An interesting situation can arise when a customer of the firm who maintains an account with the firm is on the firm specific do not call list. In these cases, the representative may not contact the customer unless it is to verify account information such as the mailing address. The customer may not be contacted to discuss holdings in the account or to make a recommendation.

DO NOT CALL LIST EXEMPTIONS

The following are exempt from the prohibited calls listed above:

- Calls to existing customers who have executed a transaction or who have had an account containing cash or securities on deposit within the last 18 months or to a person who has contacted the member within the last 3 months.
- Calls to a person where the caller has a personal relationship with the recipient.
- Calls to a person who has given written permission to be contacted by the firm and the number where the person may be contacted.
- Inadvertent calls to a number that now appears on the national do not call list but were not included on the do not call list used by the member so long as that list was not more than 31 days old.

THE PENNY STOCK COLD CALL RULE

The penny stock cold call rule was enacted in order to ensure that investors do not purchase penny stocks without knowing the risks. A penny stock is an unlisted security that trades below $5 per share. Prior to purchasing a penny stock:

- The agent must make sure that the purchase is suitable.
- The customer must sign a suitability statement.
- The firm must supply a current quote.

- The firm must disclose the amount of commission earned by the firm and the agent.

 TAKE**NOTE!**

Established customers are exempt from the penny stock cold call rule. An established customer is one that has made three transactions in three different penny stocks on three different days. An established customer is also one that has had cash or securities on deposit with the firm during the previous 12 months.

THE ROLE OF THE PRINCIPAL

Prior to any firm being admitted as a FINRA member, it must have at least two principals to supervise the firm's activities. All firms are required to have a written policy and procedures manual to ensure compliance with the firm's rules as well as the rules of the industry. The manual must be updated to reflect the adoption of new policies, a change in personnel, or new industry rules. It is the principal's responsibility to ensure that all rules in the policy and procedure manual are followed by all of the firm's employees. It is the responsibility of the principal to review and approve all of the following:

- New accounts
- Retail communication
- Transactions

VIOLATIONS AND COMPLAINTS

FINRA's code of procedure sets forth guidelines for the investigation of alleged violations and complaints against a member firm or a registered representative. The FINRA staff originates many complaints against member firms and associated persons during their routine examinations of member firms. Complaints and allegations of wrongdoing may also originate from a customer of the member firm or from another member. If a FINRA staff member has received the complaint that alleges a violation of securities regulations, it is up to FINRA to determine if the complaint is meritorious. FINRA will begin an investigation of the complaint by notifying the member and/or the associated person that a complaint has been received and will request the member or an associated person to respond in writing. All requests for information must be met within 25 days from the day that the request was made.

RESOLUTION OF ALLEGATIONS

Should FINRA find that the allegations are baseless, it may dismiss it without action. However, if FINRA finds that the allegation has merit, it may be resolved through summary complaint procedure or through a formal hearing process.

MINOR RULE VIOLATION

A minor rule violation letter is traditionally used in cases that involve only small violations. FINRA has outlined a number of rule violations that qualify to be resolved using a minor rule violation (MRV) procedure. It is offered to respondents in an effort to avoid a costly hearing. Under MRV procedure, the maximum penalty is a censure and a $2,500 fine. If the MRV procedure is offered, the member or associated person has 10 business days to accept it. By signing the MRV letter, the respondent does not admit or deny the allegations and gives up his or her right to appeal the decision. Should the offer of MRV procedure not be accepted, the Department of Enforcement will proceed with a formal hearing to determine if a violation has occurred. Possible penalties after having been found to have violated one or more of the association's rules include:

- Censure
- Suspension for up to one year
- Expulsion for up to 10 years
- Barred for life
- Fined any amount
- Any other penalty deemed appropriate, such as restitution

Decisions of the Department of Enforcement may be appealed within 15 days to the National Adjudicatory Counsel (NAC). If no action is taken, the decision of the Department of Enforcement becomes final in 45 days. Should the NAC determine that the appeal is meritorious, it must start a review within a 45-day period. The decision of the NAC may be appealed to the SEC and finally to the court system. Upon final determination, all fines, penalties, and costs must be paid promptly.

CODE OF ARBITRATION

FINRA's arbitration procedure provides parties with a forum to resolve disputes. Most claims submitted to arbitration are financial in nature, although other claims may be submitted. Sexual harassment and discrimination claims are not required to be resolved in arbitration unless both parties specifically agree to arbitrate. Class action claims are also not resolved in arbitration. Class action status is awarded by the court system. Arbitration provides a cost-effective alternative to dispute resolution, and many disputes will be resolved much sooner than they otherwise may have been in court. All industry members are required to settle all disputes through arbitration. A public customer, however, must agree in writing to settle any dispute through arbitration. When a customer opens an account with a broker dealer, the broker dealer will often have the customer sign a customer agreement, although not required by industry standards. The customer agreement usually contains a predispute arbitration cause where the customer agrees to settle any dispute that may arise in arbitration rather than in court. Should the customer request a copy of the predispute arbitration clause the member has 10 business days to provide it to the customer.

THE ARBITRATION PROCESS

Arbitration begins when an aggrieved party, known as the claimant, files a statement of claim, along with a submission agreement and payment for the arbitration fee, with FINRA. The party alleged to have caused the claimant harm (known as the respondent), must respond to the statement of claim within 45 calendar days. The response is sent to both the arbitration director and the claimant, and the claimant then has 10 calendar days to reply to both the arbitration director and respondent. Dispute resolution through arbitration is available for matters involving:

- Member vs. member
- Bank vs. member
- Member vs. bank
- Member vs. registered representative
- Registered representative vs. member
- Customer vs. member
- Member vs. customer

SIMPLIFIED ARBITRATION

Simplified arbitration is available for disputes involving amounts in dispute of $50,000 or less. Traditionally, simplified arbitration provides no opportunity for a hearing. Parties submit their case in writing only. One arbitrator reviews the case and renders a decision. If a public customer is involved in the arbitration in a matter of $50,000 or less excluding interest and expenses, the customer can request a hearing in front of a single arbitrator. For amounts that exceed $50,000, a hearing must be held.

LARGER DISPUTES

Larger disputes will be submitted to a panel of up to three arbitrators to render a decision on the matter. A hearing will take place and evidence and testimony will be presented to the panel. The number of arbitrators must always be odd, so the panel will be made up of one or three arbitrators from both the public and the industry. An arbitrator will be deemed to be a nonpublic or industry arbitrator if the person is or was in the securities industry at any point in the last 5 years. Included in this definition are persons associated with hedge funds and accountants and attorneys whose practice is dedicated at least 20% of the time to industry clients within the last two years. An accountant or attorney will be deemed to be a public arbitrator if 10% or less of the business of such professional was dedicated to industry clients in the last two years and the revenue received was less than $50,000.

AWARDS UNDER ARBITRATION

Awards under arbitration are final and binding; there is no appeal. If a monetary payment has been awarded, the party required to pay has 30 days to comply with the decision. A member or a registered representative who fails to pay an award under arbitration is subject to suspension. All pending arbitrations, arbitrations settled prior to final judgement, and arbitrations settled in favor of the customer will be disclosed on BrokerCheck. If an arbitration is settled in favor of the firm or representative it will be removed from BrokerCheck. Any sanction by a regulator which carries a penalty of $15,000 or more will also be disclosed on BrokerCheck.

MEDIATION

Mediation is an informal attempt by two parties to try to resolve a dispute prior to entering into the formal arbitration process. During the mediation process the two parties meet to discuss the contested issue, and the dialog is monitored by a mediator. The mediator is a neutral person with industry knowledge suggested by FINRA who tries to help the parties reach an agreement. If the mediator is not acceptable, the parties may select another mediator from a list of approved mediators or provide their own independent mediator. Prior to entering into the mediation process, both parties must agree to try to resolve the issue in mediation and must split the mediator's fee. The mediation process begins with an initial joint meeting where both parties lay out their claims for the mediator and the other party. During the second phase of the process, each side meets with the mediator individually in meetings known as caucuses. The mediator is a neutral party and will not disclose information provided during the caucus sessions to the opposing side. The mediation process will continue until an agreement is reached, the mediator declares an impasse with no possible resolution, or one of the parties or the mediator withdraws from the process in writing. The mediation process may provide a resolution for all or some of the contested issues. Mediation may take place while the parties are moving forward with the arbitration process. Issues that are not resolved in mediation may be resolved through formal arbitration. The party who served as the mediator may not serve as an arbitrator for the same dispute.

CURRENCY TRANSACTIONS

The Bank Secrecy Act requires all member firms must guard against money laundering. Every member must report any currency receipt of $10,000 or more from any one customer on a single day. The firm must fill out and submit a currency transaction report, also known as Form 4789, to the IRS within 15 days of the receipt of the currency. Multiple deposits that total $10,000 or more will also require the firm to file a currency transaction report (CTR). Additionally, the firm is required to maintain a record of all international wire transfers of $3,000 or greater.

THE PATRIOT ACT

The Patriot Act, as part of the Bank Secrecy Act, requires broker dealers to have written policies and procedures designed to detect suspicious activity. The firm must designate a principal to ensure compliance with the firm's policies and to train firm personnel. The firm is required to file a Suspicious Activity Report (SAR) for any transaction of more than $5,000 that appears questionable. The firm must file the report within 30 days of identifying any suspicious activity. Anti-money-laundering rules require that all firms implement a customer identification program to ensure that the firm knows the true identity of its customers. All customers who open an account with the firm, as well as individuals with trading authority, are subject to this rule. The firm must ensure that its customers do not appear on any list of known or suspected terrorists. A firm's anti-money-laundering program must be approved by senior management. Should the approving member of management leave the firm the plan should be reapproved by the new member of senior management.

All records relating to the SAR filing, including a copy of the SAR report, must be maintained by the firm for 5 years. FINRA Rule 3310 requires member firms to identify to FINRA the name of the person in charge of the firm's AML program as well as the name and full contact details of the person(s) who are to oversee the day-to-day operation of the AML program. Any changes to AML persons identified to FINRA must be updated within 30 days. Members must also conduct an annual independent test of the program. The person conducting the test may not perform the daily AML duties at the firm or report to anyone in charge of the program. The person should have substantial knowledge of the Bank Secrecy Act and its related rules and regulations.

The money-laundering process begins with the placement of the funds. This is when the money is deposited in an account with the broker dealer. The second step of the laundering process is known as layering. The layering process consists of multiple deposits in amounts less than $10,000. The funds will often be drawn from different financial institutions; which is known as structuring. The launderers will then purchase and sell securities in the account. The integration of the proceeds back into the banking system completes the process. At this point, the launderers may use the money, which now appears to have come from legitimate sources, to purchase goods and services. Firms must also identify the customers who open the account and must make sure that they are not conducting business with anyone on the OFAC list. This list is maintained by the Treasury Department Office of Foreign Assets Control. It consists of known and suspected terrorists, criminals, and members of pariah nations. Individuals and entities who appear on this list are known as Specially Designated Nationals and Blocked Persons. Conducting business with anyone on this list is strictly prohibited. Registered representatives who aid in the laundering of money are subject to prosecution and face up to 20 years in prison and a $500,000 fine per transaction. The representative does not even have to be involved in the scheme or even know about it to be prosecuted.

FinCEN is a bureau of the U.S. Department of the Treasury. FinCEN's mission is to safeguard the financial system and guard against money laundering and promote national security. FinCEN collects, receives, and maintains financial transactions data; analyzes and disseminates that data for law enforcement purposes; and builds global cooperation with counterpart organizations in other countries and with international bodies. FinCEN will email a list of individuals and entities to a designated principal every few weeks. The principal is required to check the list against the firm's customer list. If a match is found the firm must notify FinCEN within 14 calendar days.

U.S. ACCOUNTS

Every member must obtain the following from U.S. customers:

- A social security number/documentation number
- Date of birth
- Address
- Place of business

FOREIGN ACCOUNTS

All non-U.S. customers must provide at least one of the following:

- A passport number and country of issuance.
- An alien ID number.
- A U.S. tax ID number.
- A number from another form of government-issued ID and the name of the issuing country.

ANNUAL COMPLIANCE REVIEW

At least once per year the member must conduct a compliance review of each OSJ, supervising branch office, and each registered representative. Nonsupervising branch offices should be directly reviewed every three years. When the member reviews the OSJ, the member is automatically inspecting the activities of the branch offices under the jurisdiction of the OSJ. Each member must designate a principal to test the firm's supervisory and compliance controls. This principal must file a report with senior management detailing the results of these tests. Controls must be in place to provide daily supervision of any producing managers.

BUSINESS CONTINUITY PLAN

One of the regulations developed as a result of the attack on 9/11 is the requirement for FINRA member firms to develop and maintain plans and backup facilities to ensure that the firm can meet its obligations to its customers and counterparties in the event that its main facilities are damaged, destroyed, or inaccessible. The plan must provide for alternative means of communication between the firm, its employees, customers, and regulators as well as a data backup. The plan must provide for data back up in both hard copy and electronic format. The plan must be approved and reviewed annually by a senior member of the firm's management team and provide plans to ensure that customers have access to their funds. The plan must be provided to FINRA upon request. The plan must identify two members of senior management as emergency contacts, one of whom must be a registered principal with the firm. Should one of the contact people change FINRA must be notified in 30 days. Customers of the firm must be advised of the business continuity plan at the time the account is open and in writing upon request. The plan must also be posted on the firms website. Small firms with one office should provide a contact number to the clearing firm. Specific language is required to be included in the plan provided to customers stating that in certain events the firm may have no alternative but to go out of business.

SARBANES-OXLEY ACT

The Sarbanes-Oxley Act, also known as the Public Company Accounting Reform and Investor Protection Act of 2002, was enacted to help restore confidence in the financial reports and accounting standards of publicly traded companies. The act created the Public Company Accounting Oversight Board to oversee, regulate, and discipline accounting firms' activities when performing auditing functions for publicly traded companies. Section 302 of the Sarbanes-Oxley Act requires the management of publicly traded companies to affirm the accuracy of the company's financial reports and to accept responsibility for the content of the reports by signing all annual and quarterly reports filed under the Securities Exchange Act of 1934. The principal executive officer as well as the principal financial officer must:

- Sign an acknowledgment that they have read the report.
- Certify to their knowledge that the financial reports do not contain any untrue or misleading statements.
- Certify that to their knowledge the reports do not omit any material fact and accurately represent the company's financial condition for the period covered by the report.
- Establish internal controls to ensure the accurate reporting of all of the issuer's subsidiaries.

- Have evaluated the effectiveness of the internal controls within 90 days prior to the filing of the report and must file a report relating to the effectiveness of the internal controls.
- Disclose to the audit committee and the board of directors any deficiencies with internal controls or any act of fraud involving management or any employee significantly involved in the company's internal controls.
- Disclose any material changes to the internal controls or any weaknesses or corrective actions taken.

Section 401 of the Sarbanes-Oxley Act requires financial reports to contain detailed information regarding any off-balance-sheet transactions, obligations, and liabilities the company may have engaged in or have outstanding. The statement may not contain any false or misleading information.

Section 402 of the Sarbanes-Oxley Act enhanced conflict-of-interest rules regarding loans made by the company to any officer. Section 402 of the act made it unlawful for any company to extend or maintain personal loans either directly or indirectly through a subsidiary to or for any officer of the company.

Section 403 of the Sarbanes-Oxley Act requires that the company's management as well as any owner of 10% or more of the company's securities file reports regarding holdings and transactions in the company's securities. These reports must be filed within 10 days of the person becoming an officer or 10% holder. If any person subject to the reporting requirements of Section 403 purchases or sells the company's securities or enters into a security-based swap agreement, a report of the transaction must be filed within two business days. Such reports may be filed electronically.

Section 404 of the Sarbanes-Oxley Act requires that management file with the annual report a report detailing the company's internal controls over financial reporting. The company's independent auditor is required to certify management's report regarding its internal controls.

THE UNIFORM SECURITIES ACT

In the early half of the twentieth century, state securities regulators developed their state's rules and regulations for transacting securities business within their state. The result was a nation of states with regulations that varied widely from state to state. The Uniform Securities Act (USA) laid out model legislation for all states in an effort to make each state's rules and regulations more uniform and easier to address. The USA, also known as "The Act," sets minimum qualification standards for each state securities administrator. The state securities administrator is the top securities regulator within the state.

The state securities administrator may be the attorney general of that state or may be an individual appointed specifically to that post.

The USA also:

- Prohibits the state securities administrator from using the post for personal benefit or from disclosing information.
- Gives the state securities administrator authority to enforce the rules of the USA within that state.
- Gives the administrator the ability to set certain registration requirements for broker dealers, agents, and investment advisers.
- Administrators may set fee and testing requirements.
- Administrators may suspend or revoke the state registration of a broker dealer, agent, investment adviser, or a security or a security's exemption from registration.
- The USA also sets civil and criminal penalties for violators.

The state-based laws set forth by the USA are also known as blue-sky laws.

TENDER OFFERS

A tender offer is made by a person or firm who is seeking to purchase all or part of the outstanding securities of an issuer at a specific price. The SEC has issued strict guidelines that must be followed by both the person making the tender and investors who tender their securities. The guidelines to be followed by parties making a tender offer include:

- The offer must be open for 20 business days from the day it is announced.
- If any of the terms of the tender are changed, the tender must remain open for at least 10 business days from the day the change in the terms was announced.
- A party making a tender offer for stock may not buy the stock or the convertible securities of the issuer during the term of the tender. However, the party may purchase nonconvertible bonds.
- If the duration of the offer is extended, the announcement extending the offer must be released no later than the opening of the exchange on the business day following the original expiration date for exchange-listed securities. The announcement must include the amount of securities tendered to date.

- If a tender offer is extended for securities that are not listed on an exchange, the announcement must be made no later than 9:00 a.m. EST the business day following the original expiration and must also include the amount of securities tendered to date.
- Shareholders must be notified of the tender offer not later than 10 business days after the tender is announced.
- Management of the company subject to the tender offer must advise shareholders as to management's opinion on the offer (i.e., accept, decline, or neutral).
- A party making a tender offer must pay the price offered for the securities to the extent the offer was made.

Investors may only tender securities that they actually own. An investor may not sell short into a tender, which is known as short tendering. Investors are considered long the security if they have possession of the security or have issued exercise or conversion instructions for an option, warrant, or convertible security. Additionally, investors may only tender their securities to the extent of their net long position. If an investor is short against the box or has written calls with a strike price lower than the tender price, then the investor's net long position will be reduced.

EXAMPLE   If an investor owns 1,000 XYZ and has written 5 XYZ June 40 calls when a tender offer is announced at $42 for XYZ, the investor could only tender 500 shares.

During a partial tender the exact amount of securities to be accepted from all tendering parities is not known. As a result, an investor who has a convertible security may tender an amount equal to the amount to be received upon conversion. If the investor is informed that its tender has been accepted, it must convert the securities and deliver the subject securities.

Another type of tender offer you may see on your exam is known as a Dutch auction. During a Dutch auction the issuer will announce a range of prices at which it is willing to repurchase its own securities. For example, TRY Inc. announces that it is willing to repurchase 10 million of its class A common shares between $45 and $50 per share. Investors who are interested in selling their shares will tender their shares at a stated price. Based on the prices received during the Dutch auction, the issuer will set a final price for the tender. All shares tendered at or below the final price will be purchased by the issuer up to the maximum number of shares stated in the tender.

Investors who tendered shares at a price above the final price will have their shares returned to them.

STOCKHOLDERS OWNING 5% OF AN ISSUER'S EQUITY SECURITIES

The Securities Exchange Act requires that individuals or entities who acquire 5% or more of an issuer's equity securities to file Form 13D with the SEC. Rule 13D requires that the SEC, the exchange where the securities are listed, and the issuer be informed of the size of the investor's holdings and the purpose for the investment. Rule 13D does not require that the stockholders be informed directly by the investor. An entity may acquire more than 5% of the issuer's securities for investment purposes, for control, or for acquisition.

Other entities must also disclose their large holdings in an issuer's securities. Investment companies who acquire 5% or more of an issuer will file a notice of their ownership on Form 13G. Investment advisers who have discretion over $100 million or more in assets must disclose their holding within 45 days of the end of each calendar quarter on Form 13F.

Pretest

SECURITIES INDUSTRY RULES AND REGULATIONS

1. You are the owner of a restaurant and you would like to have a guitarist play in the lounge on Saturday evenings. You have known your representative for 15 years and know her to be a great jazz guitarist. You think she would like to play and ask her if she is available to do so. She would have to notify from which of the following before accepting your offer?
   a. Her firm
   b. No one, because it is not securities related and is on her own time.
   c. FINRA
   d. NYSE

2. A firm has been taken to arbitration by a customer. The disputed amount is $47,400. Which of the following is true?
   a. There will be a hearing, and the decision may be appealed.
   b. There will not be a hearing, and the decision may not be appealed.
   c. There will be a hearing, and the arbitrator's decision is final.
   d. There will be a hearing with up to three arbitrators.

3. The Securities Exchange Act of 1934 regulates which of the following markets?
   a. Third
   b. Fourth
   c. Primary
   d. Secondary

4. Which of the following is an associated person of a member firm?

   I. Registered representative

   II. Trader

   III. Director

   IV. Manager

   a. I and III

   b. I and II

   c. I, II, and IV

   d. I, II, III, and IV

5. In the securities industry, which of the following is the ultimate industry authority regulating conduct?

   a. NYSE

   b. SRO

   c. SEC

   d. FINRA

6. A testimonial by a compensated expert, citing the results she realized following a member's recommendations, must include which of the following?

   I. A statement detailing the expert's credentials

   II. A statement that past performance is not a guarantee of future performance

   III. A statement that the individual is a compensated spokesperson

   IV. The name of the principal who approved the ad

   a. I, II, and III

   b. II and IV

   c. I and II

   d. I, II, III, and IV

7. FINRA's gift rule applies to all of the following, EXCEPT:

   a. noncash gifts.

   b. cash gratuities.

   c. entertainment.

   d. employment contracts to provide temporary services to another member.

8. At a member firm, which of the following must be registered?

    a. A corporate officer whose sole function is to act as liaison between the board of directors and management

    b. A part-time sales assistant who occasionally takes verbal orders from customers

    c. A back-office margin clerk who assists the head of the margin department

    d. A receptionist who takes messages from customers inquiring about their accounts

9. FINRA has taken disciplinary action against a member. The decision of the Department of Enforcement becomes final in:

    a. 30 days

    b. 45 days

    c. 60 days

    d. 90 days

10. A FINRA member has failed to receive a stock certificate in good form from the selling FINRA firm. Which FINRA bylaw defines good delivery?

    a. Rules of Fair Practice

    b. Code of Procedure

    c. Code of Arbitration

    d. Uniform Practice Code

11. Which act gave the NASD (now part of FINRA) the authority to regulate the OTC market?

    a. The NASD Act of 1929

    b. The Securities Act of 1933

    c. The Securities Act of 1934

    d. The Maloney Act of 1938

12. FINRA considers which of the following to be considered retail communication?

    I. Video displays
    II. Listings in phone directories
    III. Circulars
    IV. Telemarketing scripts

    a. II and III
    b. I and II
    c. I, II, III, and IV
    d. I and III

13. A principal must do all of the following, EXCEPT:

    a. report violations of professional conduct by broker dealers to the SEC.
    b. supervise all of the actions of a firm and its employees.
    c. report violations of state and federal laws to the proper authorities.
    d. approve all transactions before they are executed to ensure suitability and to prevent violations.

14. Your brokerage firm has placed an ad in the local newspaper, advertising its new line of services being offered to investors. The firm must maintain the ad for how long?

    a. 24 months
    b. 36 months
    c. 12 months
    d. 18 months

15. According to Rule 135, as it relates to generic advertising, which of the following is NOT true?

    a. The ad may contain information about the services a company offers.
    b. The ad may describe the nature of the investment company's business.
    c. The ad may contain information about exchange privileges.
    d. The ad may contain information about the performance of past recommendations.

16. Sanctions imposed by FINRA are effective within how many days of a written decision?

    a. 45 days

    b. 15 days

    c. 30 days

    d. 60 days

17. During registration of a new issue, false information is included in the prospectus to buyers. Which of the following may be held liable to investors?

    I. Officers of the issuer

    II. Accountants

    III. Syndicate members

    IV. People who signed the registration statement

    a. I and III

    b. I and II

    c. I, II, and III

    d. I, II, III, and IV

18. As it relates to a member firm conducting business with the public, all of the following are violations, EXCEPT:

    a. charging a customer a larger than normal commission for executing a specific order.

    b. failing to execute a customer's order for a speculative security.

    c. stating that a new issue has been approved for sale by the SEC.

    d. printing "FINRA" in large type on business cards.

19. A syndicate has published a tombstone ad prior to an issue becoming effective. Which of the following must appear in the tombstone?

    I. A statement that the registration has not yet become effective.

    II. A statement that the tombstone ad is not an offer to sell the securities.

    III. Contact information.

    IV. A no commitment statement.

    a. III and IV

    b. II and III

    c. I and II

    d. I, II, III, and IV

Answer Keys

1. (D) A non-recourse loan is one which will not allow the creditor or lender to seek repayment from the partners in a limited partnership. A recourse loan is one for which a limited partner would be contingently liable for its payment.

2. (D) The higher the capitalization rate, the greater the risk associated with the investment. Paying a higher capitalization rate indicates that the purchaser is paying a greater multiple for the revenue stream to be received. By paying a higher multiple the investor assumes a greater amount of risk. An investor would be willing to pay a higher multiple or capitalization rate if the investor expected a higher rate of return from the property in the future.

3. (B) A non recourse loan would not increase an investor's value at risk.

4. (D) The partnership in question is an oil and gas limited partnership. Therefore, the non-cash charge taken by the partnership would be depletion. However, the question is asking to describe cash flow which is cash from operations minus expenses and prior deducting depletion expenses.

5. (A) The closing date for a limited partnership is the date when an investor's interest in the partnership becomes effective.

6. (B) A Delaware statutory trust allows an owner of real property to exchange a property for an interest in the trust without being subject to capital gains on the exchange.

7. (A) A dissenting limited partner is one who opposes the combination of two or more partnerships through a DPP roll-up transaction.

8. (C) The unincorporated entity formed by ABC and XYZ is a joint venture. With a joint venture two or more parties share in the ownership, management, returns and risks of the operation.

9. (B) A master limited partnership is a limited partnership that allows the entity to have its interest listed on the stock exchange in order to provide liquidity to its investors. A master limited partnership like other types of limited partnerships provides for the flow through of tax benefits.

10. (C) The mining operator who acquired the property and formed a limited partnership is known as the sponsor.

CHAPTER 2: DIRECT PARTICIPATION PROGRAMS

1. (C) This type of sharing arrangement is known as a reversionary working interest.
2. (D) Historic rehabilitation programs generate the most tax advantages.
3. (C) This is known as the crossover point, and it is bad for investors.
4. (C) A limited partner may not advise the general partner. If a limited partner advises the general partner, it risks losing its limited partner status and could be considered a general partner.
5. (C) The holder of an overriding royalty interest has no partnership risks but receives a royalty from the partnership.
6. (A) A recourse loan could require the limited partners to make additional payments.
7. (C) A recourse loan means that the lender has recourse to the limited partners. They can be held liable for the debt service, and it can increase their cost base.
8. (B) DPPs are generally very illiquid and fairly speculative. The main concern is profitability and tax considerations.
9. (D) Raw land may never be depreciated.
10. (C) Intangible drilling costs, such as geological surveys, will generate the largest tax credits.

CHAPTER 3: ADDITIONAL TYPES OF DPPs

1. (C) The three distinct stages of a direct participation program include the organizational or offering stage, followed by the operational stage and all direct participation programs conclude with a liquidation stage.
2. (D) Because timber is not a perishable product and can be harvested at any time, programs that invest in timber have a substantial amount of flexibility in determining when to sell. As a result the program can harvest and sell the timber at a time when prices are the most favorable.
3. (B) For feedlot programs raising $1million or more to operate, the sponsor of the program must maintain a participation of at least $100,000.
4. (B) Forest management companies do not provide the services of an underwriter or distributor and are not involved in the formation of the

programs. Forest management companies will typically provide appraisal services, management services, harvesting, selling and reforesting on behalf of the program.

5. (A) The maximum fee that may be charged in the first year of a feedlot program is 12.5% of the gross receipts.

6. (D) Specifically excluded from the definition of a sponsor would be an entity who merely manages and maintains the equipment for the benefit of the program provided that this person is independent and is paid a fee for the management services.

7. (C) One of the advantages of investing in a timber program is the fact that the trees are growing over time and as a result increasing in value. A timber program could be a suitable investment choice for an individual seeking capital appreciation.

8. C) Either the sponsor or its Chief Operating Officer for an equipment lease program must have a minimum of 3 years experience to establish the program.

9. (B) A feedlot sponsor who charges the markup on feed may charge a handling charge on the cattle it grows provided the markup and handling charge are limited to 20% total.

10. (B) A business development program is specifically designed to make loans to small businesses. The objective of the business development program is to earn interest income on its loan portfolio.

CHAPTER 4: ISSUING CORPORATE SECURITIES

1. (D) All of the items listed must appear in the tombstone ad.

2. (D) All of the parties listed may be held liable to the purchasers of the new issue.

3. (B) A syndicate may only enter a stabilizing bid at or below the offering price.

4. (A) A corporation must issue common stock before it issues any preferred stock.

5. (C) The issuance of prior lien bonds requires the approval of shareholders.

6. (C) A greenshoe provision allows the syndicate to purchase up to an additional 15% of the offering from the issuer.

7. (A) All of the choices listed are types of offerings, except Rule 149.

8. (B) A business must first hire an underwriter to advise the issuer about the type of securities to issue.

9. (C) The number of nonaccredited investors is limited to 35 in any 12-month period.

10. (D) A company doing a preemptive rights offering will use a standby underwriting agreement where the underwriter will "standby" ready to purchase any shares not purchased by shareholders.

11. (B) Only one syndicate bid may be entered to the benefit of the syndicate.

12. (A) When existing stockholders are offered their "right," they may buy stock at the subscription price, which is generally below market value and to their benefit, also preserving their percentage holding in the company.

13. (C) When the SEC wants more information; it will most likely issue a deficiency letter.

14. (A) Primary commitment is not a type of underwriting commitment.

15. (B) Purchasers of stock that has just gone public must get a prospectus for 90 days.

16. (A) All of the answers listed will appear in the preliminary prospectus, except the offering price and the proceeds to the company.

17. (A) A selling group member has no liability to the syndicate if securities remain unsold.

CHAPTER 5: DPP OFFERING AND SUITABILITY

1. (C) FINRA member firms who engage in private placements must file the private placement memorandum with FINRA within 15 days of the first sale.

2. (B) FINRA considers organizational and offering expenses that exceed 15% of the gross proceeds to be excessive. The only partnership listed in the answer key where the organizational and offering expenses exceed 15% of gross proceeds is XYZ real estate limited partnership. XYZ real estate limited partnership has gross proceeds of $50 million and organizational offering expenses of $8 million which is greater than 15%.

3. (D) A trustee is the only individual who may sign the acknowledgements in the subscription agreement for a limited partnership. Otherwise the acknowledgements must be signed by the purchaser.

4. (A) An investor may never be required to sign any acknowledgement that misrepresents the status of the participant nor may they be required to sign a waiver of any rights under state or federal law. Examples of prohibited acknowledgements may be included in the disclosure section of the subscription agreement in the effort to detail the participant's rights.

5. (A) In order to be classified as a covered person an individual would have to own 20% or more of the issuer's voting stock. Therefore, an owner of 10% would not meet the definition of a covered person.

6. (D) Mandatory assessments are allowed to be included as a condition of ownership. However, the amount of the mandatory assessments must be included in the offering price. In this case there are five mandatory assessments of $2 each, making the total offering price $510 per unit.

7. (C) The investor will be subject to a 6-month holding period based on the time when the investor's funds were deposited into the escrow account.

8. (D) All the choices would be required to be disclosed in the offering documents for an oil and gas program except the lifetime performance of the sponsor. The sponsor of the program must disclose their performance history for 10 years not for the lifetime of the sponsor.

9. (C) The tabular representation of the commission's and proceeds to the issuer must appear on the front cover of the prospectus.

10. (A) Any additional interest over and above the general partner's contribution to the partnership would be referred to as an applicable partnership interest or carried interest. This is the additional compensation that the general partner will receive for managing the partnership's business.

CHAPTER 6: CUSTOMER ACCOUNTS

1. (C) A registered representative may only accept orders from the client.

2. (A) In a custodial account, the custodian is the nominal owner of the account and carries on all transactions for the minor, the real beneficial owner of the account.

3. (D) An adult may never have a joint account with a minor.

4. (A) The assets of the decedent will be distributed according to the decedent's will.

5. (C) An account set up by a guardian must be accompanied by declaration papers.

6. (B) In a fiduciary account, the trustee enters all orders for the owners of the account.

7. (D) There is no limit to the size of the gift that may be given to anyone, but $15,000 per year is the tax-free limit.

8. (A) The nominal owner of a UGMA account is the custodian.

9. (B) A representative may only borrow from a client if the client is in the business of making loans (i.e., a bank or credit union).

10. (D) The registered representative's father-in-law may be able to purchase a hot issue, provided strict conditions are met.

11. (B) Although the minor's social security number is listed on the account, it does not appear in the account title.

12. (C) The customer is not required to sign anything when opening a new account.

13. (D) The rule is one custodian and one minor for each UGMA account. There is not a rule regarding who must be custodian.

14. (A) A client may have a numbered account if his signature as owner is on file; broker dealers may give gifts to the employees of other broker dealers with certain restrictions. To obtain outside employment, a representative must first obtain approval from the member firm where he works.

15. (C) The customer's educational information is not required on the new account form.

16. (A) This is a joint account with rights of survivorship. All assets become the property of the surviving party.

17. (A) Before opening a new account for any new customer, a registered representative must fill out and submit a new account form, which does not require the signature of the new customer.

18. (B) If a client dies without a will, the client's assets will be distributed by the administrator.

CHAPTER 7: RETIREMENT PLANS

1. (B) Of the choices listed, only II and IV are correct. A 401k may not be easily rolled over. Remember that a rollover allows the participant to take possession of the money. A plan participant is only vested immediately in his or her own contributions. The participant will become vested in the employer's contributions based on a vesting schedule.

2. (B) Only the Keogh plan and the TDA are funded with pre-tax dollars. The rest are funded with after-tax dollars.

3. (D) The money has been deposited into a nonqualified plan, and the $11,000 has therefore been placed into the plan with after-tax dollars. Only the growth in the account is taxable, or in this case: $5,200 \times 30\% = $1,560.

4. (D) The penalty for an excess Keogh contribution is 10%.

5. (B) An investor may roll over an IRA once per year and has 60 days to get the money into a qualified plan.

6. (D) A Keogh plan allows individuals, sole proprietors, and unincorporated small businesses to establish a retirement plan for themselves and their employees.

7. (A) IRS approval is required for participation in a qualified plan. IRS approval is not required for a nonqualified plan.

8. (C) The retirement account is qualified. Because the investors have deposited the money pre-tax, all of the money is taxed when it is withdrawn.

9. (D) A deferred compensation plan is nonfunded. There is no money set aside for the participant in the plan.

CHAPTER 8: CUSTOMER RECOMMENDATIONS, PROFESSIONAL CONDUCT, AND TAXATION

1. (B) This is known as painting the tape matched purchases or matched sales.

2. (D) This client is concerned about legislative risk, which is the risk that the government will do something that adversely affects an investment.

3. (A) The investor has a large position in a thinly traded stock; as a result, the investor is subject to a large amount of liquidity risk.

4. (B) An investor who is concerned with the changes in interest rates would be least likely to purchase long-term bonds. As interest rates change, the price of the long-term bonds will fluctuate the most.

5. (D) Using the pending dividend to create an urgency on the part of the investor to purchase this stock is a perfect example of this violation, and the results are listed in answers A, B, and C.

6. (B) This is a violation known as trading ahead.

7. (D) Showing a client the past performance for a mutual fund that has only been around for three years is in line with the regulations. All of the other choices are violations.

8. (A) If an investor may lose part or all of his capital, it is called capital risk.

CHAPTER 9: SECURITIES INDUSTRY RULES AND REGULATIONS

1. (A) The representative would have to notify from her employer before working outside the office in any capacity.

2. (B) There will be no hearing unless specifically requested by a public customer, and the decision of the arbitrator is final and binding. Claims under $50,000 will be resolved in simplified arbitration.

3. (D) The Securities Exchange Act of 1934 regulates the secondary market.

4. (D) All of the choices listed are associated people.

5. (C) The SEC is the ultimate industry authority in regulating conduct.

6. (A) All of the choices listed must be included, except for the name of the principal who approved the ad for use.

7. (D) The FINRA rule regarding gifts or payments to employees of another member covers all of those things listed, except contract employees of another member firm who are exempt from the gift rule.

8. (B) The part-time sales assistant who takes orders from customers must be registered because she is taking orders.

9. (B) The decision of the DOE becomes final in 45 days if not appealed.

10. (D) The Uniform Practice Code regulates the way that members conduct business with other members.

11. (D) The Maloney Act of 1938 was an amendment to the Securities Exchange Act of 1934 and established the NASD (now part of FINRA) as the self-regulatory organization for the over-the-counter market.

12. (C) All of the choices listed would be considered to be retail communication if any part of the communications listed could be seen by an individual investor.

13. (D) A principal is designated to supervise all of the actions of a firm and its employees; a principal must prevent any violation of industry, state, or federal laws or regulations. However, the principal need not approve all transactions prior to their execution.

14. (B) Brokerage firms must maintain their advertising for at least three years.

15. (D) Generic advertising may not contain information about past recommendations.

16. (C) The decisions are final after 30 days.

17. (D) All of the parties listed may be held liable to the purchasers of the new issue.

18. (A) A member firm may charge a customer a larger than ordinary commission for the execution of a specific order so long as it is disclosed to the customer. A member firm must always execute a customer's order.

19. (D) All of the items listed must appear in the tombstone ad.

Glossary of Exam Terms

A

AAA/Aaa	The highest investment-grade rating for bond issuers awarded by Standard & Poor's and Moody's ratings agencies.
acceptance waiver and consent (AWAC)	A process used when a respondent does not contest an allegation made by FINRA. The respondent accepts the findings without admitting any wrongdoing and agrees to accept any penalty for the violation.
account executive (AE)	An individual who is duly licensed to represent a broker dealer in securities transactions or investment banking business. Also known as a registered representative.
accredited investor	Any individual or institution that meets one or more of the following: (1) a net worth exceeding $1 million, excluding the primary residence, or (2) is single and has an annual income of $200,000 or more or $300,000 jointly with a spouse.
accretion	An accounting method used to step up an investor's cost base for a bond purchased at a discount.
accrued interest	The portion of a debt securities future interest payment that has been earned by the seller of the security. The purchaser must pay this amount of accrued interest to the seller at the time of the transaction's settlement. Interest accrues from the date of the last interest payment date up to, but not including, the transaction's settlement date.
accumulation stage	The period during which an annuitant is making contributions to an annuity contract.
accumulation unit	A measure used to determine the annuitant's proportional ownership interest in the insurance company's separate account during the accumulation stage. During the accumulation stage, the number of accumulation units owned by the annuitant changes and their value varies.
acid-test ratio	A measure of corporate liquidity found by subtracting inventory from current assets and dividing the result by the current liabilities.
ACT	*See* Automated Comparison Transaction (ACT) service.
ad valorem tax	A tax based on the value of the subject property.
adjusted basis	The value assigned to an asset after all deductions or additions for improvements have been taken into consideration.
adjusted gross income (AGI)	An accounting measure employed by the IRS to help determine tax liability. AGI = earned income + investment income (portfolio income) + capital gains + net passive income.
administrator	(1) An individual authorized to oversee the liquidation of an intestate decedent's estate. (2) An individual or agency that administers securities' laws within a state.
ADR/ADS	*See* American depositary receipt (ADR).
advance/decline line	Measures the health of the overall market by calculating advancing issues and subtracting the number of declining issues.

advance refunding	The early refinancing of municipal securities. A new issue of bonds is sold to retire the old issue at its first available call date or maturity.
advertisement	Any material that is distributed by a broker dealer or issuer for the purpose of increasing business or public awareness for the firm or issuer. The broker dealer or issuer must distribute advertisements to an audience that is not controlled. Advertisements are distributed through any of the following: newspapers/magazines, radio, TV, billboards, telephone.
affiliate	An individual who owns 10% or more of the company's voting stock. In the case of a direct participation program (DPP), this is anyone who controls the partnership or is controlled by the partnership.
agency issue	A debt security issued by any authorized entity of the U.S. government. The debt security is an obligation of the issuing entity, not an obligation of the U.S. government (with the exception of Ginnie Mae and the Federal Import Export Bank issues).
agency transaction	A transaction made by a firm for the benefit of a customer. The firm merely executes a customer's order and charges a fee for the service, which is known as a commission.
agent	A firm or an individual who executes securities transactions for customers and charges a service fee known as a commission. Also known as a broker.
aggregate indebtedness	The total amount of the firm's customer-related debts.
allied member	An owner-director or 5% owner of an NYSE member firm. Allied members may not trade on the floor.
all-or-none (AON) order	A non-time-sensitive order that stipulates that the customer wants to buy or sell all of the securities in the order.
all-or-none underwriting	A type of underwriting that states that the issuer wants to sell all of the securities being offered or none of the securities being offered. The proceeds from the issue will be held in escrow until all securities are sold.
alpha	A measure of the projected change in the security's price as a result of fundamental factors relating only to that company.
alternative minimum tax (AMT)	A method used to calculate the tax liability for some high-income earners that adds back the deductions taken for certain tax preference items.
AMBAC Indemnity Corporation	Insures the interest and principal payments for municipal bonds.
American depositary receipt (ADR)/American depositary security (ADS)	A receipt representing the beneficial ownership of foreign securities being held in trust overseas by a foreign branch of a U.S. bank. ADRs/ADSs facilitate the trading and ownership of foreign securities and trade in the United States on an exchange or in the over-the-counter markets.
American Stock Exchange (AMEX)	An exchange located in New York using the dual-auction method and specialist system to facilitate trading in stocks, options, exchange-traded funds, and portfolios. AMEX was acquired by the NYSE Euronext and is now part of NYSE Alternext.

amortization	An accounting method that reduces the value of an asset over its projected useful life. Also the way that loan principal is systematically paid off over the life of a loan.
annual compliance review	All firms must hold at least one compliance meeting per year with all of its agents.
annuitant	An individual who receives scheduled payments from an annuity contract.
annuitize	A process by which an individual converts from the accumulation stage to the payout stage of an annuity contract. This is accomplished by exchanging accumulation units for annuity units. Once a payout option is selected, it cannot be changed.
annuity	A contract between an individual and an insurance company that is designed to provide the annuitant with lifetime income in exchange for either a lump sum or periodic deposits into the contract.
annuity unit	An accounting measure used to determine an individual's proportionate ownership of the separate account during the payout stage of the contract. The number of annuity units owned by an individual remains constant, and their value, which may vary, is used to determine the amount of the individual's annuity payment.
appreciation	An asset's increase in value over time.
arbitrage	An investment strategy used to profit from market inefficiencies.
arbitration	A forum provided by both the NYSE and FINRA to resolve disputes between two parties. Only a public customer may not be forced to settle a dispute through arbitration. The public customer must agree to arbitration in writing. All industry participants must settle disputes through arbitration.
ask	*See* offer.
assessed value	A base value assigned to property for the purpose of determining tax liability.
assessment	An additional amount of taxes due as a result of a municipal project that the homeowner benefits from. Also an additional call for capital by a direct participation program.
asset	Anything of value owned by an individual or a corporation.
asset allocation fund	A mutual fund that spreads its investments among different asset classes (i.e., stocks, bonds, and other investments) based on a predetermined formula.
assignee	A person to whom the ownership of an asset is being transferred.
assignment	(1) The transfer of ownership or rights through a signature. (2) The notification given to investors who are short an option that the option holder has exercised its right and they must now meet their obligations as detailed in the option contract.
associated person	Any individual under the control of a broker dealer, issuer, or bank, including employees, officers, and directors, as well as those individuals who control or have common control of a broker dealer, issuer, or bank.

assumed interest rate (AIR)	(1) A benchmark used to determine the minimum rate of return that must be realized by a variable annuity's separate account during the payout phase in order to keep the annuitant's payments consistent. (2) In the case of a variable life insurance policy, the minimum rate of return that must be achieved in order to maintain the policy's variable death benefit.
at-the-close order	An order that stipulates that the security is to be bought or sold only at the close of the market, or as close to the close as is reasonable, or not at all.
at the money	A term used to describe an option when the underlying security price is equal to the exercise price of the option.
at-the-opening order	An order that stipulates that the security is to be bought or sold only at the opening of the market, or as close to the opening as is reasonable, or not at all.
auction market	The method of trading employed by stock exchanges that allows buyers and sellers to compete with one another in a centralized location.
authorized stock	The maximum number of shares that a corporation can sell in an effort to raise capital. The number of authorized shares may only be changed by a vote of the shareholders.
Automated Comparison Transaction (ACT) service	ACT is the service that clears and locks Nasdaq trades.
average cost	A method used to determine the cost of an investment for an investor who has made multiple purchases of the same security at different times and prices. An investor's average cost may be used to determine a cost base for tax purposes or to evaluate the profitability of an investment program, such as dollar-cost averaging. Average cost is determined by dividing the total dollars invested by the number of shares purchased.
average price	A method used to determine the average price paid by an investor for a security that has been purchased at different times and prices, such as through dollar-cost averaging. An investor's average price is determined by dividing the total of the purchase prices by the number of purchases.

B

BBB/Baa	The lowest ratings assigned by Standard & Poor's and Moody's for debt in the investment-grade category.
back-end load	A mutual fund sales charge that is assessed upon the redemption of the shares. The amount of the sales charge to be assessed upon redemption decreases the longer the shares are held. Also known as a contingent deferred sales charge.
backing away	The failure of an over-the-counter market maker to honor firm quotes. It is a violation of FINRA rules.
balanced fund	A mutual fund whose investment policy requires that the portfolio's holdings are diversified among asset classes and invested in common and preferred stock, bonds, and other debt instruments. The exact asset distribution among the asset classes will be predetermined by a set formula that is designed to balance out the investment return of the fund.

balance of payments	The net balance of all international transactions for a country in a given time.
balance of trade	The net flow of goods into or out of a country for a given period. Net exports result in a surplus or credit; net exports result in a deficit or net debit.
balance sheet	A corporate report that shows a company's financial condition at the time the balance sheet was created.
balance sheet equation	Assets = liabilities + shareholders equity.
balloon maturity	A bond maturity schedule that requires the largest portion of the principal to be repaid on the last maturity date.
bankers' acceptance (BA)	A letter of credit that facilitates foreign trade. BAs are traded in the money market and have a maximum maturity of 270 days.
basis	The cost that is assigned to an asset.
basis book	A table used to calculate bond prices for bonds quoted on a yield basis and to calculate yields for bonds quoted on a price basis.
basis point	Measures a bond's yield; 1 basis point is equal to 1/100 of 1%.
basis quote	A bond quote based on the bond's yield.
bearer bond	A bond that is issued without the owner's name being registered on the bond certificate or the books of the issuer. Whoever has possession of (bears) the certificate is deemed to be the rightful owner.
bearish	An investor's belief that prices will decline.
bear market	A market condition that is characterized by continuing falling prices and a series of lower lows in overall prices.
best efforts underwriting	A type of underwriting that does not guarantee the issuer that any of its securities will be sold.
beta	A measure of a security's or portfolio's volatility relative to the market as a whole. A security or portfolio whose beta is greater than 1 will experience a greater change in price than overall market prices. A security or portfolio with a beta of less than 1 will experience a price change that is less than the price changes realized by the market as a whole.
bid	A price that an investor or broker dealer is willing to pay for a security. It is also a price at which an investor may sell a security immediately and the price at which a market maker will buy a security.
blind pool	A type of direct participation program where less than 75% of the assets to be acquired have been identified.
block trade	A trade involving 10,000 shares or market value of over $200,000.
blotter	A daily record of broker dealer transactions.
blue chip stock	Stock of a company whose earnings and dividends are stable regardless of the economy.
Blue List	A daily publication of municipal bond offerings and secondary market interest.
blue sky	A term used to describe the state registration process for a security offering.
blue-sky laws	Term used to describe the state-based laws enacted under the Uniform Securities Act.
board broker	See order book official.

board of directors	A group of directors elected by the stockholders of a corporation to appoint and oversee corporate management.
Board of Governors	The governing body of FINRA. The board is made up of 27 members elected by FINRA's membership and the board itself.
bona fide quote	*See* firm quote.
bond	The legal obligation of a corporation or government to repay the principal amount of debt along with interest at a predetermined schedule.
bond anticipation note	Short-term municipal financing sold in anticipation of long-term financing.
bond buyer indexes	A group of yield-based municipal bond indexes published daily in the *Daily Bond Buyer.*
bond counsel	An attorney for the issuer of municipal securities who renders the legal opinion.
bond fund	A fund whose portfolio is made up of debt instruments issued by corporations, governments, and/or their agencies. The fund's investment objective is usually current income.
bond interest coverage ratio	A measure of the issuer's liquidity. It demonstrates how many times the issuer's earnings will cover its bond interest expense.
bond quotes	Corporate and government bond quotes are based on a percentage of par. Municipal bonds are usually quoted on a yield-to-maturity basis.
bond rating	A rating that assesses the financial soundness of issuers and their ability to make interest and principal payments in a timely manner. Standard & Poor's and Moody's are the two largest ratings agencies. Issuers must request and pay for the service to rate their bonds.
bond ratio	A measure used to determine how much of the corporation's capitalization was obtained through the issuance of bonds.
bond swap	The sale and purchase of two different bonds to allow the investor to claim a loss on the bond being sold without violating wash sale rules.
book entry	Securities that are issued in book entry form do not offer any physical certificates as evidence of ownership. The owner's name is registered on the books of the issuer, and the only evidence of ownership is the trade confirmation.
book value	A corporation's book value is the theoretical liquidation value of the company. Book value is in theory what someone would be willing to pay for the entire company.
book value per bond	A measure used to determine the amount of the corporation's tangible value for each bond issued.
book value per share	Used to determine the tangible value of each common share. It is found by subtracting intangible assets and the par value of preferred stock from the corporation's total net worth and dividing that figure by the number of common shares outstanding.
branch office	A branch office of a member firm is required to display the name of the member firm and is any office in which the member conducts securities business outside of its main office.

breadth	A measure of the broad market's health. It measures how many stocks are increasing and how many are declining.
breakdown	A technical term used to describe the price action of a security when it falls below support to a lower level and into a new trading range.
breakeven point	The point at which the value of a security or portfolio is exactly equal to the investor's cost for that security or portfolio.
breakout	A technical term used to describe the price action of a security when it increases past resistance to a higher level and into a new trading range.
breakpoint sale	The practice of selling mutual fund shares in dollar amounts that are just below the point where an investor would be entitled to a sales charge reduction. A breakpoint sale is designed for the purpose of trying to earn a larger commission. This is a violation of the Rules of Fair Practice and should never be done.
breakpoint schedule	A breakpoint schedule offers mutual fund investors reduced sales charges for larger dollar investments.
broad-based index	An index that represents a large cross-section of the market as a whole. The price movement of the index reflects the price movement of a large portion of the market, such as the S&P 500 or the Wilshire 5000.
broker	*See* agent.
broker dealer	A person or firm who buys and sells securities for its own account and for the accounts of others. When acting as a broker or agent for a customer, the broker dealer is merely executing the customer's orders and charging the customer a fee known as a commission. When acting as a dealer or principal, the broker dealer is trading for its own account and participating in the customer's transaction by taking the other side of the trade and charging the customer a markup or markdown. A firm also is acting as a principal or dealer when it is trading for its own account and making markets in OTC securities.
broker's broker	(1) A municipal bond dealer who specializes in executing orders for other dealers who are not active in the municipal bond market. (2) A specialist on the exchange executing orders for other members or an OTC market.
bullish	An investor who believes that the price of a security or prices as a whole will rise is said to be bullish.
bull market	A market condition that is characterized by rising prices and a series of higher highs.
business cycle	The normal economic pattern that is characterized by four stages: expansion, peak, contraction, and trough. The business cycle constantly repeats itself and the economy is always in flux.
business day	The business day in the securities industry is defined as the time when the financial markets are open for trading.
buyer's option	A settlement option that allows the buyer to determine when the transaction will settle.
buy in	An order executed in the event of a customer's or firm's failure to deliver the securities it sold. The buyer repurchases the securities in the open market and charges the seller for any loss.

buying power	The amount of money available to buy securities.
buy stop order	A buy stop order is used to protect against a loss or to protect a profit on a short sale of stock.

C

call	(1) A type of option that gives the holder the right to purchase a specified amount of the underlying security at a stated price for a specified period of time. (2) The act of exercising a call option.
callable bond	A bond that may be called in or retired by the issuer prior to its maturity date.
callable preferred	A preferred share issued with a feature allowing the issuing corporation to retire it under certain conditions.
call date	A specific date after which the securities in question become callable by the issuer.
call feature	A condition attached to some bonds and preferred stocks that allows the issuer to call in or redeem the securities prior to their maturity date and according to certain conditions.
call price	The price that will be paid by the issuer to retire the callable securities in question. The call price is usually set at a price above the par value of the bond or preferred stock, which is the subject of the call.
call protection	A period of time, usually right after the securities' issuance, when the securities may not be called by the issuer. Call protection usually ranges from 5 to 10 years.
call provision	*See* call feature.
call risk	The risk borne by the owner of callable securities that may require that the investor accept a lower rate of return once the securities have been called. Callable bonds and preferred stock are more likely to be called when interest rates are low or are falling.
call spread	An option position consisting of one long and one short call on the same underlying security with different strike prices, expirations, or both.
call writer	An investor who has sold a call.
capital	Money and assets available to use in an attempt to earn more money or to accumulate more assets.
capital appreciation	An increase in an asset's value over time.
capital assets	Tangible assets, including securities, real estate, equipment, and other assets, owned for the long term.
capital gain	A profit realized on the sale of an asset at a price that exceeds its cost.
capitalization	The composition of a company's financial structure. It is the sum of paid-in capital + paid-in surplus + long-term debt + retained earnings.
capital loss	A loss realized on the sale of an asset at a price that is lower than its cost.
capital market	The securities markets that deal in equity and debt securities with more than 1 year to maturity.
capital risk	The risk that the value of an asset will decline and cause an investor to lose all or part of the invested capital.
capital stock	The sum of the par value of all of a corporation's outstanding common and preferred stock.

capital structure	*See* capitalization.
capital surplus	The amount of money received by an issuer in excess of the par value of the stock at the time of its initial sale to the public.
capped index option	An index option that trades like a spread and is automatically exercised if it goes 30 points in the money.
capping	A manipulative practice of selling stock to depress the price.
carried interest	A sharing arrangement for an oil and gas direct participation program where the general partner shares in the tangible drilling costs with the limited partners.
cash account	An account in which the investor must deposit the full purchase price of the securities by the fourth business day after the trade date. The investor is not required by industry regulations to sign anything to open a cash account.
cash assets ratio	The most liquid measure of a company's solvency. The cash asset ratio is found by dividing cash and equivalents by current liabilities.
cash dividend	The distribution of corporate profits to shareholders of record. Cash dividends must be declared by the company's board of directors.
cash equivalent	Short-term liquid securities that can quickly be converted into cash. Money market instruments and funds are the most common examples.
cash flow	A company's cash flow equals net income plus depreciation.
cashiering department	The department in a brokerage firm that is responsible for the receipt and delivery of cash and securities.
cash management bill	Short-term federal financing issued in minimum denominations of $10 million.
cash settlement	A transaction that settles for cash requires the delivery of the securities from the seller as well as the delivery of cash from the buyer on the same day of the trade. A trade done for cash settles the same day.
catastrophe call	The redemption of a bond by an issuer due to the destruction of the facility that was financed by the issue. Issuers will carry insurance to cover such events and to pay off the bondholders.
certificate of deposit (CD)	An unsecured promissory note issued as evidence of ownership of a time deposit that has been guaranteed by the issuing bank.
certificates of accrual on Treasury securities	Zero-coupon bonds issued by brokerage firms and collateralized by Treasury securities.
change	The difference between the current price and the previous day's closing price.
Chicago Board of Trade (CBOT)	A commodity exchange that provides a marketplace for agricultural and financial futures.
Chicago Board Options Exchange (CBOE)	The premier option exchange in the United States for listed options.
Chinese wall	The physical separation that is required between investment banking and trading and retail divisions of a brokerage firm. Now known as a firewall.

churning	Executing transactions that are excessive in their frequency or size in light of the resources of the account for the purpose of generating commissions. Churning is a violation of the Rules of Fair Practice.
class A share	A mutual fund share that charges a front-end load.
class B share	A mutual fund share that charges a back-end load.
class C share	A mutual fund share that charges a level load.
class D share	A mutual fund share that charges a level load and a back-end load.
classical economics	A theory stating that the economy will do the best when the government does not interfere.
clearing firm	A firm that carries its customers' cash and securities and/or provides the service to customers of other firms.
clearinghouse	An agency that guarantees and settles futures and option transactions.
close	The last price at which a security traded for the day.
closed-end indenture	A bond indenture that will not allow additional bonds to be issued with the same claim on the issuer's assets.
closed-end investment company	A management company that issues a fixed number of shares to investors in a managed portfolio and whose shares are traded in the secondary market.
closing date	The date when sales of interest in a direct participation plan will cease.
closing purchase	An order executed to close out a short option position.
Code of Arbitration Procedure	The FINRA bylaw that provides for a forum for dispute resolution relating to industry matters. All industry participants must arbitrate in public and the customer must agree to arbitration in writing.
Code of Procedure	The FINRA bylaw that sets guidelines for the investigation of trade practice complaints and alleged rule violations.
coincident indicator	An economic indicator that moves simultaneously with the movement of the underlying economy.
collateral	Assets pledged to a lender. If the borrower defaults, the lender will take possession of the collateral.
collateral trust certificate	A bond backed by the pledge of securities the issuer owns in another entity.
collateralized mortgage obligation (CMO)	A corporate debt security that is secured by an underlying pool of mortgages.
collection ratio	A measure of a municipality's ability to collect the taxes it has assessed.
collect on delivery (COD)	A method of trade settlement that requires the physical delivery of the securities to receive payment.
combination	An option position with a call and put on the same underlying security with different strike prices and expiration months on both.
combination fund	A mutual fund that tries to achieve growth and current income by combining portfolios of common stock with portfolios of high-yielding equities.
combination preferred stock	A preferred share with multiple features, such as cumulative and participating.

combination privileges	A feature offered by a mutual fund family that allows an investor to combine two simultaneous purchases of different portfolios in order to receive a reduced sales charge on the total amount invested.
combined account	A margin account that contains both long and short positions.
commercial paper	Short-term unsecured promissory notes issued by large financially stable corporations to obtain short-term financing. Commercial paper does not pay interest and is issued at a discount from its face value. All commercial paper matures in 270 days or less and matures at its face value.
commingling	A FINRA violation resulting from the mixing of customer and firm assets in the same account.
commission	A fee charged by a broker or agent for executing a securities transaction.
commission house broker	A floor broker who executes orders for the firm's account and for the accounts of the firm's customers on an exchange.
common stock	A security that represents the ownership of a corporation. Common stockholders vote to elect the board of directors and to institute major corporate policies.
common stock ratio	A measure of how much of a company's capitalization was obtained through the sale of common stock. The ratio is found by summing the par value of the common stock, excess paid in capital, and retained earnings, and then dividing that number by the total capitalization.
competitive bid underwriting	A method of underwriter selection that solicits bids from multiple underwriters. The underwriter submitting the best terms will be awarded the issue.
compliance department	The department of a broker dealer that ensures that the firm adheres to industry rules and regulations.
concession	The amount of an underwriting discount that is allocated to a syndicate member or a selling group member for selling new securities.
conduct rules	The Rules of Fair Practice.
conduit theory	The IRS classification that allows a regulated investment company to avoid paying taxes on investment income it distributes to its shareholders.
confirmation	The receipt for a securities transaction that must be sent to all customers either on or before the completion of a transaction. The confirmation must show the trade date, settlement date, and total amount due to or from the customer. A transaction is considered to be complete on settlement date.
consolidated tape	The consolidated tape A displays transactions for NYSE securities that take place on the NYSE, all regional exchanges, and the third markets. The consolidated tape B reports transactions for AMEX stocks that take place on the American Stock Exchange, all regional exchanges, and in the third market.
consolidation	A chart pattern that results from a narrowing of a security's trading range.

constant dollar plan	An investment plan designed to keep a specific amount of money invested in the market regardless of the market's condition. An investor will sell when the value of the account rises and buy when the value of the account falls.
constant ratio plan	An investment plan designed to keep the investor's portfolio invested at a constant ratio of equity and debt securities.
construction loan note	A short-term municipal note designed to provide financing for construction projects.
constructive receipt	The time when the IRS determines that the taxpayer has effectively received payment.
consumer price index (CPI)	A price-based index made up of a basket of goods and services that are used by consumers in their daily lives. An increase in the CPI indicates a rise in overall prices, while a decline in the index represents a fall in overall prices.
consumption	A term used to describe the purchase of newly produced household goods.
contemporaneous trader	A trader who enters an order on the other side of the market at the same time as a trader with inside information enters an order. Contemporaneous traders can sue traders who act on inside information to recover losses.
contingent deferred sales charge	*See* back-end load.
contraction	A period of declining economic output. Also known as a recession.
contractual plan	A mutual fund accumulation plan under which the investor agrees to contribute a fixed sum of money over time. If the investor does not complete or terminates the contract early, the investor may be subject to penalties.
control	The ability to influence the actions of an organization or individual.
control person	A director or officer of an issuer or broker dealer or a 10% stockholder of a corporation.
control stock	Stock that is acquired or owned by an officer, director, or person owning 10% or more of the outstanding stock of a company.
conversion price	The set price at which a convertible security may be exchanged for another security.
conversion privilege	The right offered to a mutual fund investor that allows the investor to move money between different portfolios offered by the same mutual fund family without paying another sales charge.
conversion ratio	The number of shares that can be received by the holder of a convertible security if it were converted into the underlying common stock.
convertible bond	A bond that may be converted or exchanged for common shares of the corporation at a predetermined price.
convertible preferred stock	A preferred stock that may be converted or exchanged for common shares of the corporation at a predetermined price.
cooling-off period	The period of time between the filing of a registration statement and its effective date. During this time, the SEC is reviewing the registration statement and no sales may take place. The cooling-off period is at least 20 days.

coordination	A method of securities registration during which a new issue is registered simultaneously at both the federal and state levels.
corporate account	An investment account for the benefit of a company that requires a corporate resolution listing the names of individuals who may transact business in the company's name.
corporate bond	A legally binding obligation of a corporation to repay a principal amount of debt along with interest at a predetermined rate and schedule.
corporation	A perpetual entity that survives after the death of its officers, directors, and stockholders. It is the most common form of business entity.
correspondent broker dealer	A broker dealer who introduces customer accounts to a clearing broker dealer.
cost basis	The cost of an asset, including any acquisition costs. It is used to determine capital gains and losses.
cost depletion	A method used to determine the tax deductions for investors in oil and gas programs.
cost of carry	All costs incurred by an investor for maintaining a position in a security, including margin interest and opportunity costs.
coterminous	Municipalities that share the same borders and have overlapping debt.
coupon bond	*See* bearer bond.
coupon yield	*See* nominal yield.
covenant	A promise made by an issuer of debt that describes the issuer's obligations and the bondholders' rights.
covered call	The sale of a call against a long position in the underlying security.
covered put	The sale of a put against a short position in the underlying security or against cash that will allow the person to purchase the security if the put is exercised.
CPI	*See* consumer price index (CPI).
credit agreement	The portion of the margin agreement that describes the terms and conditions under which credit will be extended to the customer.
credit balance	The cash balance in a customer's account.
credit department	*See* margin department.
credit risk	The risk that the issuer of debt securities will default on its obligation to pay interest or principal on a timely basis.
credit spread	An option position that results in a net premium or credit received by the investor from the simultaneous purchase and sale of two calls or two puts on the same security.
crossed market	A market condition that results when a broker enters a bid for a stock that exceeds the offering price for that stock. Also a condition that may result when a broker enters an offer that is lower than the bid price for that stock.
crossing stock	The pairing off of two offsetting customer orders by the same floor broker. The floor broker executing the cross must first show the order to the crowd for possible price improvement before crossing the orders.

crossover point	The point at which all tax credits have been used up by a limited partnership; results in a tax liability for the partners.
cum rights	A stock that is the subject of a rights offering and is trading with the rights attached to the common stock.
cumulative preferred stock	A preferred stock that entitles the holder to receive unpaid dividends prior to the payment of any dividends to common stockholders. Dividends that accumulate in arrears on cumulative issues are always the first dividends to be paid by a corporation.
cumulative voting	A method of voting that allows stockholders to cast all of their votes for one director or to distribute them among the candidates they wish to vote for. Cumulative voting favors smaller investors by allowing them to have a larger say in the election of the board of directors.
current assets	Cash, securities, accounts receivable, and other assets that can be converted into cash within 12 months.
current liabilities	Corporate obligations, including accounts payable, that must be paid within 12 months.
current market value (CMV)/current market price (CMP)	The present value of a marketable security or of a portfolio of marketable securities.
current ratio	A measure of a corporation's short-term liquidity found by dividing its current assets by its current liabilities.
current yield	A relationship between a securities annual income relative to its current market price. Determined by dividing annual income by the current market price.
CUSIP (Committee on Uniform Securities Identification Procedures)	A committee that assigns identification numbers to securities to help identify them.
custodial account	An account operated by a custodian for the benefit of a minor.
custodian	A party responsible for managing an account for another party. In acting as a custodian, the individual or corporation must adhere to the prudent man rule and only take such actions as a prudent person would do for him- or herself.
customer	Any individual or entity that maintains an account with a broker dealer.
customer agreement	An agreement signed by a customer at the time the account is opened, detailing the conditions of the customer's relationship with the firm. The customer agreement usually contains a predispute arbitration clause.
customer ledger	A ledger that lists all customer cash and margin accounts.
customer protection rule	Rule 15C3-3 requires that customer assets be kept segregated from the firm assets.
cyclical industry	An industry whose prospects fluctuate with the business cycle.

D

Daily Bond Buyer	A daily publication for the municipal securities industry that publishes information related to the municipal bond market and official notices of sales.
dated date	The day when interest starts to accrue for bonds.
dealer	(1) A person or firm who transacts securities business for its own account. (2) A brokerage firm acting as a principal when executing a customer's transaction or making markets over the counter.
dealer paper	Commercial paper sold to the public by a dealer, rather than placed with investors directly by the issuer.
debenture	An unsecured promissory note issued by a corporation backed only by the issuer's credit and promise to pay.
debit balance	The amount of money a customer owes a broker dealer.
debit spread	An option position that results in a net premium paid by the investor from the simultaneous purchase and sale of two calls or two puts on the same security.
debt securities	A security that represents a loan to the issuer. The owner of a debt security is a creditor of the issuing entity, be it a corporation or a government.
debt service	The scheduled interest payments and repayment of principal for debt securities.
debt service account	An account set up by a municipal issuer to pay the debt service of municipal revenue bonds.
debt service ratio	Indicates the issuer's ability to pay its interest and principal payments.
debt-to-equity ratio	A ratio that shows how highly leveraged the company is. It is found by dividing total long-term debt by total shareholder equity.
declaration date	The day chosen by the board of directors of a corporation to pay a dividend to shareholders.
deduction	An adjustment taken from gross income to reduce tax liability.
default	The failure of an issuer of debt securities to make interest and principal payments when they are due.
default risk	*See* credit risk.
defeasance	Results in the elimination of the issuer's debt obligations by issuing a new debt instrument to pay off the outstanding issue. The old issue is removed from the issuer's balance sheet and the proceeds of the new issue are placed in an escrow account to pay off the now-defeased issue.
defensive industry	A term used to describe a business whose economic prospects are independent from the business cycle. Pharmaceutical companies, utilities, and food producers are examples of defensive industries.
deferred annuity	A contract between an individual and an insurance company that delays payments to the annuitant until some future date.
deferred compensation plan	A contractual agreement between an employer and an employee under which the employee elects to defer receiving money owed until after retirement. Deferred compensation plans are typically unfunded, and the employee could lose all the money due under the agreement if the company goes out of business.

deficiency letter	A letter sent to a corporate issuer by the SEC, requesting additional information regarding the issuer's registration statement.
defined benefit plan	A qualified retirement plan established to provide a specific amount of retirement income for the plan participants. Unlike a defined contribution plan, the individual's retirement benefits are known prior to reaching retirement.
defined contribution plan	A qualified retirement plan that details the amount of money that the employer will contribute to the plan for the benefit of the employee. This amount is usually expressed as a percentage of the employee's gross annual income. The actual retirement benefits are not known until the employee reaches retirement, and the amount of the retirement benefit is a result of the contributions to the plan, along with the investment experience of the plan.
deflation	The economic condition that is characterized by a persistent decline in overall prices.
delivery	As used in the settlement process, results in the change of ownership of cash or securities.
delivery vs. payment	A type of settlement option that requires that the securities be physically received at the time payment is made.
delta	A measure of an option's price change in relation to a price change in the underlying security.
demand deposit	A deposit that a customer has with a bank or other financial institution that will allow the customer to withdraw the money at any time or on demand.
Department of Enforcement	The FINRA committee that has original jurisdiction over complaints and violations.
depletion	A tax deduction taken for the reduction in the amount of natural resources (e.g., gas, gold, oil) available to a business or partnership.
depreciation	A tax deduction taken for the reduction of value in a capital asset.
depreciation expense	A noncash expense that results in a reduction in taxable income.
depression	An economic condition that is characterized by a protracted decline in economic output and a rising level of unemployment.
derivative	A security that derives its value in whole or in part based on the price of another security. Options and futures are examples of derivative securities.
designated order	An order entered by an institution for a new issue of municipal bonds that states what firm and what agent is going to get the sales credit for the order.
devaluation	A significant fall in the value of a country's currency relative to other currencies. Devaluation could be the result of poor economic prospects in the home country. In extreme circumstances, it can be the result of government intervention.
developmental drilling program	An oil or gas program that drills for wells in areas of proven reserves.
developmental fee	A fee paid to organizers of a direct participation plan for the development of plans, obtaining financing or zoning authorizations, and other services.
diagonal spread	A spread that is created through the simultaneous purchase and sale of two calls or two puts on the same underlying security that differ in both strike price and expiration months.

dilution	A reduction in a stockholder's proportional ownership of a corporation as a result of the issuance of more shares. Earnings per share may also be diluted as a result of the issuance of additional shares.
direct debt	The total amount of a municipality's debt that has been issued by the municipality for its own benefit and for which the municipality is responsible to repay.
direct paper	Commercial paper sold to investors directly from the issuer without the use of a dealer.
direct participation program (DPP)	An entity that allows all taxable events to be passed through to investors, including limited partnerships and subchapter S corporations.
discount	The amount by which the price of a security is lower than its par value.
discount bond	A bond that is selling for a price that is lower than its par value.
discount rate	The rate that is charged to Federal Reserve member banks on loans directly from the Federal Reserve. This rate is largely symbolic, and member banks only borrow directly from the Federal Reserve as a last resort.
discretion	Authorization given to a firm or a representative to determine which securities are to be purchased and sold for the benefit of the customer without the customer's prior knowledge or approval.
discretionary account	An account where the owner has given the firm or the representative authority to transact business without the customer's prior knowledge or approval. All discretionary accounts must be approved and monitored closely by a principal of the firm.
disintermediation	The flow of money from traditional bank accounts to alternative higher yielding investments. This is more likely to occur as the Federal Reserve tightens monetary policy and interest rates rise.
disposable income	The sum of money an individual has left after paying taxes and required expenditures.
disproportional allocation	A method used by FINRA to determine if a free-riding violation has occurred with respect to a hot issuer. A firm is only allowed to sell up to 10% of a new issue to conditionally approved purchasers.
disproportionate sharing	An oil and gas sharing arrangement where the general partner pays a portion of the cost but receives a larger portion of the program's revenues.
distribution	Cash or property sent to shareholders or partners.
distribution stage	The period of time during which an annuitant is receiving payments from an annuity contract.
diversification	The distribution of investment capital among different investment choices. By purchasing several different investments, investors may be able to reduce their overall risk by minimizing the impact of any one security's adverse performance.
diversified fund/ diversified management company	A mutual fund that distributes its investment capital among a wide variety of investments. In order for a mutual fund to market itself as a diversified mutual fund it must meet the 75-5-10 rule: 75% of the fund's assets must be invested in securities issued by other entities, no more than 5% of the fund's assets may be invested in any one issuer, and the fund may own no more than 10% of any one company's outstanding securities.

dividend	A distribution of corporate assets to shareholders. A dividend may be paid in cash, stock, or property or product.
dividend department	The department in a brokerage firm that is responsible for the collecting of dividends and crediting them to customer accounts.
dividend disbursement agent	An agent of the issuer who pays out the dividends to shareholders of record.
dividend payout ratio	The amount of a company's earnings that were paid out to shareholders relative to the total earnings that were available to be paid out to shareholders. It can be calculated by dividing dividends per share by earnings per share.
dividend yield	Also known as a stock's current yield. It is a relationship between the annual dividends paid to shareholders relative to the stock's current market price. To determine a stock's dividend yield, divide annual dividends by the current market price.
DJIA	*See* Dow Jones Industrial Average.
doctrine of mutual reciprocity	An agreement that the federal government would not tax interest income received by investors in municipal bonds and that reciprocally the states would not tax interest income received by investors in federal debt obligations.
dollar bonds	A term issue of municipal bonds that are quoted as a percentage of par rather than on a yield basis.
dollar-cost averaging	A strategy of investing a fixed sum of money on a regular basis into a fluctuating market price. Over time an investor should be able to achieve an average cost per share that is below the average price per share. Dollar-cost averaging is a popular investment strategy with mutual fund investors.
donor	A person who gives a gift of cash or securities to another person. Once the gift has been made, the donor no longer has any rights or claim to the security. All gifts to a minor are irrevocable.
do not reduce (DNR)	An order qualifier for an order placed under the market that stipulates that the price of the order is not to be reduced for the distribution of ordinary dividends.
don't know (DK)	A term used to describe a dealer's response to a confirmation for a trade they "don't know" doing.
Dow Jones Composite Average	An index composed of 65 stocks that is used as an indicator of market performance.
Dow Jones Industrial Average (DJIA)	An index composed of 30 industrial companies. The Dow Jones is the most widely quoted market index.
Dow Jones Transportation Average	An index composed of 20 transportation stocks.
Dow Jones Utility Average	An index composed of 15 utility stocks.
Dow theory	A theory that believes that the health both of the market and of the economy may be predicted by the performance of the Dow Jones Industrial Average.
dry hole	A term used to describe a nonproducing well.
dual-purpose fund	A mutual fund that offers two classes of shares to investors. One class is sold to investors seeking income and the other class is sold to investors seeking capital appreciation.

E

early withdrawal penalty	A penalty tax charged to an investor for withdrawing money from a qualified retirement plan prior to age 59-1/2, usually 10% on top of ordinary income taxes.
earned income	Money received by an individual in return for performing services.
earnings per share	The net amount of a corporation's earnings available to common shareholders divided by the number of common shares outstanding.
earnings per share fully diluted	The net amount of a corporation's earnings available to common shareholders after taking into consideration the potential conversion of all convertible securities.
eastern account	A type of syndicate account that requires all members to be responsible for their own allocation as well as for their proportional share of any member's unsold securities.
economic risk	The risk of loss of principal associated with the purchase of securities.
EE savings bonds	Nonmarketable U.S. government zero-coupon bonds that must be purchased from the government and redeemed to the government.
effective date	The day when a new issue's registration with the SEC becomes effective. Once the issue's registration statement has become effective, the securities may then be sold to investors.
efficient market theory	A theory that states that the market operates and processes information efficiently and prices in all information as soon as it becomes known.
Employee Retirement Income Security Act of 1974 (ERISA)	The legislation that governs the operation of private-sector pension plans. Corporate pension plans organized under ERISA guidelines qualify for beneficial tax treatment by the IRS.
endorsement	The signature on the back of a security that allows its ownership to be transferred.
EPS	*See* earnings per share.
equipment leasing limited partnership	A limited partnership that is organized to purchase equipment and lease it to corporations to earn lease income and to shelter passive income for investors.
equipment trust certificate	A bond backed by a pledge of large equipment, such as airplanes, railroad cars, and ships.
equity	A security that represents the ownership in a corporation. Both preferred and common equity holders have an ownership interest in the corporation.
equity financing	The sale of common or preferred equity by a corporation in an effort to raise capital.
equity option	An option to purchase or sell common stock.
ERISA	*See* Employee Retirement Income Security Act of 1974.
erroneous report	A report of an execution given in error to a client. The report is not binding on the firm or on the agent.
escrow agreement	Evidence of ownership of a security provided to a broker dealer as proof of ownership of the underlying security for covered call writers.
Eurobond	A bond issued in domestic currency of the issuer but sold outside of the issuer's country.

Eurodollar	A deposit held outside of the United States denominated in U.S. dollars.
Eurodollar bonds	A bond issued by a foreign issuer denominated in U.S. dollars.
Euroyen bonds	Bonds issued outside of Japan but denominated in yen.
excess equity (EE)	The value of an account's equity in excess of Regulation T.
exchange	A market, whether physical or electronic, that provides a forum for trading securities through a dual-auction process.
exchange distribution	A distribution of a large block of stock on the floor of the exchange that is crossed with offsetting orders.
exchange privilege	The right offered by many mutual funds that allows an investor to transfer or move money between different portfolios offered through the same fund company. An investor may redeem shares of the fund, which is being sold at the NAV, and purchase shares of the new portfolio at the NAV without paying another sales charge.
ex date/ex-dividend date	The first day when purchasers of a security will no longer be entitled to receive a previously declared dividend.
executor/executrix	An individual with the authority to manage the affairs of a decedent's estate.
exempt security	A security that is exempt from the registration requirements of the Securities Act of 1933.
exempt transaction	A transaction that is not subject to state registration.
exercise	An investor's election to take advantage of the rights offered through the terms of an option, a right, or a warrant.
exercise price	The price at which an option investor may purchase or sell a security. Also the price at which an investor may purchase a security through a warrant or right.
existing property program	A type of real estate direct participation program that purchases existing property for the established rental income.
expansion	A period marked by a general increase in business activity and an increase in gross domestic product.
expansionary policy	A monetary policy enacted through the Federal Reserve Board that increases money supply and reduces interest rates in an effort to stimulate the economy.
expense ratio	The amount of a mutual fund's expenses relative to its assets. The higher the expense ratio, the lower the investor's return. A mutual fund's expense ratio tells an investor how efficiently a mutual fund operates, not how profitable the mutual fund is.
expiration cycle	A 4-month cycle for option expiration: January, April, July, and October; February, May, August, and November; or March, June, September, and December.
expiration date	The date on which an option ceases to exist.
exploratory drilling program	A direct participation program that engages in the drilling for oil or gas in new areas seeking to find new wells.
exploratory well	Also known as wildcatting. The drilling for oil or gas in new areas in an effort to find new wells.

ex rights	The common stock subject to a rights offering trade without the rights attached.
ex rights date	The first day when the common stock is subject to a rights offering trade without the rights attached.
ex warrants	Common trading without the warrants attached.

F

face-amount certificate company (FAC)	A type of investment company that requires an investor to make fixed payments over time or to deposit a lump sum, and that will return to the investor a stated sum known as the face amount on a specific date.
face amount/face value	*See* par.
fail to deliver	An event where the broker on the sell side of the transaction fails to deliver the security.
fail to receive	An event where the broker on the buy side of the transaction fails to receive the security from the broker on the sell side.
Fannie Mae	*See* Federal National Mortgage Association.
Farm Credit Administrator	The agency that oversees all of the activities of the banks in the Federal Farm Credit System.
Federal Deposit Insurance Corporation (FDIC)	The government insurance agency that provides insurance for bank depositors in case of bank failure.
Federal Farm Credit System	An organization of banks that is designed to provide financing to farmers for mortgages, feed and grain, and equipment.
federal funds rate	The rate banks charge each other on overnight loans.
Federal Home Loan Mortgage Corporation (FHLMC; Freddie Mac)	A publicly traded for-profit corporation that provides liquidity to the secondary mortgage market by purchasing pools of mortgages from lenders and, in turn, issues mortgage-backed securities.
Federal Intermediate Credit Bank	Provides short-term financing to farmers for equipment.
Federal National Mortgage Association (FNMA; Fannie Mae)	A publicly traded for-profit corporation that provides liquidity to the secondary mortgage market by purchasing pools of mortgages and issuing mortgage-backed securities.
Federal Open Market Committee (FOMC)	The committee of the Federal Reserve Board that makes policy decisions relating to the nation's money supply.
Federal Reserve Board	A seven-member board that directs the policies of the Federal Reserve System. The members are appointed by the President and approved by Congress.
Federal Reserve System	The nation's central banking system, the purpose of which is to regulate money supply and the extension of credit. The Federal Reserve System is composed of 12 central banks and 24 regional banks, along with hundreds of national and state chartered banks.
fictitious quote	A quote that is not representative of an actual bid or offer for a security.
fidelity bond	A bond that must be posted by all broker dealers to ensure the public against employee dishonesty.
fill or kill (FK)	A type of order that requires that all of the securities in the order be purchased or sold immediately or not at all.

final prospectus	The official offering document for a security that contains the security's final offering price along with all information required by law for an investor to make an informed decision.
firm commitment underwriting	Guarantees the issuer all of the money right away. The underwriters purchase all of the securities from the issuer regardless of whether they can sell the securities to their customers.
firm quote	A quote displayed at which the dealer is obligated to buy or sell at least one round lot at the quoted price.
fiscal policy	Government policy designed to influence the economy through government tax and spending programs. The President and Congress control fiscal policy.
5% markup policy	FINRA's guideline that requires all prices paid by customers to be reasonably related to a security's market price. The 5% policy is a guideline, not a rule, and it does not apply to securities sold through a prospectus.
fixed annuity	An insurance contract where the insurance company guarantees fixed payments to the annuitant, usually until the annuitant's death.
fixed assets	Assets used by a corporation to conduct its business, such as plant and equipment.
flat	A term used to describe a bond that trades without accrued interest, such as a zero-coupon bond or a bond that is in default.
floor broker	An individual member of an exchange who may execute orders on the floor.
floor trader	Members of the exchange who trade for their own accounts. Members of the NYSE may not trade from the floor for their own accounts.
flow of funds	A schedule of expenses and interested parties that prioritizes how payments will be made from the revenue generated by a facility financed by a municipal revenue bond.
forced conversion	The calling in of convertible bonds at a price that is less than the market value of the underlying common stock into which the bonds may be converted.
foreign currency	Currency of another country.
foreign currency option	An option to purchase or sell a specified amount of another country's currency.
Form 10-K	An annual report filed by a corporation detailing its financial performance for the year.
Form 10-Q	A quarterly report filed by a corporation detailing its financial performance for the quarter.
form letter	A letter sent out by a brokerage firm or a registered representative to more than 25 people in a 90-day period. Form letters are subject to approval and recordkeeping requirements.
forward pricing	The way in which open-end mutual funds are valued for investors who wish to purchase or redeem shares of the fund. Mutual funds usually price their shares at the end of the business day. The price to be paid or received by the investor will be the price that is next calculated after the fund receives the order.

401K	A qualified retirement plan offered by an employer.
403B	A qualified retirement plan offered to teachers and employees of nonprofit organizations.
fourth market	A transaction between two large institutions without the use of a broker dealer.
fractional share	A portion of a whole share that represents ownership of an open-end mutual fund.
fraud	Any attempt to gain an unfair advantage over another party through the use of deception, concealment, or misrepresentation.
free credit balance	Cash reserves in a customer's account that have not been invested. Customers must be notified of their free credit balances at least quarterly.
free look	A privilege offered to purchasers of contractual plans and insurance policies that will allow the individual to cancel the contract within the free-look period, usually 45 days.
freeriding	The purchase and sale of a security without depositing the money required to cover the purchase price as required by Regulation T.
freeriding and withholding	The withholding of new issue securities offered by a broker dealer for the benefit of the brokerage firm or an employee.
front-end load	(1) A sales charge paid by investors in open-end mutual funds that is paid at the time of purchase. (2) A contractual plan that seeks to assess sales charges in the first years of the plan and may charge up to 50% of the first year's payments as sales charges.
frozen account	An account where the owner is required to deposit cash or securities up front, prior to any purchase or sale taking place. An account is usually frozen as a result of a customer's failure to pay or deliver securities.
full power of attorney	A type of discretionary authority that allows a third party to purchase and sell securities as well as to withdraw cash and securities without the owner's prior consent or knowledge. This type of authority is usually reserved to trustees and attorneys.
fully registered bonds	A type of bond issuance where the issuer has a complete record of the owners of the bonds and who is entitled to receive interest and principal payments. The owners of fully registered bonds are not required to clip coupons.
functional allocation	An arrangement for oil and gas programs where the general partner pays the tangible drilling costs and the limited partner absorbs the intangible drilling costs.
fundamental analyst	A method of valuing the company that takes into consideration the financial performance of the corporation, the value of its assets, and the quality of its management.
funded debt	Long-term debt obligations of corporations or municipalities.
fungible	Easily exchangeable items with the same conditions.

G

general account	An insurance company's account that holds the money and investments for fixed contracts and traditional life insurance policies.
general obligation bond	A municipal bond that is backed by the taxing power of the state or municipality.
general partner	The partner in a general partnership who manages the business and is responsible for any debt of the program.
general securities principal	An individual who has passed the Series 24 exam and may supervise the activities of the firm and its agents.
generic advertising	Advertising designed to promote name recognition for a firm and securities as investments, but does not recommend specific securities.
good 'til cancel (GTC)	An order that remains on the books until it is executed or canceled.
goodwill	An intangible asset of a corporation, such as its name recognition and reputation, that adds to its value.
Government National Mortgage Association (GNMA; Ginnie Mae)	A government corporation that provides liquidity to the mortgage markets by purchasing pools of mortgages that have been insured by the Federal Housing Administration and the Veterans Administration. Ginnie Mae issues pass-through certificates to investors backed by the pools of mortgages.
government security	A security that is an obligation of the U.S. government and that is backed by the full faith and credit of the U.S. government, such as Treasury bills, notes, and bonds.
grant anticipation note (GAN)	Short-term municipal financing issued in anticipation of receiving a grant from the federal government or one of its agencies.
greenshoe option	An option given to an underwriter of common stock that will allow it to purchase up to an additional 15% of the offering from the issuer at the original offering price to cover over-allotments for securities that are in high demand.
gross domestic product (GDP)	The value of all goods and services produced by a country within a period of time. GDP includes government purchases, investments, and exports minus imports.
gross income	All income received by a taxpayer before deductions for taxes.
gross revenue pledge	A flow-of-funds pledge for a municipal revenue bond that states that debt service will be paid first.
growth fund	A fund whose objective is capital appreciation. Growth funds invest in common stocks to achieve their objective.
growth stock	The stock of a company whose earnings grow at a rate that is faster than the growth rate of the economy as a whole. Growth stocks are characterized by increased opportunities for appreciation and little or no dividends.
guardian	An individual who has a fiduciary responsibility for another, usually a minor.

H

halt	A temporary stop in the trading of a security. If a common stock is halted, all derivatives and convertibles will be halted as well.
head and shoulders	A chart pattern that indicates a reversal of a trend. A head-and-shoulders top indicates a reversal of an uptrend and is considered bearish. A head-and-shoulders bottom is the reversal of a downtrend and is considered bullish.
hedge	A position taken in a security to offset or reduce the risk associated with the risk of another security.
HH bond	A nonmarketable government security that pays semiannual interest. Series HH bonds are issued with a $500 minimum value and may only be purchased by trading matured Series EE bonds; they may not be purchased with cash.
high	The highest price paid for a security during a trading session or during a 52-week period.
holder	An individual or corporation that owns a security. The holder of a security is also known as being long the security.
holding period	The length of time during which an investor owns a security. The holding period is important for calculating tax liability.
hold in street name	The registration of customer securities in the name of the broker dealer. Most customers register securities in the name of the broker dealer to make the transfer of ownership easier.
horizontal spread	Also known as a calendar spread. The simultaneous purchase and sale of two calls or two puts on the same underlying security with the same exercise price but with different expiration months.
hot issue	A new issue of securities that trades at an immediate premium to its offering price in the secondary market.
HR 10 plan	*See* Keogh plan.
hypothecation	The customer's pledge of securities as collateral for a margin loan.

I

immediate annuity	An annuity contract purchased with a single payment that entitles the holder to receive immediate payments from the contract. The annuitant purchases annuity units and usually begins receiving payments within 60 days.
immediate family	An individual's immediate family includes parents, parents-in-law, children, spouse, and any relative financially dependent upon the individual.
immediate or cancel (IOC)	An order that is to be executed as fully as possible immediately and whatever is not executed will be canceled.
income bond	A highly speculative bond that is issued at a discount from par and only pays interest if the issuer has enough income to do so. The issuer of the income bond only promises to pay principal at maturity. Income bonds trade flat without accrued interest.

income fund	A mutual fund whose investment objective is to achieve current income for its shareholders by investing in bonds and preferred stocks.
income program	A type of oil and gas program that purchases producing wells to receive the income received from the sale of the proven reserves.
income statement	A financial statement that shows a corporation's revenue and expenses for the time period in question.
indefeasible title	A record of ownership that cannot be challenged.
index	A representation of the price action of a given group of securities. Indexes are used to measure the condition of the market as a whole, such as with the S&P 500, or can be used to measure the condition of an industry group, such as with the Biotech index.
index option	An option on an underlying financial index. Index options settle in cash.
indication of interest	An investor's expression of a willingness to purchase a new issue of securities after receiving a preliminary prospectus. The investor's indication of interest is not binding on either the investor or the firm.
Individual Retirement Account (IRA)	A self-directed retirement account that allows individuals with earned income to contribute the lesser of 100% of earned income or the annual maximum per year. The contributions may be made with pre- or after-tax dollars, depending on the individual's level of income and whether he or she is eligible to participate in an employer's sponsored plan.
industrial development bond	A private-purpose municipal bond whose proceeds are used to build a facility that is leased to a corporation. The debt service on the bonds is supported by the lease payments.
inflation	The persistent upward pressure on the price of goods and services over time.
initial margin requirement	The initial amount of equity that a customer must deposit to establish a position. The initial margin requirement is set by the Federal Reserve Board under Regulation T.
initial public offering (IPO)	The first offering of common stock to the general investing public.
in part call	A partial call of a bond issue for redemption.
inside information	Information that is not known to people outside of the corporation. Information becomes public only after it is released by the corporation through a recognized media source. Inside information may be both material and immaterial. It is only illegal to trade on inside material information.
inside market	The highest bid and the lowest offer for a security.
insider	A company's officers, directors, large stockholders of 10% or more of the company, and anyone who is in possession of nonpublic material information, along with the immediate family members of the same.

Insider Trading and Securities Fraud Enforcement Act of 1988	Federal legislation that made the penalties for people trading on material nonpublic information more severe. Penalties for insider traders are up to the greater of 300% of the amount of money made or the loss avoided or $1 million and up to 5 years in prison. People who disseminate inside information may be imprisoned and fined up to $1 million.
INSTINET	A computer network that facilitates trading of large blocks of stocks between institutions without the use of a broker dealer.
institutional account	An account in the name of an institution but operated for the benefit of others (i.e., banks and mutual funds). There is no minimum size for an institutional account.
institutional communication	Any communication that is distributed exclusively to institutional investors. Institutional communication does not require the preapproval of a principal but must be maintained for 3 years by the firm.
institutional investor	An investor who trades for its own account or for the accounts of others in large quantities and is covered by fewer protective laws.
insurance covenant	The promise of an issuer of revenue bonds to maintain insurance on the financed project.
intangible asset	Nonphysical property of a corporation, such as trademarks and copyrights.
intangible drilling cost (IDC)	Costs for an oil and gas program that are expensed in the year in which they are incurred for such things as wages, surveys, and well casings.
interbank market	An international currency market.
interest	The cost for borrowing money, usually charged at an annual percentage rate.
interest rate option	An option based on U.S. government securities. The options are either rate-based or priced-based options.
interest rate risk	The risk borne by investors in interest-bearing securities, which subjects the holder to a loss of principal should interest rates rise.
interlocking directorate	Corporate boards that share one or more directors.
Intermarket Trading System/ Computer-Assisted Execution System (ITS/ CAES)	A computer system that links the third market for securities with the exchanges.
Internal Revenue Code (IRC)	The codes that define tax liabilities for U.S. taxpayers.
interpositioning	The placing of another broker dealer in between the customer and the best market. Interpositioning is prohibited unless it can be demonstrated that the customer received a better price because of it.
interstate offering	A multistate offering of securities that requires that the issuer register with the SEC as well as with the states in which the securities will be sold.
in the money	A relationship between the strike price of an option and the underlying security's price. A call is in the money when the strike price is lower than the security's price. A put is in the money when the strike price is higher than the security's price.
intrastate offering	*See* Rule 147.

intrinsic value	The amount by which an option is in the money.
introducing broker	*See* correspondent broker dealer.
inverted yield curve	A yield curve where the cost of short-term financing exceeds the cost of long-term financing.
investment adviser	Anyone who charges a fee for investment advice or who holds himself out to the public as being in the business of giving investment advice for a fee.
Investment Advisers Act of 1940	The federal legislation that sets forth guidelines for business requirements and activities of investment advisers.
investment banker	A financial institution that is in the business of raising capital for companies and municipalities by underwriting securities.
investment company	A company that sells undivided interests in a pool of securities and manages the portfolio for the benefit of the investors. Investment companies include management companies, unit investment trusts, and face-amount companies.
Investment Company Act of 1940	Federal legislation that regulates the operation and registration of investment companies.
investment-grade security	A security that has been assigned a rating in the highest rating tier by a recognized ratings agency.
investment objective	An investor's set of goals as to how he or she is seeking to make money, such as capital appreciation or current income.
investor	The purchaser of a security who seeks to realize a profit.
IRA rollover	The temporary distribution of assets from an IRA and the subsequent reinvestment of the assets into another IRA within 60 days. An IRA may be rolled over only once per year and is subject to a 10% penalty and ordinary income taxes if the investor is under 59-1/2 and if the assets are not deposited in another qualified account within 60 days.
IRA transfer	The movement of assets from one qualified account to another without the account holder taking possession of the assets. Investors may transfer an IRA as often as they like.
issued stock	Stock that has actually been sold to the investing public.
issuer	Any entity that issues or proposes to issue securities.

J

joint account	An account that is owned by two or more parties. Joint accounts allow either party to enter transactions for the account. Both parties must sign a joint account agreement. All joint accounts must be designated as joint tenants in common or with rights of survivorship.
joint tenants in common (JTIC)	A joint account where the assets of a party who has died transfer to the decedent's estate, not the other tenant.
joint tenants with rights of survivorship (JTWROS)	A joint account where the assets of a party who has died transfer to the surviving party, not the decedent's estate.
joint venture	An interest in an operation shared by two or more parties. The parties have no other relationship beyond the joint venture.

junk bond	A bond with a high degree of default risk that has been assigned a speculative rating by the ratings agencies.
junk bond fund	A speculative bond fund that invests in high-yield bonds in order to achieve a high degree of current income.

K

Keogh plan	A qualified retirement account for self-employed individuals. Contributions are limited to the lesser of 20% of their gross income or $51,000.
Keynesian economics	An economic theory that states that government intervention in the marketplace helps sustain economic growth.
know-your-customer rule	Industry regulation that requires a registered representative to be familiar with the customer's financial objectives and needs prior to making a recommendation; also known as Rule 405.

L

lagging indicator	A measurement of economic activity that changes after a change has taken place in economic activity. Lagging indicators are useful confirmation tools when determining the strength of an economic trend. Lagging indicators include corporate profits, average duration of unemployment, and labor costs.
last in, first out (LIFO)	An accounting method used that states that the last item that was produced is the first item sold.
leading indicator	A measurement of economic activity that changes prior to a change in economic activity. Leading economic indicators are useful in predicting a coming trend in economic activity. Leading economic indicators include housing permits, new orders for durable goods, and the S&P 500.
LEAPS (long-term equity anticipation securities)	A long-term option on a security that has an expiration of up to 39 months.
lease rental bonds	A municipal bond that is issued to finance the building of a facility that will be rented out. The lease payments on the facility will support the bond's debt service.
legal list	A list of securities that have been approved by certain state securities regulators for purchase by fiduciaries.
legal opinion	An opinion issued by a bond attorney stating that the issue is a legally binding obligation of the state or municipality. The legal opinion also contains a statement regarding the tax status of the interest payments received by investors.
legislative risk	The risk that the government may do something that adversely affects an investment.

letter of intent (LOI)	A letter signed by the purchaser of mutual fund shares that states the investor's intention to invest a certain amount of money over a 13-month period. By agreeing to invest this sum, the investor is entitled to receive a lower sales charge on all purchases covered by the letter of intent. The letter of intent may be backdated up to 90 days from an initial purchase. Should the investor fail to invest the stated sum, a sales charge adjustment will be charged.
level load	A mutual fund share that charges a flat annual fee, such as a 12B-1 fee.
level one	A Nasdaq workstation service that allows the agent to see the inside market only.
level two	A Nasdaq workstation service that allows the order-entry firm to see the inside market, to view the quotes entered by all market makers, and to execute orders.
level three	A Nasdaq workstation service that allows market-making firms to see the inside market, to view the quotes entered by all market makers, to execute orders, and to enter their own quotes for the security. This is the highest level of Nasdaq service.
leverage	The use of borrowed funds to try to obtain a rate of return that exceeds the cost of the funds.
liability	A legal obligation to pay a debt either incurred through borrowing or through the normal course of business.
life annuity/straight life	An annuity payout option that provides payments over the life of the annuitant.
life annuity with period certain	An annuity payout option that provides payments to the annuitant for life or to the annuitant's estate for the period certain, whichever is longer.
life contingency	An annuity payout option that provides a death benefit in case the annuitant dies during the accumulation stage.
limit order	An order that sets a maximum price that the investor will pay in the case of a buy order or the minimum price the investor will accept in the case of a sell order.
limited liability	A protection afforded to investors in securities that limits their liability to the amount of money invested in the securities.
limited partner	A passive investor in a direct participation program who has no role in the project's management.
limited partnership (LP)	An association of two or more partners with at least one partner being the general partner who is responsible for the management of the partnership.
limited partnership agreement	The foundation of all limited partnerships. The agreement is the contract between all partners, and it spells out the authority of the general partner and the rights of all limited partners.
limited power of attorney/limited trading authorization	Legal authorization for a representative or a firm to effect purchases and sales for a customer's account without the customer's prior knowledge. The authorization is limited to buying and selling securities and may not be given to another party.

limited principal	An individual who has passed the Series 26 exam and may supervise Series 6 limited representatives.
limited representative	An individual who has passed the Series 6 exam and may represent a broker dealer in the sale of mutual fund shares and variable contracts.
limited tax bond	A type of general obligation bond that is issued by a municipality that may not increase its tax rate to pay the debt service of the issue.
liquidity	The ability of an investment to be readily converted into cash.
liquidity risk	The risk that an investor may not be able to sell a security when needed or that selling a security when needed will adversely affect the price.
listed option	A standardized option contract that is traded on an exchange.
listed security	A security that trades on one of the exchanges. Only securities that trade on an exchange are known as listed securities.
loan consent agreement	A portion of the margin agreement that allows the broker dealer to loan out the customer's securities to another customer who wishes to borrow them to sell the security short.
locked market	A market condition that results when the bid and the offer for a security are equal.
LOI	*See* letter of intent.
London Interbank Offered Rate (LIBOR)	The interbank rates for dollar-denominated deposits in England.
long	A term used to describe an investor who owns a security.
long market value	The total long market value of a customer's account.
long-term gain	A profit realized through the sale of a security at a price that is higher than its purchase price after a being held for more than 12 months.
long-term loss	A loss realized through the sale of a security at a price that is lower than its purchase price after being held for more than 12 months.
loss carry forward	A capital loss realized on the sale of an asset in 1 year that is carried forward in whole or part to subsequent tax years.
low	The lowest price at which a security has traded in any given period, usually measured during a trading day or for 52 weeks.

M

M1	The most liquid measure of the money supply. It includes all currency and demand and NOW deposits (checking accounts).
M2	A measure of the money supply that includes M1 plus all time deposits, savings accounts, and noninstitutional money market accounts.
M3	A measure of the money supply that includes M2 and large time deposits, institutional money market funds, short-term repurchase agreements, and other large liquid assets.
maintenance call	A demand for additional cash or collateral made by a broker dealer when a margin customer's account equity has fallen below the minimum requirement of the NYSE or that is set by the broker dealer.
maintenance covenant	A promise made by an issuer of a municipal revenue bond to maintain the facility in good repair.

Major Market Index (XMI)	An index created by the Amex to AMEX 15 of the 30 largest stocks in the Dow Jones Industrial Average.
Maloney Act of 1938	An amendment to the Securities Exchange Act of 1934 that gave the NASD (now part of FINRA) the authority to regulate the over-the-counter market.
managed underwriting	An underwriting conducted by a syndicate led by the managing underwriter.
management company	A type of investment company that actively manages a portfolio of securities in order to meet a stated investment objective. Management companies are also known as mutual funds.
management fee	(1) The fee received by the lead or managing underwriter of a syndicate. (2) The fee received by a sponsor of a direct participation program.
managing partner	The general partner in a direct participation program.
managing underwriter	The lead underwriter in a syndicate who is responsible for negotiating with the issuer, forming the syndicate, and settling the syndicate account.
margin	The amount of customer equity that is required to hold a position in a security.
margin account	An account that allows the customer to borrow money from the brokerage firm to buy securities.
margin call	A demand for cash or collateral mandated by the Federal Reserve Board under Regulation T.
margin department	The department in a broker dealer that calculates money owed by the customer or money due the customer.
margin maintenance call	*See* maintenance call.
mark to the market	The monitoring of a the current value of a position relative to the price at which the trade was executed for securities purchased on margin or on a when-issued basis.
markdown	The profit earned by a dealer on a transaction when purchasing securities for its own account from a customer.
marketability	The ability of an investment to be exchanged between two investors. A security with an active secondary market has a higher level of marketability than one whose market is not as active.
market arbitrage	A type of arbitrage that consists of purchasing a security in one marketplace and selling it in another to take advantage of price inefficiencies.
market letter	A regular publication, usually issued by an investment adviser, that offers information and/or advice regarding a security, market conditions, or the economy as a whole.
market maker	A Nasdaq firm that is required to quote a continuous two-sided market for the securities in which it trades.
market not held	A type of order that gives the floor broker discretion over the time and price of execution.

market on close	An order that will be executed at whatever price the market is at, either on the closing print or just prior to the closing print.
market on open	An order that will be executed at whatever price the market is at, either on the opening print or just after the opening print.
market order	A type of order that will be executed immediately at the best available price once it is presented to the market.
market-out clause	A clause in an underwriting agreement that gives the syndicate the ability to cancel the underwriting if it finds a material problem with the information or condition of the issuer.
market risk/systematic risk	The risk inherent in any investment in the market that states an investor may lose money simply because the market is going down.
market value	The value of a security that is determined in the marketplace by the investors who enter bids and offers for a security.
markup	The compensation paid to a securities dealer for selling a security to a customer from its inventory.
markup policy	FINRA's guideline that states that the price that is paid or received by an investor must be reasonably related to the market price for that security. FINRA offers 5% as a guideline for what is reasonable to charge investors when they purchase or sell securities.
material information	Information that would affect a company's current or future prospects or an investor's decision to invest in the company.
maturity date	The date on which a bond's principal amount becomes payable to its holders.
member	A member of FINRA or one of the 1,366 members of the NYSE.
member firm	A firm that is a member of the NYSE, FINRA, or another self-regulatory organization.
member order	A retail order entered by a member of a municipal bond syndicate for which the member will receive all of the sales credit.
mini maxi underwriting	A type of best efforts underwriting that states that the offering will not become effective until a minimum amount is sold and sets a maximum amount that may be sold.
minimum death benefit	The minimum guaranteed death benefit that will be paid to the beneficiaries if the holder of a variable life insurance policy dies.
minus tick	A trade in an exchange-listed security that is at a price that is lower than the previous trade.
modern portfolio theory	An investing approach that looks at the overall return and risk of a portfolio as a whole, not as a collection of single investments.
modified accelerated cost recovery system (MACRS)	An accounting method that allows the owner to recover a larger portion of the asset's value in the early years of its life.
monetarist theory	A theory that states that the money supply is the driving force in the economy and that a well-managed money supply will benefit the economy.
monetary policy	Economic policy that is controlled by the Federal Reserve Board and controls the amount of money in circulation and the level of interest rates.

money market	The secondary market where short-term highly liquid securities are traded. Securities traded in the money market include T-bills, negotiable CDs, bankers' acceptances, commercial paper, and other short-term securities with less than 12 months to maturity.
money market mutual fund	A mutual fund that invests in money market instruments to generate monthly interest for its shareholders. Money market mutual funds have a stable NAV that is equal to $1, but it is not guaranteed.
money supply	The total amount of currency, loans, and credit in the economy. The money supply is measured by M1, M2, M3, and L.
moral obligation bond	A type of municipal revenue bond that will allow the state or municipality to vote to cover a shortfall in the debt service.
multiplier effect	The ability of the money supply to grow simply through the normal course of banking. When banks and other financial institutions accept deposits and subsequently loan out those deposits to earn interest, the amount of money in the system grows.
municipal bond	A bond issued by a state or political subdivision of a state in an effort to finance its operations. Interest earned by investors in municipal bonds is almost always free from federal income taxes.
municipal bond fund	A mutual fund that invests in a portfolio of municipal debt in an effort to produce income that is free from federal income taxes for its investors.
Municipal Bond Investors Assurance Corp. (MBIA)	An independent insurance company that will, for a fee received from the issuer, insure the interest and principal payments on a municipal bond.
municipal note	A short-term municipal issue sold to manage the issuer's cash flow, usually in anticipation of the offering of long-term financing.
Municipal Securities Rulemaking Board (MSRB)	The self-regulatory organization that oversees the issuance and trading of municipal bonds. The MSRB's rules are enforced by other industry SROs.
Munifacts	A service that provides real-time secondary market quotes. Munifacts is now known as Thomson Muni Market Monitor.
mutual fund	An investment company that invests in and manages a portfolio of securities for its shareholders. Open-end mutual funds sell their shares to investors on a continuous basis and must stand ready to redeem their shares upon the shareholder's request.
mutual fund custodian	A qualified financial institution that maintains physical custody of a mutual fund's cash and securities. Custodians are usually banks, trust companies, or exchange member firms.

N

naked	The sale of a call option without owning the underlying security or the sale of a put option without being short the stock or having cash on deposit that is sufficient to purchase the underlying security.

narrow-based index	An index that is based on a market sector or a limited number of securities.
NASD (National Association of Securities Dealers)	The industry self-regulatory agency that was authorized by the Maloney Act of 1938 and empowered to regulate the over-the-counter market. The NASD is now part of FINRA.
NASD bylaws	The rules that define the operation of the NASD and how it regulates the over-the-counter market. The four major bylaws are the Rules of Fair Practice, the Uniform Practice Code, the Code of Procedure, and the Code of Arbitration. Now known as FINRA bylaws.
NASD Manual	An NASD publication that outlines the rules and regulations of NASD membership. Now known as the FINRA Manual.
National Securities Clearing Corporation (NSCC)	The clearing intermediary through which clearing member firms reconcile their securities accounts.
NAV (net asset value)	The net value of a mutual fund after deducting all its liabilities. A mutual fund must calculate its NAV at least once per business day. To determine NAV per share, simply divide the mutual fund's NAV by the total number of shares outstanding.
negotiability	The ability of an investment to be freely exchanged between noninterested parties.
negotiable certificate of deposit	A certificate issued by a bank for a time deposit in excess of $100,000 that can be exchanged between parties prior to its maturity date. FDIC insurance only covers the first $250,000 of the principal amount should the bank fail.
NOW (negotiable order of withdrawal) Account	A type of demand deposit that allows the holder to write checks against an interest-bearing account.
net change	The difference between the previous day's closing price and the price of the most recently reported trade for a security.
net current assets per share	A calculation of the value per share that excludes fixed assets and intangibles.
net debt per capita	A measure of a municipal issuer's ability to meet its obligations. It measures the debt level of the issuer in relation to the population.
net debt to assessed valuation	A measure of the issuer's ability to meet its obligations and to raise additional revenue through property taxes.
net direct debt	The total amount of general obligation debt, including notes and short-term financing, issued by a municipality or state.
net interest cost (NIC)	A calculation that measures the interest cost of a municipal issue over the life of all bonds. Most competitive underwritings for municipal securities are awarded to the syndicate that submits the bid with the lowest NIC.
net investment income	The total sum of investment income derived from dividend and interest income after subtracting expenses.
net revenue pledge	A pledge from a revenue bond that pays maintenance and operation expenses first, then debt service.
net total debt	The total of a municipality's direct debt plus its overlapping debt.

net worth	The value of a corporation after subtracting all of its liabilities. A corporation's net worth is also equal to shareholder's equity.
new account form	Paperwork that must be filled out and signed by the representative and a principal of the firm prior to the opening of any account being opened for a customer.
new construction program	A real estate program that seeks to achieve capital appreciation by building new properties.
new housing authority (NHA)	A municipal bond issued to build low-income housing. NHA bonds are guaranteed by the U.S. government and are considered the safest type of municipal bonds. NHA bonds are not considered to be double-barreled bonds.
new issue	*See* initial public offering (IPO).
New York Stock Exchange (NYSE)	A membership organization that provides a marketplace for securities to be exchanged in one centralized location through a dual-auction process.
no-load fund	A fund that does not charge the investor a sales charge to invest in the fund. Shares of no-load mutual funds are sold directly from the fund company to the investor.
nominal owner	An individual or entity registered as the owner of record of securities for the benefit of another party.
nominal quote	A quote given for informational purposes only. A trader who identifies a quote as being nominal cannot be held to trading at the prices that were clearly identified as being nominal.
nominal yield	The yield that is stated or named on the security. The nominal yield, once it has been set, never changes, regardless of the market price of the security.
noncompetitive bid	A bid submitted for Treasury bills where the purchaser agrees to accept the average of all yields accepted at the auction. Noncompetitive tenders are always the first orders filled at the auction.
noncumulative preferred	A type of preferred stock whose dividends do not accumulate in arrears if the issuer misses the payment.
nondiscrimination	A clause that states that all eligible individuals must be allowed to participate in a qualified retirement plan.
nondiversification	An investment strategy that concentrates its investments among a small group of securities or issuers.
nondiversified management company	An investment company that concentrates its investments among a few issuers or securities and does not meet the diversification requirements of the Investment Company Act of 1940.
nonfixed UIT	A type of UIT that allows changes in the portfolio and traditionally invests in mutual fund shares.
nonqualified retirement plan	A retirement plan that does not allow contributions to be made with pre-tax dollars; that is, the retirement plan does not qualify for beneficial tax treatment from the IRS for its contributions.
nonsystematic risk	A risk that is specific to an issuer or an industry.

note	An intermediate-term interest-bearing security that represents an obligation of its issuer.
not-held (NH) order	An order that gives the floor broker discretion as to the time and price of execution.
numbered account	An account that has been designated a number for identification purposes in order to maintain anonymity for its owner. The owner must sign a statement acknowledging ownership.

O

odd lot	A transaction that is for less than 100 shares of stock or for less than 5 bonds.
odd lot differential	An additional fee that may be charged to an investor for the handling of odd lot transactions (usually waived).
odd lot theory	A contrarian theory that states that small investors will invariably buy and sell at the wrong time.
offer	A price published at which an investor or broker dealer is willing to sell a security.
offering circular	The offering document that is prepared by a corporation selling securities under a Regulation A offering.
office of supervisory jurisdiction (OSJ)	An office identified by the broker dealer as having supervisory responsibilities for agents. It has final approval of new accounts, makes markets, and structures offerings.
Office of the Comptroller of the Currency	An office of the U.S. Treasury that is responsible for regulating the practices of national banks.
official notice of sale	The notice of sale published in the *Daily Bond Buyer* by a municipal issuer that is used to obtain an underwriter for municipal bonds.
official statement	The offering document for a municipal issuer that must be provided to every purchaser if the issuer prepares one.
oil and gas direct participation program	A type of direct participation program designed to invest in oil and gas production or exploration.
oil depletion allowance	An accounting method used to reduce the amount of reserves available from a producing well.
omnibus account	An account used by an introducing member to execute and clear all of its customers' trades.
open-end covenant	A type of bond indenture that allows for the issuance of additional bonds with the same claim on the collateral as the original issue.
open-end investment company	See mutual fund.
option	A contract between two investors to purchase or sell a security at a given price for a certain period of time.
option agreement	A form that must be signed and returned by an option investor within 15 days of the account's approval to trade options.

option disclosure document	A document that must be furnished to all option investors at the time the account is approved for options trading. It is published by the Options Clearing Corporation (OCC), and it details the risks and features of standardized options.
Options Clearing Corporation (OCC)	The organization that issues and guarantees the performance of standardized options.
order book official (OBO)	Employees of the CBOE who are responsible for maintaining a fair and orderly market in the options assigned to them and for executing orders that have been left with them.
order department	The department of a broker dealer that is responsible for routing orders to the markets for execution.
order memorandum/ order ticket	The written document filled out by a registered representative that identifies, among other things, the security, the amount, the customer, and the account number for which the order is being entered.
original issue discount (OID)	A bond that has been issued to the public at a discount to its par value. The OID on a corporate bond is taxed as if it was earned annually. The OID on a municipal bond is exempt from taxation.
OTC market	*See* over-the-counter (OTC) market.
out of the money	The relationship of an option's strike price to the underlying security's price when exercising the option would not make economic sense. A call is out of the money when the security's price is below the option's strike price. A put is out of the money when the security's price is above the option's strike price.
outstanding stock	The total amount of a security that has been sold to the investing public and that remains in the hands of the investing public.
overlapping debt	The portion of another taxing authority's debt that a municipality is responsible for.
overriding royalty interest	A type of sharing arrangement that offers an individual with no risk a portion of the revenue in exchange for something of value, such as the right to drill on the owner's land.
over-the-counter (OTC) market	An interdealer market that consists of a computer and phone network through which broker dealers trade securities.

P

par	The stated principal amount of a security. Par value is of great importance for fixed-income securities such as bonds or preferred stock. Par value for bonds is traditionally $1,000, whereas par for a preferred stock is normally $100. Par value is of little importance when looking at common stock.
parity	A condition that results when the value of an underlying common stock to be received upon conversion equals the value of the convertible security.
partial call	A call of a portion of an issuer's callable securities.

participation	The code set forth in the Employee Retirement Income Security Act of 1974 that states who is eligible to participate in an employer sponsored retirement plan.
passive income	Income received by an individual for which no work was performed, such as rental income received from a rental property.
passive loss	A loss realized on an investment in a limited partnership or rental property that can be used to offset passive income.
pass-through certificate	A security that passes through income and principal payments made to an underlying portfolio of mortgages. Ginnie Mae is one of the biggest issuers of this type of security.
payment date	The day when a dividend will actually be sent to investors. The payment date is set by the corporation's board of directors at the time when they initially declare the dividend.
payout stage	The period during which an annuitant receives payments from an annuity contract.
payroll deduction plan	A nonqualified retirement plan where employees authorize the employer to take regular deductions from their paychecks to invest in a retirement account.
pension plan	A contractual retirement plan between an employee and an employer that is designed to provide regular income for the employee after retirement.
percentage depletion	An accounting method that allows for a tax deduction for the reduction of reserves.
periodic payment plan	A contract to purchase mutual fund shares over an extended period of time, usually in exchange for the fund company waiving its minimum investment requirement.
person	Any individual or entity that can enter into a legally binding contract for the purchase and sale of securities.
personal income	Income earned by an individual from providing services and through investments.
phantom income	(1) A term used to describe the taxable appreciation on a zero-coupon bond. (2) The term used to describe taxable income generated by a limited partnership that is not producing positive cash flow.
Philadelphia Automated Communication Execution System (PACE)	The computerized order-routing system for the Philadelphia Stock Exchange.
pink sheets	An electronic quote service containing quotes for unlisted securities that is published by the National Quotation Bureau; operated as the PINK over-the-counter market.
placement ratio	A ratio that details the percentage of municipal bonds sold, relative to the number of bonds offered in the last week, published by the *Daily Bond Buyer*.

plus tick	A transaction in an exchange-listed security that is higher than the previous transaction.
point	An increment of change in the price of a security: 1 bond point equals 1% of par or 1% of $1,000, or $10.
POP	*See* public offering price (POP).
portfolio income	Interest and dividends earned through investing in securities.
portfolio manager	An entity that is hired to manage the investment portfolios of a mutual fund. The portfolio manager is paid a fee that is based on the net assets of the fund.
position	The amount of a security in which an investor has an interest by either being long (owning) or short (owing) the security.
power of substitution	*See* stock power.
preemptive right	The right of a common stockholder to maintain proportional ownership interest in a security. A corporation may not issue additional shares of common stock without first offering those shares to existing stockholders.
preferred stock	An equity security issued with a stated dividend rate. Preferred stockholders have a higher claim on a corporation's dividends and assets than common holders.
preferred stock ratio	A ratio detailing the amount of an issuer's total capitalization that is made up of preferred stock. The ratio is found by dividing the total par value of preferred stock by the issuer's total capitalization.
preliminary prospectus/ red herring	A document used to solicit indications of interest during the cooling-off period for a new issue of securities. All of the information in the preliminary prospectus is subject to revision and change. The cover of a preliminary prospectus must have a statement saying that the securities have not yet become registered and that they may not be sold until the registration becomes effective. This statement is written in red ink, and this is where the term red herring comes from.
price-earnings ratio (PE)	A measure of value used by analysts. It is calculated by dividing the issuer's stock price by its earnings per share.
price spread	A term used to describe an option spread where the long and short options differ only in their exercise prices.
primary earnings per share	The amount of earnings available per common share prior to the conversion of any outstanding convertible securities.
prime rate	The interest rate that banks charge their best corporate customers on loans.
principal	(1) The face amount of a bond. (2) A broker dealer trading for its own account. (3) An individual who has successfully completed a principal exam and may supervise representatives.
principal transaction	A transaction where a broker dealer participates in a trade by buying or selling securities for its own account.
priority	The acceptance of bids and offers for exchange-listed securities on a first-come, first-served (FCFS) basis.

private placement	The private sale of securities to a limited number of investors. Also known as a Regulation D offering.
profit sharing plan	A plan that allows the employer to distribute a percentage of its profits to its employees at a predetermined rate. The money may be paid directly to the employee or deposited into a retirement account.
progressive tax	A tax structure where the tax rate increases as the income level of the individual or entity increases.
project note	A municipal bond issued as interim financing in anticipation of the issuance of new housing authority bonds.
prospectus	*See* final prospectus.
proxy	A limited authority given by stockholders to another party to vote their shares in a corporate election. The stockholder may specify how the votes are cast or may give the party discretion.
proxy department	The department in a brokerage firm that is responsible for forwarding proxies and financial information to investors whose stock is held in street name.
prudent man rule	A rule that governs investments made by fiduciaries for the benefit of a third party. The rule states that the investments must be similar to those that a prudent person would make for him- or herself.
public offering	The sale of securities by an issuer to public investors.
public offering price (POP)	The price paid by an investor to purchase open-end mutual fund shares. Also the price set for a security the first time it is sold to the investing public.
put	An option contract that allows the buyer to sell a security at a set price for a specific period of time. The seller of a put is obligated to purchase the security at a set price for a specific period of time, should the buyer exercise the option.
put buyer	A bearish investor who pays a premium for the right to sell a security at a set price for a certain period of time.
put spread	An option position created by the simultaneous purchase and sale of two put options on the same underlying security that differ in strike prices, expiration months, or both.
put writer	A bullish investor who sells a put option in order to receive the option premium. The writer is obligated to purchase the security if the buyer exercises the option.

Q

qualified legal opinion	A legal opinion containing conditions or reservations relating to the issue. A legal opinion is issued by a bond counsel for a municipal issuer.
qualified retirement plan	A retirement plan that qualifies for favorable tax treatment by the IRS for contributions made into the plan.
quick assets	A measure of liquidity that subtracts the value of a corporation's unsold inventory from its current assets.

quick ratio   *See* acid-test ratio.

quote   A bid and offer broadcast from the exchange or through the Nasdaq system that displays the prices at which a security may be purchased and sold and in what quantities.

R

range	The price difference between the high and low for a security.
rate covenant	A promise in the trust indenture of a municipal revenue bond to keep the user fees high enough to support the debt service.
rating	A judgment of an issuer's ability to meet its credit obligations. The higher the credit quality of the issuer is, the higher the credit rating. The lower the credit quality is, the lower the credit rating, and the higher the risk associated with the securities.
rating service	Major financial organizations that evaluate the credit quality of issuers. Issuers have to request and pay for the service. Standard and Poor's, Moody's, and Fitch are the most widely followed rating services.
raw land program	A type of real estate limited partnership that invests in land for capital appreciation.
real estate investment trust (REIT)	An entity that is organized to invest in or manage real estate. REITs offer investors certain tax advantages that are beyond the scope of the exam.
real estate limited partnership	A type of direct participation program that invests in real estate projects to produce income or capital appreciation.
real estate mortgage investment conduit (REMIC)	An organization that pools investors' capital to purchase portfolios of mortgages.
realized gain	A profit earned on the sale of a security at a price that exceeds its purchase price.
realized loss	A loss recognized by an investor by selling a security at a price that is less than its purchase price.
reallowance	A sales concession available to dealers who sell securities subject to an offering who are not syndicate or selling group members.
recapture	An event that causes a tax liability on a previously taken deduction, such as selling an asset above its depreciated cost base.
recession	A decline in GDP that lasts for at least 6 months but not longer than 18 months.
reclamation	The right of a seller to demand or claim any loss from the buying party due to the buyer's failure to settle the transaction.
record date	A date set by a corporation's board of directors that determines which shareholders will be entitled to receive a declared dividend. Shareholders must be owners of record on this date in order to collect the dividend.
recourse loan	A loan taken out by a limited partnership that allows the lender to seek payment from the limited partners in the case of the partnership's failure to pay.
redeemable security	A security that can be redeemed by the issuer at the investor's request. Open-end mutual funds are an example of redeemable securities.
redemption	The return of an investor's capital by an issuer. Open-end mutual funds must redeem their securities within 7 days of an investor's request.
red herring	*See* preliminary prospectus.

registered	A term that describes the level of owner information that is recorded by the security's issuer.
registered as to principal only	A type of bond registration that requires the investor to clip coupons to receive the bond's interest payments. The issuer will automatically send the investor the bond's principal amount at maturity.
registered options principal (ROP)	An individual who has passed the Series 4 exam.
registered principal	A supervisor of a member firm who has passed the principal examination.
registered representative	An individual who has successfully completed a qualified examination to represent a broker dealer or issuer in securities transactions.
registrar	An independent organization that accounts for all outstanding stock and bonds of an issuer.
registration statement	The full disclosure statement that nonexempt issuers must file with the SEC prior to offering securities for sale to the public. The Securities Act of 1933 requires that a registration statement be filed.
regressive tax	A tax that is levied on all parties at the same rate, regardless of their income. An example of a regressive tax is a sales tax. A larger percentage of a low-income earner's income is taken away by the tax.
regular-way settlement	The standard number of business days in which a securities transaction is completed and paid for. Corporate securities and municipal bonds settle the regular way on the second business day after the trade date with payment due on the fourth business day. Government securities settle the next business day.
regulated investment company	An investment company that qualifies as a conduit for net investment income under Internal Revenue Code subchapter M, so long as it distributes at least 90% of its net investment income to shareholders.
Regulation A	A Regulation A offering allows a company to raise up to 75 million dollars in a tier 2 offering and up to 20 million dollars in a tier 1 offering in any 12-month period.
Regulation D	A private placement or sale of securities that allows for an exemption from registration under the Securities Act of 1933. A private placement may be sold to an unlimited number of accredited investors but may only be sold to 35 nonaccredited investors in any 12-month period.
Regulation G	Regulates the extension of credit for securities purchases by other commercial lenders.
Regulation T	Regulates the extension of credit by broker dealers for securities purchases.
Regulation U	Regulates the extension of credit by banks for securities purchases.
Regulation X	Regulates the extension of credit by overseas lenders for securities purchases.
Rehypothecation	The act of a broker dealer repledging a customer's securities as collateral at a bank to obtain a loan for the customer.
REIT	*See* real estate investment trust (REIT).
rejection	The act of a buyer of a security refusing delivery.

reorganization department	The department in a brokerage firm that handles changes in securities that result from a merger or acquisition or calls.
repurchase agreement (REPO)	A fully collateralized loan that results in a sale of securities to the lender, with the borrower agreeing to repurchase them at a higher price in the future. The higher price represents the lender's interest.
reserve maintenance fund	An account set up to provide additional funds to maintain a revenue-producing facility financed by a revenue bond.
reserve requirement	A deposit required to be placed on account with the Federal Reserve Board by banks. The requirement is a percentage of the bank's customers' deposits.
resistance	A price level to which a security appreciates and attracts sellers. The new sellers keep the security's price from rising any higher.
restricted account	(1) A long margin account that has less than 50% equity but more than 25% or a short margin account that has equity of less than 50% but more than 30%. (2) A customer account that has been subject to a sellout.
restricted stock	A nonexempt unregistered security that has been obtained by means other than a public offering.
retail communication	Any communication that may be seen in whole or in part by an individual investor. Retail communication must be approved by a principal prior to first use and maintained by the firm for 3 years.
retained earnings	The amount of a corporation's net income that has not been paid out to shareholders as dividends.
retention	The amount of a new issue that an underwriter allocates to its own clients.
retention requirement	The amount of equity that must be left in a restricted margin account when withdrawing securities.
return on equity	A measure of performance found by dividing after-tax income by common stockholders' equity.
return on investment (ROI)	The profit or loss realized by an investor from holding a security expressed as a percentage of the invested capital.
revenue anticipation note	A short-term municipal issue that is sold to manage an issuer's cash flow in anticipation of other revenue in the future.
reverse repurchase agreement	A fully collateralized loan that results in the purchase of securities with the intention of reselling them to the borrower at a higher price. The higher price represents the buyer's/lender's interest.
reverse split	A stock split that results in fewer shares outstanding, with each share being worth proportionally more.
reversionary working interest	A revenue-sharing arrangement where the general partner shares none of the cost and receives none of the revenue until the limited partners have received their payments back, plus any predetermined amount of return.
right	A short-term security issued in conjunction with a shareholder's preemptive right. The maximum length of a right is 45 days, and it is issued with a subscription price, which allows the holder to purchase the underlying security at a discount from its market price.

rights agent	An independent entity responsible for maintaining the records for rights holders.
rights of accumulation	A right offered to mutual fund investors that allows them to calculate all past contributions and growth to reach a breakpoint to receive a sales charge discount on future purchases.
rights offering	The offering of new shares by a corporation that is preceded by the offering of the new shares to existing shareholders.
riskless simultaneous transaction	The purchase of a security on a principal basis by a brokerage firm for the sole purpose of filling a customer's order that the firm has already received. The markup on riskless principal transactions has to be based on the firm's actual cost for the security.
rollover	The distribution of assets from a qualified account to an investor for the purpose of depositing the assets in another qualified account within 60 days. An investor may only roll over an IRA once every 12 months.
round lot	A standard trading unit for securities. For common and preferred stock, a round lot is 100 shares. For bonds, it is 5 bonds.
Rule 144	SEC rule that regulates the sale of restricted and control securities requiring the seller to file Form 144 at the time the order is entered to sell. Rule 144 also regulates the number of securities that may be sold.
Rule 145	SEC rule that requires a corporation to provide stockholders with full disclosure relating to reorganizations and to solicit proxies.
Rule 147	An intrastate offering that provides an exemption from SEC registration.
Rule 405	The NYSE rule that requires that all customer recommendations must be suitable and that the representative must "know" the customer.

S

sale	*See* sell.
sales charge	*See* commission.
sales literature	Written material distributed by a firm to a controlled audience for the purpose of increasing business. Sales literature includes market letters, research reports, and form letters sent to more than 25 customers.
sales load	The amount of commission charged to investors in open-end mutual funds. The amount of the sales load is added to the net asset value of the fund to determine the public offering price of the fund.
satellite office	An office not identified to the public as an office of the member, such as an agent's home office.
savings bond	A nonnegotiable U.S. government bond that must be purchased from the government and redeemed to the government. These bonds are generally known as Series EE and HH bonds.
scale	A list of maturities and yields for a new serial bond issue.

Schedule 13D	A form that must be filed with the SEC by any individual or group of individuals acquiring 5% or more of a corporation's nonexempt equity securities. Form 13D must be filed within 10 days of the acquisition.
scheduled premium policy	A variable life insurance policy with fixed premium payments.
SEC	*See* Securities and Exchange Commission (SEC).
secondary distribution	A distribution of a large number of securities by a large shareholder or group of large shareholders. The distribution may or may not be done under a prospectus.
secondary offering	An underwriting of a large block of stock being sold by large shareholders. The proceeds of the issue are received by the selling shareholders, not the corporation.
secondary market	A marketplace where securities are exchanged between investors. All transactions that take place on an exchange or on the Nasdaq are secondary market transactions.
sector fund	A mutual fund that invests in companies within a specific business area in an effort to maximize gains. Sector funds have larger risk-reward ratios because of the concentration of investments.
Securities Act of 1933	The first major piece of securities industry legislation. It regulates the primary market and requires that nonexempt issuers file a registration statement with the SEC. The act also requires that investors in new issues be given a prospectus.
Securities Act Amendments of 1975	Created the Municipal Securities Rulemaking Board (MSRB).
Securities Exchange Act of 1934	Regulates the secondary market and all broker dealers and industry participants. It created the Securities and Exchange Commission, the industry's ultimate authority. The act gave the authority to the Federal Reserve Board to regulate the extension of credit for securities purchases through Regulation T.
Securities and Exchange Commission	The ultimate securities industry authority. The SEC is a direct government body, not a self-regulatory organization. The commissioners are appointed by the U.S. President and must be approved by Congress.
Securities Investor Protection Corporation (SIPC)	The industry's nonprofit insurance company that provides protection for investors in case of broker dealer failure. All member firms must pay dues to SIPC based upon their revenue. SIPC provides coverage for each separate customer for up to $500,000, of which a maximum of $250,000 may be cash. The Securities Investor Protection Act of 1970 created SIPC.
security	Any investment that can be exchanged for value between two parties that contains risk. Securities include stocks, bonds, mutual funds, notes, rights, warrants, and options, among others.
segregation	The physical separation of customer and firm assets.

self-regulatory organization (SRO)	An industry authority that regulates its own members. FINRA, the NYSE, and the CBOE are all self-regulatory organizations that regulate their own members.
sell	The act of conveying the ownership of a security for value to another party. A sale includes any security that is attached to another security, as well as any security which the security may be converted or exchanged into.
seller's option	A type of settlement option that allows the seller to determine when delivery of the securities and final settlement of the trade will occur.
selling away	Any recommendation to a customer that involves an investment product that is not offered through the employing firm without the firm's knowledge and consent. This is a violation of industry regulations and may result in action being taken against the representative.
selling concession	*See* concession.
selling dividends .	The act of using a pending dividend to create urgency for the customer to purchase a security. This is a violation and could result in action being taken against the representative.
selling group	A group of broker dealers who may sell a new issue of securities but who are not members of the syndicate and who have no liability to the issuer.
sell out	A transaction executed by a broker dealer when a customer fails to pay for the securities.
sell-stop order	An order placed beneath the current market for a security to protect a profit, to guard against a loss, or to establish a short position.
separate account	The account established by an insurance company to invest the pooled funds of variable contract holders in the securities markets. The separate account must register as either an open-end investment company or as a unit investment trust.
separate trading of registered interest and principal securities (STRIPS)	A zero-coupon bond issued by the U.S. government. The principal payment due in the future is sold to investors at a discount and appreciates to par at maturity. The interest payment component is sold to other investors who want some current income.
serial bonds	A bond issue that has an increasing amount of principal maturing in successive years.
Series EE bond	A nonmarketable U.S. government zero-coupon bond that is issued at a discount and matures at its face value. Investors must purchase the bonds from the U.S. government and redeem them to the government at maturity.
Series HH bond	A nonmarketable U.S. government interest-bearing bond that can only be purchased by trading in matured Series EE bonds. Series HH bonds may not be purchased with cash and are issued with a $500 minimum denomination.
settlement	The completion of a securities transaction. A transaction settles and is completed when the security is delivered to the buyer and the cash is delivered to the seller.

settlement date	The date when a securities ownership changes. Settlement dates are set by FINRA's Uniform Practice Code.
75-5-10 diversification	The diversification test that must be met by mutual funds under the Investment Company Act of 1940 in order to market themselves as a diversified mutual fund: 75% of the fund's assets must be invested in other issuer's securities, no more than 5% of the fund's assets may be invested in any one company, and the fund may own no more than 10% of an issuer's outstanding securities.
shareholder's equity	*See* net worth.
share identification	The process of identifying which shares are being sold at the time the sale order is entered in order to minimize an investor's tax liability.
shelf offering	A type of securities registration that allows the issuer to sell the securities over a 2-year period. Well-known, seasoned issuers may sell securities over a 3-year period.
short	A position established by a bearish investor that is created by borrowing the security and selling in the hopes that the price of the security will fall. The investor hopes to be able to repurchase the security at a lower price, thus replacing it cheaply. If the security's price rises, the investor will suffer a loss.
short against the box	A short position established against an equal long position in the security to roll tax liabilities forward. Most of the benefits of establishing a short against the box position have been eliminated.
short straddle	The simultaneous sale of a call and a put on the same underlying security with the same strike price and expiration. A short straddle would be established by an investor who believes that the security price will move sideways.
simplified arbitration	A method of resolving disputes of $50,000 or less. There is no hearing; one arbitrator reads the submissions and renders a final decision.
Simplified Employee Pension (SEP)	A qualified retirement plan created for small employers with 25 or fewer employees that allows the employees' money to grow tax-deferred until retirement.
single account	An account operated for one individual. The individual has control of the account, and the assets go to the individual's estate in the case of his or her death.
sinking fund	An account established by an issuer of debt to place money for the exclusive purpose of paying bond principal.
special assessment bond	A municipal bond backed by assessments from the property that benefits from the improvements.
specialist	Member of an exchange responsible for maintaining a fair and orderly market in the securities that he or she specializes in and for executing orders left with him or her.
specialist book	A book of limit orders left with the specialist for execution.
special situation fund	A fund that seeks to take advantage of unusual corporate developments, such as take mergers and restructuring.

special tax bond	A type of municipal revenue bond that is supported only by revenue from certain taxes.
speculation	An investment objective where the investor is willing to accept a high degree of risk in exchange for the opportunity to realize a high return.
split offering	An offering where a portion of the proceeds from the underwriting goes to the issuer and a portion goes to the selling shareholders.
spousal account	An IRA opened for a nonworking spouse that allows a full contribution to be made for the nonworking spouse.
spread	(1) The difference between the bid and ask for a security. (2) The simultaneous purchase and sale of two calls or two puts on the same underlying security.
spread load plan	A contractual plan that seeks to spread the sales charge over a longer period of time, as detailed in the Spread Load Plan Act of 1970. The maximum sales charge over the life of the plan is 9%, while the maximum sales charge in any one year is 20%.
stabilizing	The only form of price manipulation allowed by the SEC. The managing underwriter enters a bid at or below the offering price to ensure even distribution of shares.
standby underwriting	An underwriting used in connection with a preemptive rights offering. The standby underwriter must purchase any shares not subscribed to by existing shareholders.
statutory disqualification	A set of rules that prohibit an individual who has been barred or suspended or convicted of a securities-related crime from becoming registered.
statutory voting	A method of voting that requires investors to cast their votes evenly for the directors they wish to elect.
stock ahead	A condition that causes an investor's order not to be executed, even though the stock is trading at a price that would satisfy the customer's limit order, because other limit orders have been entered prior to the customer's order.
stock certificate	Evidence of equity ownership.
stock or bond power	A form that, when signed by the owner and attached to a security, makes the security negotiable.
stock split	A change in the number of outstanding shares, the par value, and the number of authorized shares that has been approved through a vote of the shareholders. Forward-stock splits increase the number of shares outstanding and reduce the stock price in order to make the security more attractive to individual investors.
stop limit order	An order that becomes a limit order to buy or sell the stock when the stock trades at or through the stop price.
stop order	An order that becomes a market order to buy or sell the stock when the stock trades at or through the stop price.
stopping stock	A courtesy offered by a specialist to public customers, whereby the specialist guarantees a price but tries to obtain a better price for the customer.

straddle	The simultaneous purchase or sale of a call and a put on the same security with the same strike price and expiration.
straight line depreciation	An accounting method that allows an owner to take equal tax deductions over the useful life of the asset.
strangle	The purchase or sale of a call and a put on either side of the current market price. The options have the same expiration months but different strike prices.
stripped bond	A bond that has had its coupons removed by a broker dealer and that is selling at a deep discount to its principal payment in the future.
stripper well	An oil well that is in operation just to recover a very limited amount of reserves.
subchapter S corporation	A business organization that allows the tax consequences of the organization to flow through to the owners.
subscription agreement	An application signed by the purchaser of an interest in a direct participation plan. An investor in a limited partnership does not become an investor until the general partner signs the subscription agreement.
subscription right	*See* right.
suitability	A determination that the characteristics of a security are in line with an investor's objectives, financial profile, and attitudes.
Super Display Book System (SDBK)	The electronic order-routing system used by the NYSE to route orders directly to the trading post.
supervise	The actions of a principal that ensure that the actions of a firm and its representatives are in compliance with industry regulations.
support	The price to which a security will fall and attract new buyers. As the new buyers enter the market, it keeps the price from falling any lower.
surplus fund	An account set up for funds generated by a project financed by a municipal revenue bond to pay a variety of expenses.
syndicate	A group of underwriters responsible for underwriting a new issue.
systematic risk	A risk inherent in any investment in the market. An investor may lose money simply because the market is going down.

T

takedown	The price at which a syndicate purchases a new issue of securities from the issuer.
tax and revenue anticipation note	A short-term note sold by a municipal issuer as interim financing in anticipation of tax and other revenue.
tax anticipation note (TAN)	A short-term note sold by a municipal issuer as interim financing in anticipation of tax revenue.
tax-deferred annuity	A nonqualified retirement account that allows an investor's money to grow tax deferred. A tax-deferred annuity is a contract between an insurance company and an investor.

tax equivalent yield	The interest rate that must be offered by a taxable bond of similar quality in order to be equal to the rate that is offered by a municipal bond.
tax-exempt bond fund	A bond fund that seeks to produce investment income that is free from federal tax by investing in a portfolio of municipal bonds.
tax liability	The amount of money that is owed by an investor after realizing a gain on the sale of an investment or after receiving investment income.
tax preference item	An item that receives preferential tax treatment and must be added back into income when calculating an investor's alternative minimum tax.
tax-sheltered annuity (TSA)	A qualified retirement plan offered to employees of governments, school systems, or nonprofit organizations. Contributions to TSAs are made with pre-tax dollars.
technical analysis	A method of security analysis that uses past price performance to predict the future performance of a security.
Telephone Consumer Protection Act of 1991	Legislation that regulates how potential customers are contacted by phone at home.
tenants in common	*See* joint tenants in common.
tender offer	An offer to buy all or part of a company's outstanding securities for cash or cash and securities.
term bond	A bond issue that has its entire principal due on one date.
term maturity	A type of bond maturity that has all principal due on one date.
testimonial	The use of a recognized expert or leader to endorse the services of a firm.
third market	A transaction in an exchange-listed security executed over the Nasdaq workstation.
third-party account	An account that is managed for the benefit of a customer by another party, such as an investment adviser, a trustee, or an attorney.
30-day visible supply	The total par value of all new issue municipal bonds coming to market in the next 30 days.
time deposit	An account that is established by a bank customer where the customer agrees to leave the funds on deposit for an agreed upon amount of time.
time value	The value of an option that exceeds its intrinsic value or its in-the-money amount.
tombstone ad	An announcement published in financial papers advertising the offering of securities by a group of underwriters. Only basic information may be contained in the tombstone ad, and all offers must be made through the prospectus only.
top heavy rule	The rule that states the maximum salary for which a Keogh contribution may be based. This is in effect to limit the disparity between high- and low-salary employees.
trade confirmation	The printed notification of a securities transaction. A confirmation must be sent to a customer on or before the completion of a transaction. The completion of a transaction is considered to be the settlement date.
trade date	The day when an investor's order is executed.

tranche	A class of collateralized mortgage obligation (CMO) that has a predicted maturity and interest rate.
transfer agent	An independent entity that handles name changes, records the names of security holders of record, and ensures that all certificates are properly endorsed.
transfer and hold in safekeeping	A request by customers for the brokerage firm to transfer their securities into the firm's name and to hold them in safekeeping at the firm. A brokerage may charge a fee for holding a customer's securities that have been registered in its name.
transfer and ship	A request by customers for the brokerage firm to transfer their securities into their name and to ship them to their address of record.
Treasury bill	A U.S. government security that is issued at a discount and matures at par in 4, 13, 26, and 52 weeks.
Treasury bond	A long-term U.S. government security that pays semiannual interest and matures in 10 to 30 years.
Treasury note	An intermediate-term U.S. government security that pays semiannual interest and matures in 1 to 10 years.
Treasury receipt	A zero-coupon bond created by a brokerage firm that is backed by U.S. government securities. It is issued at a discount and matures at par.
treasury stock	Stock that has been issued by a corporation and that has subsequently been repurchased by the corporation. Treasury stock does not vote or receive dividends. It is not used in the calculation of earnings per share.
trendline	A line used to predict the future price movement for a security. Drawing a line under the successive lows or successive highs creates a trendline.
trough	The bottoming out of the business cycle just prior to an new upward movement in activity.
true interest cost (TIC)	A calculation for the cost of a municipal issuer's interest expense that includes the time value of money.
Trust Indenture Act of 1940	Regulates the issuance of corporate debt in excess of $5 million and with a term exceeding 1 year. It requires an indenture between the issuer and the trustee.
trustee	A person who legally acts for the benefit of another party.
12B-1 fee	An asset-based distribution fee that is assessed annually and paid out quarterly to cover advertising and distribution costs. All 12B-1 fees must be reasonable.
two-dollar broker	An independent exchange member who executes orders for commission house brokers and other customers for a fee.
type	A classification method for an option as either a call or a put.

U

uncovered	*See* naked.

underlying security	A security for which an investor has an option to buy or sell.
underwriting	The process of marketing a new issue of securities to the investing public. A broker dealer forwards the proceeds of the sale to the issuer minus its fee for selling the securities.
unearned income	Any income received by an individual from an investment, such as dividends and interest income.
uniform delivery ticket	A document that must be attached to every security delivered by the seller, making the security "good delivery."
Uniform Gifts to Minors Act (UGMA)	Sets forth guidelines for the gifting of cash and securities to minors and for the operation of accounts managed for the benefit of minors. Once a gift is given to a minor, it is irrevocable.
Uniform Practice Code	The FINRA bylaw that sets guidelines for how industry members transact business with other members. The Uniform Practice Code establishes such things as settlement dates, rules of good delivery, and ex-dividend dates.
Uniform Securities Act (USA)	The framework for state-based securities legislation. The act is a model that can be adapted to each state's particular needs.
Uniform Transfer to Minors Act (UTMA)	Legislation that has been adopted in certain states, in lieu of the Uniform Gifts to Minors Act. UTMA allows the custodian to determine the age at which the assets become the property of the minor. The maximum age for transfer of ownership is 25.
unit investment trust (UIT)	A type of investment company organized as a trust to invest in a portfolio of securities. The UIT sells redeemable securities to investors in the form of shares or units of beneficial interest.
unit of beneficial interest	The redeemable share issued to investors in a unit investment trust.
unit refund annuity	An annuity payout option that will make payments to the annuitant for life. If the annuitant dies prior to receiving an amount that is equal to his or her account value, the balance of the account will be paid to the annuitant's beneficiaries.
unqualified legal opinion	A legal opinion issued by a bond attorney for the issue where there are no reservations relating to the issue.
unrealized	A paper profit or loss on a security that is still owned.

V

variable annuity	A contract issued by an insurance company that is both a security and an insurance product. The annuitant's contributions are invested through the separate account into a portfolio of securities. The annuitant's payments depend largely on the investment results of the separate account.
variable death benefit	The amount of a death benefit paid to a beneficiary that is based on the investment results of the insurance company's separate account. This amount is over the contract's minimum guaranteed death benefit.

variable life insurance	A life insurance policy that provides for a minimum guaranteed death benefit, as well as an additional death benefit, based on the investment results of the separate account.
variable rate municipal security	Interim municipal financing issued with a variable rate.
vertical spread	The simultaneous purchase and sale of two calls or two puts on the same underlying security that differ only in strike price.
vesting	The process by which an employer's contributions to an employee's retirement account become the property of the employee.
visible supply	*See* 30-day visible supply.
voluntary accumulation plan	A method, such as dollar-cost averaging, by which an investor regularly makes contributions to acquire mutual fund shares.
voting right	The right of a corporation's stockholders to cast their votes for the election of the corporation's board of directors as well as for certain major corporate issues.

W

warrant	A long-term security that gives the holder the right to purchase the common shares of a corporation for up to 10 years. The warrant's subscription price is always higher than the price of the underlying common shares when the warrant is initially issued.
wash sale	The sale of a security at a loss and the subsequent repurchase of that security or of a security that is substantially the same within 30 days of the sale. The repurchase disallows the claim of the loss for tax purposes.
western account	A type of municipal security syndicate account where only the member with unsold bonds is responsible for the unsold bonds.
when-issued security	A security that has been sold prior to the certificates being available for delivery.
wildcatting	An exploratory oil- and gas-drilling program.
wire room	*See* order department.
withdrawal plan	The systematic removal of funds from a mutual fund account over time. Withdrawal plans vary in type and availability among fund companies.
workable indication	An indication of the prices and yields that a municipal securities dealer may be willing to buy or sell bonds.
working capital	A measure of a corporation's liquidity that is found by subtracting current liabilities from current assets.
working interest	An interest that requires the holder to bear the proportional expenses and allows the holder to share in the revenue produced by an oil or gas project in relation to the interest.
workout quote	A nonfirm quote that requires handling and settlement conditions to be worked out between the parties prior to the trade.
writer	An investor who sells an option to receive the premium income.

writing the scale	The procedure of assigning prospective yields to a new issuer of serial municipal bonds.

Y

Yellow Sheets	A daily publication published by the national quotation bureau providing quotes for corporate bonds.
yield	The annual amount of income generated by a security relative to its price; expressed as a percentage.
yield-based option	An interest rate option that allows the holder to receive the in-the-money amount in cash upon exercise or expiration.
yield curve	The rate at which interest rates vary among investments of similar quality with different maturities. Longer-term securities generally offer higher yields.
yield to call	An investor's overall return for owning a bond should it be called in prior to maturity by the issuer.
yield to maturity	An investor's overall return for owning a bond if the bond is held until maturity.

Z

zero-coupon bond	A bond that is issued at a discount from its par value and makes no regular interest payments. An investor's interest is reflected by the security's appreciation toward par at maturity. The appreciation is taxable each year even though it is not actually received by the investor (phantom income).
zero-minus tick	A trade in an exchange-listed security that occurs at the same price as the previous transaction, but at a price that is lower than the last transaction that was different.
zero-plus tick	A trade in an exchange-listed security that occurs at the same price as the previous transaction, but at a price that is higher than the last transaction that was different.

Made in the USA
Middletown, DE
11 March 2022

62484338R00183